BUSINESS TORTS
A Practical Guide to Litigation

BRADLEY P. NELSON

JEFFREY R. TEETERS

Editors

FIRST
CHAIR
·PRESS·

Business Torts & Unfair Competition Committee

Cover design by Mary Anne Kulchawik/ABA Publishing.

Printed in the United States of America.

18 17 16 15 14   5 4 3 2 1

Library of Congress Cataloging-in-Publication Data

Business torts : a practical guide to litigation / Bradley P. Nelson, Jeffrey R. Teeters Editors; American Bar Association, Section of Litigation, Business Torts and Unfair Competition Committee.
    pages cm
  "First Chair Press."
  ISBN 978-1-62722-612-7 (alk. paper)
  1. Torts--United States. 2. Commercial law--United States. 3. Actions and defenses--United States. 4. Trial practice--United States. I. Nelson, Bradley P., 1960- editor of compilation. II. Teeters, Jeffrey R., editor of compilation. III. American Bar Association. Business Torts and Unfair Competition Committee, sponsoring body.
  KF1250.B845 2014
  346.7303'1--dc23   2014006082

Discounts are available for books ordered in bulk. Special consideration is given to state bars, CLE programs, and other bar-related organizations. Inquire at Book Publishing, ABA Publishing, American Bar Association, 321 N. Clark Street, Chicago, Illinois 60654-7598.

www.ShopABA.org

CONTENTS

10 Trial Preparation

PREFACE

The goal of the Business Torts & Unfair Competition Committee of the American Bar Association's Section of Litigation is to keep business litigators fully up to date in burgeoning business torts such as fiduciary duties, fraud, unfair trade practices, tortious interference, trademarks and trade secrets, remedies, and evidence, as well as technological issues and developments impacting our practice. The committee recognized that a significant number of publications already address the substantive law in these areas, but much less guidance is available on the nuances of taking those cases from investigation through trial.

The practical reality is that business torts lawsuits often implicate clients' competitive commercial interests. That means they also raise unique problems and require unique strategies and solutions. Our book addresses those problems, strategies, and solutions directly. Recognizing that business torts litigators are rarely only on the plaintiff side or only on the defense side, the book attempts to avoid any particular plaintiff or defense approach. Rather, views from seasoned litigators, consultants, and the bench offer valuable insight regardless of which side of the "v." you find yourself on.

We are fortunate that more than a dozen experienced attorneys from across the country have contributed to this task. Each chapter breaks down a particular component of the process. We start with considerations, resources, and strategies for pre-suit investigation to best prepare your case for the battle ahead. And we conclude with tips and techniques for crafting trial themes, selection and presentation of witnesses, and the always elusive voir dire. In between, chapters offer everything from rules and case authority for litigating injunctions to strategies for engaging in discovery, preparing and responding to dispositive motions, and contemplating alternative dispute resolution.

We applaud the individual authors for their thoughtfulness and time commitment toward making this book a success and for their contributions to the profession. We also extend special thanks to C. Pierce Campbell, Elizabeth Fenton, Amy Stewart, and Jack Brady, who provided valuable leadership as Co-Chairs of the Business Torts & Unfair Competition Committee.

Bradley P. Nelson, Schopf & Weiss, Chicago, IL
Jeffrey R. Teeters, Buckley King LPA, Cincinnati, OH
Co-Editors

ABOUT THE EDITORS

Bradley P. Nelson is a partner at Schopf & Weiss LLP, a national litigation firm based in Chicago, Illinois. He is an experienced trial lawyer, member of the firm's Executive Committee, and Co-Chair of its Intellectual Property Litigation Group. His practice focuses on complex commercial and business litigation, including patent infringement, intellectual property, financial services, breach of contract, fraud, insurance coverage, and professional liability matters. Mr. Nelson is recognized by Illinois' "Super Lawyers" in business litigation and has been recommended by peers for Leading Lawyers Network. He is a member of the American Bar Association's Intellectual Property and Litigation Sections, the American Intellectual Property Law Association, and the Intellectual Property Law Association of Chicago, and is also active on the ABA's Business Torts and Unfair Competition Committee. Mr. Nelson graduated from the University of Wisconsin–Oshkosh in 1983 (summa cum laude) and is a 1986 cum laude graduate of the University of Wisconsin Law School.

Schopf & Weiss LLP, One South Wacker Drive, 28th Floor, Chicago, Illinois 60606; (312) 701-9300; nelson@sw.com; www.sw.com.

Jeffrey R. Teeters is a partner in the law firm of Buckley King LPA. He serves as Partner-in-Charge of the firm's Cincinnati, Ohio, office and chairs the firm's Litigation Practice Group. His litigation and appellate practice focuses on assisting businesses in interactions with their competitors, including business and commercial disputes, trade secrets and noncompetition agreements, employment, professional liability, and antitrust. He is a frequent author and lecturer on noncompetition agreements, trade secrets, and unfair competition. Mr. Teeters is recognized among the Best Lawyers in America® in the field of commercial litigation and Ohio's "Super Lawyers" in business litigation. He served for five years as an editor of the ABA Litigation Section's *Litigation News*, including most recently as its Editor-in-Chief.

In addition, he served as co-editor of the Litigation Section's *Business Torts Journal* for over four years. Mr. Teeters graduated from the University of Dayton in 1990 (magna cum laude) and the University of Cincinnati College of Law in 1993.

Buckley King LPA, 600 Vine Street, Suite 2010, Cincinnati, Ohio 45202; (513) 412-5400; teeters@buckleyking.com; www.buckleyking.com.

ABOUT THE AUTHORS

Peter J. Boyer is a partner at Hyland Levin LLP, 6000 Sagemore Drive, Suite 6301, Marlton, NJ 08053-3900, (856) 355-2900, boyer@hylandlevin.com, www.hylandlevin.com. Mr. Boyer handles business and commercial litigation matters in state and federal courts in New Jersey and Pennsylvania, as well as in arbitration proceedings.

Catherine Cameron, CA, CPA, CMA, ABV, CFF, CGMA, is the president of Ness Consulting LLC, 261 East Vinedo Lane, Tempe, AZ 85284, (480) 247-9099, ccameron@nessexpert.com, www.nessexpert.com. Ness Consulting LLC is a company that provides consulting and expert witness services in forensic accounting, damage analysis, and business valuation.

Daniel P. Carter is the principal of The Law Office of Daniel P. Carter LLC of Cleveland, OH, (216) 392-4509, dpc@dpcarterlaw.com. His practice includes business matters and disputes involving contracts, intellectual property, insurance coverage, licensing, and trade secrets. He regularly represents clients in the firearms industry and in election law matters.

Deborah L. Edney is a partner at Parker Poe Adams & Bernstein, LLP, 401 South Tryon Street, Suite 3000, Charlotte, NC 28202, (704) 335-9856, debbieedney@parkerpoe.com, www.parkerpoe.com. She specializes in managing, trying, and arbitrating cases involving trade secret misappropriation, covenants not to compete, tortious interference, breach of fiduciary duty, antitrust claims, and unfair competition. Additionally, Ms. Edney works with clients in commercial contract and other general commercial disputes.

Peter J. Glennon, Esq., is a litigation attorney with The Glennon Law Firm, PC, 160 Linden Oaks, Rochester, NY 14625, (585) 210-2150, PGlennon@GlennonLawFirm.com, www.GlennonLawFirm.com. Mr. Glennon's practice focuses on complex commercial and business disputes, executive employment law, franchise law, and aviation law. Heather Neu, Esq., and John Kreckel, Esq., assisted with the preparation of this chapter.

David B. Graeven, PhD, is President and Senior Consultant at Trial Behavior Consulting, 505 Sansome Street, #1701, San Francisco, CA 94111, (415) 781-5879, DGraeven@trialbehavior.com, www.trialbehavior.com. He conducts jury research, works with witnesses, and helps select juries for complex cases throughout the country.

Chadwick A. McTighe is a member of Stites & Harbison, PLLC, 400 Market St., Suite 1800, Louisville, KY 40202, (502) 681-0392; cmctighe@stites.com; www.stites.com. Mr. McTighe's practice includes a wide range of business and commercial litigation matters, including extensive practice in class action litigation, shareholder and membership disputes, and fiduciary duty litigation.

Nelson A. F. Mixon is an attorney at The Cavanagh Law Firm, PA, 1850 North Central Avenue #2400, Phoenix, Arizona 85004, (602) 322-4000, nmixon@cavanaghlaw.com, www.cavanaghlaw.com. He devotes a substantial portion of his practice to representing businesses and individuals in business tort cases.

Andrea Donovan Napp is Counsel with Robinson & Cole LLP; (860) 275-8206; anapp@rc.com; www.rc.com. Ms. Napp's practice focuses on litigation of commercial disputes with an emphasis on e-discovery, information management, and data privacy and security.

Matthew J. O'Hara is a partner at Hinshaw & Culbertson LLP, 222 North LaSalle Street, Suite 300, Chicago, IL 60601, (312) 704-3246, mohara@hinshawlaw.com, www.hinshawlaw.com, and co-leader of its Lawyers Professional Liability Practice Group. He concentrates his practice in the litigation and trial of complex commercial matters in federal and state courts.

Hon. Steven Platt (Ret.) is Managing Member of The Platt Group, Inc., (410) 280-0908; info@theplattgroup.com; http://theplattgroup.com. Judge Platt is engaged in mediation, arbitration, and neutral case evaluation of complex civil litigation including legal malpractice cases, medical malpractice cases, product liability cases, business disputes, real estate matters, and other civil cases.

Daniel D. Quick is an attorney with Dickinson Wright, PLLC, in Troy, MI, where he is chair of the firm's Commercial Litigation practice; (248) 433-7242, dquick@dickinsonwright.com. Mr. Quick tries a broad array of commercial litigation matters, including UCC disputes, non-competes, trade secrets, and business divorce cases.

Heath Szymczak, Esq., is a partner with Jaeckle Fleischmann & Mugel, LLP, (716) 843-3909; hszymczak@jaeckle.com. Mr. Szymczak's practice focuses on business-related torts, complex commercial litigation, and other civil litigation.

CHAPTER 1

Pre-Suit Investigation

Andrea Donovan Napp

Prosecuting or defending a lawsuit requires a significant investment of time and resources, both yours and your client's. Regardless of whether you represent the plaintiff or the defendant, careful planning, organization, investigation, and strategizing are crucial to obtaining a favorable outcome for your client, whether that means a jury verdict or a settlement that addresses important business concerns. This process of planning and evaluating at the outset of litigation is typically referred to as a "pre-suit investigation." This chapter explores the practical and legal significance of a pre-suit investigation in a business torts case, discusses the components of a comprehensive investigation, and addresses the importance of documenting your methodology.

I. THE IMPORTANCE OF PRE-SUIT INVESTIGATIONS IN BUSINESS TORTS CASES

Conducting a thorough pre-suit investigation is important for many reasons, some pragmatic, some tactical, and some required by law. As a matter of basic practice, plaintiffs must conduct an investigation sufficient to support the allegations of their complaint. Indeed, Federal Rule of Civil Procedure 11 requires that the individual signing the complaint ensure that "(2) the claims, defenses, and other legal contentions are warranted by existing law or by a nonfrivolous argument for extending, modifying, or reversing existing law or for establishing new law; (3) the factual contentions have evidentiary support or, if specifically so identified, will likely have evidentiary support after a reasonable opportunity for further investigation or discovery."[1] Rule 11 likewise requires defendants to certify that "the denials of factual contentions are warranted on the evidence or, if specifically so identified, are reasonably based on belief or a lack of information."[2] Neither plaintiffs nor defendants can reliably make the required representations of accuracy and nonfrivolousness without conducting some form of factual or legal investigation.

The penalties for failure to comply with Rule 11 are severe. A court may impose sanctions on you and your client, either on a party's motion or sua sponte, including, but not limited to, dismissal, payment of the opposing party's attorneys' fees, or a monetary fine. Imposition of sanctions can also expose counsel to a potential malpractice claim. Thus, you should conduct an in-depth investigation before signing any pleadings.[3]

Even if a rule or statute in the jurisdiction in which you practice does not expressly require a pre-suit investigation, conducting an investigation before bringing or defending a lawsuit has several practical and tactical advantages. Pre-suit investigations enable attorneys to represent their clients better in a variety of ways, including (1) identifying a proactive litigation strategy, (2) managing the client's expectations, (3) preparing for early motion practice or discovery, and (4) seeking or opposing a prejudgment remedy or injunction.

A. Mapping a Litigation Strategy

First and foremost, conducting a pre-suit investigation is an invaluable tool in mapping out a clear litigation strategy at the outset of a matter. Operating under the time constraints and pressure inherent to the profession, too many attorneys dive into litigation without identifying a specific end goal or strategizing as to how to get there. Failure to do so thrusts counsel into a precarious reactionary role, merely responding to the opposing

---

1. FED. R. CIV. P. 11.
2. *Id.*
3. While this book focuses on business torts, certain types of cases may be subject to additional, specific pre-suit investigation requirements, such as federal patent cases or medical malpractice actions in many jurisdictions.

party's actions rather than proactively taking steps to best position his or her client for the desired outcome. This leads to errors and frustrations and frequently costs the client additional money. Conducting a pre-suit investigation—really thinking about the facts and the law that will be in play—allows you to identify your client's goals and develop a step-by-step strategy to achieve those goals. For instance, many business torts cases are not intended to ever reach a jury but rather are filed to leverage settlement. Other cases involve clear legal issues that should be disposed of through early motion practice. Lastly, some cases will ultimately need to be decided by a judge or jury. Identifying which of these very different outcomes best suits your client will allow you to plan your litigation strategy accordingly. It will also enable you to assess your chances of success, anticipate and analyze any likely defenses or counterclaims, and properly advise your client.

While a pre-suit investigation frequently yields dividends for counsel, its importance to the client should not be underestimated. In the business torts context, whether to initiate litigation is a significant business decision that is typically arrived at in the face of a specific dispute and with an eye toward a desired business outcome. The more you know about the facts and law, the better able you will be to advise your client as to the available options at the outset. This includes creating a budget for various scenarios, articulating the viability of each available approach, and clearly communicating the chances of success of each option. Perhaps the cost of litigation outweighs the financial gain of even the best-case scenario? Maybe the parties are close enough together that a mediation or negotiation will help them bridge the gap? Simply put, investing the time up front to learn the key facts and familiarize yourself with the operative law will allow you to better advise your client.

B. Managing Client Expectations

Additionally, the investigation will help you manage your client's expectations. For instance, while a tortious interference claim levied against your client in an unfamiliar jurisdiction may seem hollow at first blush, further factual investigation or research into the nuances of the law could reveal that the claim has merit and that there is the potential that your client may be found liable. Knowing enough to advise your client of this fact as early

3

as possible, before committing to a vigorous defense or making assurances of victory, will prevent your client from growing frustrated or unhappy with your representation.

C. Preparing for Early Motion Practice

Conducting a pre-suit investigation is particularly important in business torts cases where early motion practice, early discovery, prejudgment remedies, and temporary injunctions are a common practice. The knowledge, both factual and legal, gained through a comprehensive investigation can aid in expeditiously drafting or defending a motion to dismiss for lack of jurisdiction or an *Iqbal/Twombley* challenge without requesting numerous extensions, which can alienate the judge, provoke the ire of opposing counsel, or cause the client to doubt your experience.[4] Similarly, if you have previously investigated the facts available to you, such as by interviewing the witnesses under your control, and researched the elements necessary to prove your case, you will be better positioned to timely issue targeted discovery requests that are less likely to draw broad objections. Another benefit of a pre-suit investigation in discovery is that it can allow you to assess the scope of e-discovery, both offensively and defensively. As will be discussed in greater detail later in this chapter, e-discovery is becoming increasingly important in overall litigation strategy and litigation budgeting. The sooner you can get a handle on the amount of data that may be subject to discovery, the better you'll be able to prepare.

D. Remedies

Early mastery of the facts and law is of paramount importance in business torts matters involving prejudgment remedies and temporary injunctions. Plaintiffs frequently file the papers for a prejudgment remedy or temporary injunction simultaneously with the complaint. When asking the court to impose what many have deemed "extraordinary" remedies with due process considerations, without any real sense of the scope of the dispute, specificity

---

4. Ashcroft v. Iqbal, 556 U.S. 662 (2009); Bell Atlantic Corp. v. Twombly, 550 U.S. 544 (2007).

lends credibility to your allegations. Moreover, if you are the party seeking a prejudgment remedy or temporary injunction, timeliness is paramount. Any delay in filing required to marshal the facts or law will be weighed against your claim of imminent harm. Lastly, hearings on such matters are typically scheduled expeditiously. Whether you are arguing for or against these remedies, you will need to have solid command of the facts and the law to craft your argument and effectively counter the other side's claims.

In summary, no matter how big or small a matter, whether plaintiff or defendant, some form of pre-suit investigation into the facts and law at issue will benefit both counsel and the client in all business torts matters.

II. THE COMPONENTS OF A PRE-SUIT INVESTIGATION

A pre-suit investigation can take many forms and should be tailored to the needs of a specific case. There are, however, certain components that should almost always be undertaken before filing or undertaking to defend a business torts case. Generally, these tasks break down into two broad categories: factual and legal considerations. Factual considerations refer to an investigation of the facts that are likely to be at issue in the matter, while legal considerations involve research and analysis into the applicable law. Typically, the factual components of a pre-suit investigation include:

1. identification of key facts,
2. identification of key documents,
3. identification of potential witnesses, and
4. research into the opponent or key players.

The legal factors that need to be identified include:

1. the substantive legal issues implicated by the cause of action you are asserting,
2. the procedural issues that could bear on the action,
3. the need for expert witnesses,
4. the legal strategy, and
5. an analysis of any expected defenses and counterclaims.

5

Some matters require a more intense factual investigation before deciding how to proceed, such as a complex business deal where the actions taken by the parties will be key to determining liability. In other cases, where the facts are largely undisputed, a more rigorous legal investigation will be required to determine the ramifications of the undisputed facts. Still other matters will require a thorough factual *and* legal analysis before continuing. The components of each facet of a typical pre-suit investigation will be discussed herein.

A. Factual Considerations

While it seems an obvious point, a detailed preliminary investigation of the facts is often given short shrift in the rush to the courthouse or under pressure to respond to potentially damaging allegations. However, the success of a case hinges on the development of the facts as much as any other pre-suit task. Any seasoned trial lawyer will tell you that mastery of the facts is often just as important as mastery of the law. And early mastery allows counsel to begin to craft the "story" that will ultimately be told to the judge, jury, or mediator. Thus, it is important not to wait until discovery begins to dig in to the facts but instead to tackle them head on during pre-suit preparation.

1. Identification of Key Facts—Getting Started

The factual portion of a pre-suit investigation deals with the "who, what, why, when, where, and how" of a matter. For instance, in a fraud case, the allegedly fraudulent statements will take center stage. Accordingly, plaintiff's counsel should be prepared from day one to identify with specificity the allegedly fraudulent statements, who made the statements, when they were made, where or in what context they were made, the subordinate facts that make those statements untrue or misleading, and any facts indicating reliance on those statements. Conversely, a defendant responding to such allegations needs to have an equally thorough understanding of these same facts to deny or admit their truth. Assuming that the allegedly fraudulent statements were in fact made, the context of those statements as well as the subordinate facts related to their veracity could greatly impact the manner in which the allegation is answered.

6

Counsel can glean this information from many sources. In a business torts case, the most common sources will be people, physical documents, and electronic data. Your preliminary meeting with your client should provide a road map for accessing these sources as early as possible. The internet and other publicly available sources are also starting points.

(a) Preliminary Client Meeting

At the outset of any new matter, regardless of your familiarity with the client, you should schedule a preliminary meeting or phone call to provide the client the opportunity to tell you about the dispute and to allow you to probe any areas that will require further factual development. In that initial meeting, ask your client to tell you the story. Why have they called you? What is the problem that requires your assistance? Why do they believe litigation is the appropriate next step? As they tell their story, listen carefully and take notes to follow up. Who made the allegedly fraudulent statements? To whom were those statements made? Did anyone else have knowledge of the statements or related facts? Are there any writings or documents that support or undermine their version of events?

Upon leaving that initial meeting, you should have a list of the individuals within your control who may have knowledge related to the story told by your client, a list of known documents that may come into play, and a list of any other potential data sources, such as servers or electronic databases.

This list serves as the roadmap for your factual investigation. Following the preliminary meeting, you should be able to identify (1) all potential witnesses and key players, (2) key documents, both helpful and harmful, and (3) any other potential sources of data.

The importance of this initial conversation should not be underestimated. Faced with litigation or difficult business decisions, clients can be distracted, short-tempered, anxious, or any combination thereof. This can impact the manner in which they tell their story. As counsel, your job is to aid them in giving you the information that you will need to properly advise them. Do not allow the client to tell you what is relevant and what is not. Ask all questions that you deem necessary to understand the facts of the dispute. This extends to understanding the client's business, which is critical in business torts cases. Ask the client to clarify where applicable and if you don't understand how a relevant aspect of their operation works, ask the questions that you need to reach the required level of cognizance.

During the initial meeting, you should also assess whether—or more accurately, when—to issue a litigation hold. Although not explicitly articulated in the Federal Rules of Civil Procedure, parties have an unmistakable duty to preserve any information that may be relevant to a matter.[5] This duty arises "once a party reasonably anticipates litigation."[6] There is not a bright line test for when a party should reasonably anticipate litigation and the courts have found that the duty arises at varying times.[7] Notably, this duty can arise prior to the commencement of a lawsuit if the parties are aware of the existence of a dispute. Once you or your client reasonably anticipate, litigation, a litigation hold notice should be issued promptly to avoid any claims of spoliation. The litigation hold notice should be specific as to the types of materials that must be preserved and should clearly indicate that any documents, paper and electronic, covered by the hold must not be destroyed. The litigation hold notice should be provided to anyone who may have relevant documents in their possession, starting with those individuals identified by the client in your preliminary meeting. Do not forget to issue litigation holds to additional individuals as you learn of them through your investigation.

(b) The Internet and Other Sources of Facts

In addition to the facts conveyed by the client, you should also conduct your own preliminary investigation to corroborate the client's account, learn information about the client that may not have been conveyed, and identify any facts about the opposing party that may be useful. In some instances, the hiring of a private investigator is warranted. In most cases,

5. *See* FED. R. CIV. P. 37(e).
6. Zubulake v. UBS Warburg LLC, 220 F.R.D. 212, 218 (S.D.N.Y. 2003).
7. Cache LaPoudre Fees v. Land O'Lakes, 244 F.R.D. 614, 623 (D. Colo. 2007) (duty to preserve did not arise upon receipt of letter identifying potential exposure); Phillip M. Adams & Associates v. Dell, Inc., 621 F. Supp. 2d 1173 (D. Utah 2009) (duty to preserve triggered years before suit was filed based on awareness of dispute within industry).

however, attorneys and paralegals can unearth sufficient information from the internet and public records.

A basic internet search can yield a wealth of information and should be conducted as a starting point in any investigation. Simply "Googling" the names of clients, adversaries, and key witnesses may reveal information about subsidiaries, parent companies, other potentially relevant business dealings, or any number of newsworthy topics. Targeted searches may also help complete the picture. For instance, docket searches should be conducted to learn what other matters the opposing side and its principals are litigating or have litigated. Reference to the secretary of state's website may reveal corporate relationships or filing deficiencies. Other government agencies' websites may contain regulatory filings (such as the SEC) or licensing information. Social media searches of both businesses and individuals can be a treasure trove of useful information. Even a corporation's own website should be reviewed. This can be particularly helpful in disputes where venue or personal jurisdiction is at issue, potentially listing offices and locations in which an entity does business.

While internet research is easy, accessible, and cost efficient, it does have its pitfalls. Accurate, reliable information is intermingled with vast amounts of less-than-accurate information. Sites with user-generated content such as Wikipedia may be useful but be mindful of the source of the content, namely other internet users who may be far from experts on any given topic. The same is true of blogs or any other websites featuring user-generated content, which often contain pure opinion at best and sheer speculation at worst. To the extent such information will be relied upon for any purpose, verify it.

Also, the internet is a fluid, ever-evolving source of information, and the content of any web site can change between the time of an online search and the time the suit is filed. It is important to print anything relevant (and to include the date of printing) to ensure that you have a valid copy of the information. Additionally, if your case hinges on something online—such as a defamatory blog post—periodically check back to ensure that the content has not changed or been altered in any way.

Finally, while conducting Facebook or Twitter searches of publicly available information is acceptable in most circumstances, the creation of fake

9

identities, misleading friend requests, or the changing of credentials to gain access to networks that you wouldn't normally have access to are not.[8]

2. Development of Facts—Identifying Witnesses and Key Players

After marshaling the available preliminary information, the next step is to develop that information further by conducting witness interviews and gathering documents and data.

(a) Witness Interviews

Witness interviews form the backbone of a factual pre-suit investigation. While many witnesses will ultimately be deposed, do not wait until deposition preparation to sit down with the witnesses in your client's control and explore their knowledge. Early interviews are vital for several reasons.

First, in a business torts case, your client will frequently be an organization and your initial contact will often be with someone in a supervisory role, such as a manager, director, or officer. Often, these individuals will not have first-hand knowledge of the genesis of the problem but will have received reports from subordinates as the matter escalated to them. Much like the child's game of telephone, facts have a way of morphing and evolving as they are conveyed from one human being to another. Accordingly, it is important to speak directly with the actors involved before committing to a version of events in a pleading. In other words, go straight to the source and insist on early access to the individuals who will likely be key players in the litigation. You will find that the perception at the top of a company can differ dramatically from the version of events offered by the people on the ground floor.

Speaking with the actors is also important in a business torts case where industry custom or practice is at issue, such as in an unfair trade practices case. The managers of an organization are required to have vast oversight for all aspects of the business. As a result, they are understandably less familiar

---

8. *See, e.g.,* Pa. Bar Ass'n, Op. 2009-02 (2009) (concluding that fraudulent Facebook friend requests violated Pennsylvania's Professional Responsibility Rules 4.1 and 8.4(c)); N.Y. Bar Ass'n, Op. 843 (2010) (finding that deceptive or misleading friend requests violated ethical rules).

with the nitty-gritty, day-to-day operations. Where these details may be important—such as in establishing a custom or practice—you must speak directly with the people who know how business is conducted in actuality, as opposed to in theory. Frequently, practices may deviate from the written policies of an organization and it will be important to know this early.

Second, speaking with witnesses or actors while events are fresh in their minds is preferable. The passage of time, later events, suggestions from others, or simple memory loss can impact a witness's ability to recollect specific facts accurately. Interviewing people as quickly as possible presents the best chance of accurate recall.

Third, as a practical matter, employees with knowledge may no longer be with the company a year down the road when discovery heats up. It is best to understand the depths of their knowledge while they are still clearly under your control.

Lastly, witness interviews are essential in identifying relevant documents and data. In most cases, a witness interview should include questions related to what types of documents are available to support their story, what documents they are aware of that might be harmful or helpful, and their knowledge of any other data or data systems that may be relevant. Importantly, any witnesses who indicate that they have potentially relevant documents in their possession but have not yet received a litigation hold notice should be sent the litigation hold notice immediately following the interview.

Due to their import, conducting witness interviews should be approached methodically. First, make a list of individuals known to have relevant information. This should contain people identified by your client contact in the preliminary meeting. If your client is a business and you suspect that e-discovery will be a necessity, as it almost always is these days, be sure to include information technology personnel.

In addition to names, the list should contain job titles, affiliations, contact information, and whether the individual is under your control. This will help identify friendly witnesses, hostile witnesses, and third-party witnesses who are likely neutral. Witnesses under your control—i.e., employed by your client—should be easy to schedule for interviews. Third parties may initially be reluctant to become involved but may come around if they understand that they will likely be compelled to testify by subpoena at some point in the future and that this result may be avoided if they speak with you now. It is unlikely that you will have the opportunity to interview any persons affiliated with the opposing side. Indeed, if the opposing side is represented by counsel, you would need to contact him to discuss the possibility.[9] In most situations, counsel will not allow such pre-suit conversations.

Once you have identified witnesses to speak to, develop an interview template or list of questions. You will probably not ask each witness the same questions but there will be considerable overlap. To prepare your questions, consider the types of information needed to prove your claims or defenses. Also, gather relevant background information about each witness as well as facts sufficient to understand their role within the organization. Additionally, in the age of electronic discovery, it is also wise to explore the types of documents, both paper and electronic, that each witness has in their possession or uses as part of their job. When speaking with IT personnel, be sure to ask about the systems used, the locations available to store data, backup tapes, any mobile devices issued by the company, and any data retention policies. If the organization has a data map, collect it as early as possible. If the organization does not, work with the client to create one. You will need to know the location of any relevant data prior to a Rule 26(f) conference or its state court equivalent.

Many people will be nervous when speaking to "the lawyers." To the greatest extent possible, explain to them who you represent and why you are there. This will help them understand what information might be important for you to know, especially in the early stages where you may still not know what precise questions to ask. Bear in mind, however, that the attorney-client privilege may not extend to all of your conversations, particularly with third parties. Research the reach of the privilege in your jurisdiction before having conversations that you would not want to be discoverable.[10]

---

9. *See* MODEL RULES OF PROF'L CONDUCT 4.2 (2013).

10. Edna Selan Epstein's treatise, THE ATTORNEY-CLIENT PRIVILEGE AND THE WORK PRODUCT DOCTRINE (5th ed. 2007), contains helpful discussions regarding the application of the attorney-client privilege and the work product doctrine in a variety of contexts.

After you have conducted your interview, organize your notes in a memo to the file while the interview is still fresh in your mind. Make a note of any areas of follow up, such as names of other individuals who may have knowledge of the facts. In many business torts cases, it is a good practice to create a witness file for each witness. Initially, this file should include your notes from the interview, your memo, and any documents the witness may have provided at the interview.

(b) Identification of Key Documents
In addition to witness interviews, your pre-trial investigation should also focus on identifying relevant documents or other materials. This obviously includes physical, hard copy materials but also encompasses electronically stored information, commonly referred to as "ESI."

While the universe of available relevant materials will vary with the facts of each case, most business torts cases will involve emails, correspondence, contracts, and memoranda. Many others will involve spreadsheets, financial information, technical data, customer information, proprietary databases, and other forensic data, such as computer logs and other electronic access records.

This is an area that cannot be overlooked in the early stages of a matter. E-discovery is costly and time consuming. Many cases hinge on a party's ability to merely survive e-discovery. If e-discovery is going to be a significant part of your case—and it almost always is these days—you need to understand the scope early on so you can advise your client accordingly.

B. Legal Considerations

In addition to a factual investigation, the pre-suit phase of a business torts case should also include a preliminary legal analysis. This aspect of the pre-suit process typically includes identification of the substantive legal issues at play, consideration of any procedural issues that may be important, consideration of the need for expert witnesses, analysis of overall legal strategy, and identification of any challenges or pitfalls.

1. Identification of Substantive Legal Issues

Although it may seem an obvious point, early identification of the key substantive legal issues involved is crucial to success. Indeed, the threshold question to consider is whether the law provides relief for the client's predicament. Particularly in the business torts arena, not every dispute can be remedied through the legal system. When the legal process cannot provide satisfactory relief, it is imperative to advise the client before expending time and energy. Accordingly, it is wise to conduct some preliminary legal research following the initial client meeting.

Where the legal process can be of assistance, further research into the substantive legal doctrines at play is necessary. For plaintiffs, this will include research into all available causes of action and analysis of which ones will withstand a challenge for failure to state a claim. In many instances, the causes of action will be familiar: fraud, misrepresentation, tortious interference with business relations, unfair trade practices, defamation, etc. Depending on the facts of each case, there may also be less obvious causes of action that may provide relief, such as computer crimes or invasion of privacy. Less common causes of action are frequently articulated in state statutes. Also, consider what remedies are available for your client. Is there a cause of action that will allow for recovery of attorneys' fees or punitive damages? Defendants should conduct a similar exercise with an eye toward defenses and possible counterclaims. Although not as extensive, a prepared plaintiff will have undertaken the same exercise in anticipation of the defense. There may be instances in which the cause of action your client wants to bring may provoke a better, stronger counterclaim.

A good practice is to create a memorandum that identifies each cause of action, the elements of each cause of action, and the authority for those elements. This memorandum should also include available defenses, the elements of those defenses, and the authority for those defenses. This memorandum will be helpful in ingraining the important points of law that will govern your entire litigation strategy and will likely be frequent points of conversation with the court and opposing counsel.

At this stage, you will likely happen across more nuanced legal issues related to the manner in which courts interpret certain elements or the

14

proof required to establish an element. Some of these nuances will require immediate exploration, such as considerations related to insufficient pleading or motions to dismiss. Others, such as burden of proof or evidentiary issues, should be noted in the memorandum, but in-depth research likely will be tabled for a later point.

2. Identification of Procedural Issues

Equally important in the early stages of a matter are procedural issues, such as service, personal jurisdiction, venue, and choice of law. These fundamental concepts inform crucial strategy decisions, such as when and where to bring suit or what law to apply. If the parties to an action are both from the same jurisdiction, this will likely be an uncomplicated inquiry. In today's global economy, however, organizations are frequently incorporated or formed in one jurisdiction but have a principal place of business in another and have inserted themselves in the stream of commerce in yet another location. This common situation requires a careful analysis of the applicable long arm statute, minimum contacts, and other personal jurisdiction considerations, such as where a company is incorporated, headquartered, has warehouses, or advertises.[11] Your factual investigation will play a large role in this analysis.

Venue must also be considered. In federal court, venue for a corporate defendant is proper in any judicial district where it is subject to personal jurisdiction, or in a district in which "a substantial part of the events or omissions giving rise to the claim occurred, or a substantial part of property that is the subject of the action is situated."[12] A plaintiff's choice of venue is given substantial deference and can only be overcome "when the private and public interest factors clearly point towards trial in the alternative forum."[13]

The final important procedural issue to consider is the applicable law. While a court may have jurisdiction over the parties, the law of another jurisdiction may apply either as a result of the location of the events giving rise to the injury or by contract. Make sure to consider this issue prior to diving into your substantive analysis since which law applies could impact

---

11. *See* J. McIntyre Machinery, LTD v. Nicastro, 131 S. Ct. 2780 (2011).
12. 28 U.S.C. § 1391(a)–(c) (2011).
13. Piper Aircraft Co. v. Reyno, 454 U.S. 235, 255 (1981).

not only the available causes of action but the availability of prejudgment remedies, statutes of limitations, punitive damages, attorneys' fees, or statutory interest rates.

3. Identification of Likely Expert Witnesses

Many business torts cases will require expert witness testimony to establish liability or damages. Plaintiffs endeavoring to prove forms of negligence, such as breach of fiduciary duty, are likely to need an expert to establish a duty of care. In some jurisdictions, failure to present expert testimony as to the duty of care will result in a directed verdict in favor of the defendant. In other instances, expert testimony may not be required, but may be helpful to the fact finder, such as matters involving a complicated damages analysis or highly technical subject matter.

In addition to testifying experts, consider whether the case merits or requires the use of a consulting, non-testifying expert. Consulting experts are individuals with subject matter expertise who can assist counsel in understanding the nuances of a business or industry. Critically, under the Federal Rules of Evidence, communications between counsel and consulting experts are not discoverable. In many instances, a client can fill this role. However, while cost effective, a client's expertise may be embedded with biased information. Where a completely objective view is essential, hiring a consulting expert may be beneficial.

While many parties will eventually hire an expert, early consultation and retention of experts is key. Where the subject matter is complex, experts can help provide a thorough understanding of the facts at issue, allowing counsel to draft the complaint in a manner likely to withstand a challenge. Experts are also helpful in obtaining preliminary relief, such as preliminary injunctions or prejudgment remedies. Additionally, experts can also assist in focusing early discovery requests, which can result in a more efficient process or even yield information that may support settlement. As a practical matter, early identification of experts avoids the last-minute rush to complete the expert's report and allows your client the best opportunity to obtain the preeminent experts in a given field.

Accordingly, your pre-suit investigation should include the subject matters on which you anticipate needing expert assistance, analysis of whether you will need testifying or consulting experts (or both), as well as the names of potential witnesses.

4. Early Identification of Litigation Strategy
The last step in your pre-suit investigation should be to marshal the facts learned and the legal research performed to develop your overall litigation strategy. This is where you put it all together. Based on everything you have learned about the facts and the law, ask yourself the following questions:

- What is the desired outcome?
- What steps do you need to take to obtain that result?
- What are the strengths of your case?
- What are the weaknesses?
- What steps can you take to address either?

The answers to these questions will guide you in formulating your strategy and provide direction as you progress in the action.

III. DOCUMENTING YOUR EFFORTS

Many attorneys undertake several components of a pre-suit investigation without giving it much thought. We run a few Google searches, we check the elements of tortious interference, but we don't always keep a record of these efforts. Keeping detailed records of your efforts will allow you to develop a case module that centralizes and synthesizes your investigation in a single document. It will also serve as proof that you have not brought a baseless claim should such a challenge be made.

To create this document, keep your notes from each interview and put them in a file for each witness. If your notes are difficult to read, consider using them to draft a memo to the file while the conversation is fresh in your mind. Keep printouts of any internet research you performed, such as land records, dockets, or regulatory filings. Similarly, draft memos for all research performed and print out copies of key cases or statutes that you will need to refer to frequently. This will prevent you from having to duplicate your efforts in the future. Secure any documents gathered in a safe place where you will be able to locate them quickly for production.

The case module that you create based on your investigation and your analysis is attorney work product that is protected by the work product doctrine.[14] Care must be taken to preserve that protection. Accordingly, if you share the case module with your client, instruct them not to share it with any third parties. If the client is an organization, it should not be disseminated beyond the top executives or a control group, where applicable.

---

14.   *See* FED. R. CIV. P. 26(b)(3) (providing that "[o]rdinarily, a party may not discover documents and tangible things that are prepared in anticipation of litigation or for trial by or for another party or its representative" absent a showing of substantial need and undue hardship).

CHAPTER 2

Alternative Dispute Resolution

Hon. Steven Platt (Ret.)
and
Daniel P. Carter

THE DECISION TO EMPLOY ADR

The decision to employ ADR and even the choice of which ADR technique
to employ has often been made before a client comes to you with a business
problem. Parties frequently include dispute resolution clauses in commercial
documents in anticipation that problems may arise in the transaction. In a
perfect world, you would have drafted that clause, and you would know
what to expect and how to proceed. However, parties will often include a
"form" dispute resolution clause or one that they have prepared themselves
without the assistance of counsel or a full understanding of the ramifications of the clause. Thus, in many situations, the parties are bound by and
are often surprised by the parameters of the dispute resolution clause contained in their contract.

Business tort cases arise in many contexts that are neither anticipated
nor governed by a dispute resolution clause in a contract. Examples include
claims of fraud, intentional interference with business relations, malicious
abuse of civil process, and unreasonable use of land cases including nuisance
actions, product liability cases, professional liability, breach of fiduciary duty,
and bad faith claims. These claims and the defenses to them each carry a
unique potential for their own narrative that can develop into drama in the

hands of capable litigators, parties, and witnesses in a forum that favors such a presentation. Therefore, if you have a choice of dispute resolution mechanisms, it is key to keep in mind how your client and any witnesses are likely to present before different types of audiences. Will they naturally make a good impression on a judge or jury? If not, then an arbitration or mediation may be the better choice as it is easier to guide clients and witnesses in the more intimate and less formal ADR setting than in a courtroom.

I. ADR TECHNIQUES

Mediation is very different from litigation, arbitration, neutral case evaluation, and even settlement conferencing. The textbook definition of "mediation" is "a process in which the parties work with one or more impartial mediators, who without providing legal advice, assist the parties in reaching their own voluntary agreement for the resolution of all or part of a dispute."[1] That is different from a "settlement conference" where "the parties, their attorneys or both appear before an impartial individual to discuss the issues and positions of the parties in an attempt to agree on a resolution of all or part of the dispute without a trial."[2] Unlike a "pure facilitative mediation," a settlement conference may, and usually does, include neutral case evaluation and sometimes the impartial individual may recommend the terms of agreement.

The principal difference between a purely facilitative mediation and a mediation in which an impartial individual provides a neutral case evaluation and in many cases suggests possible resolution of the case or dispute lies in the role of the mediator or settlement conference officer. As you can surmise, the evaluative mediator plays an enhanced role similar to a settlement conference officer and is more aggressively involved in the substance of the attempt to resolve the dispute and the terms thereof, whereas the

---

1. Md. R. Proc. 17-102(g) (Definitions). *See also* Ariz. R. Proc. 17B A.R.S./Rule 66(4); Cal. R. Proc. 3.800(2); Colo. Rev. Stat. Ann. § 13-22-302(2.4); Fla. Stat. Ann. § 44.1011(2); Minn. Gen. R. Practice 114.02(7); N.C. Sup. Ct. R. Proc. 11(b)(2);. Vt .Stat. Ann. tit. 12, § 57B(2)

2. Md. R. Proc. 17-102(1) (Definitions). *See also* Ariz. R. Proc. 17B A.R.S. Rule 66(6); Cal. R. Proc. 3.1380; Colo. Rev. Stat. Ann. § 13-22-302(7); Minn. Gen. R. Proc. 114.02(6); N.C. Sup. Ct. Proc. 11(b)(1); Vt. Stat. Ann. tit. 12, § 571.

facilitative mediator is much more focused on the relationship of the parties and facilitating their ability to resolve their case or dispute on their own.

In business tort cases, the dispute resolution techniques most often effectively used are evaluative mediation or even settlement conferencing. The reasons are readily apparent and largely are driven by the relative transactional costs of each process. A purely facilitative mediation will always take longer and therefore cost more than an evaluative mediation because these disputes usually involve significant financial stakes that often overwhelm whatever business or even personal relationship the parties may have had or could have in the future. To resolve the dispute, the economic, psychological, and legal reality and the associated risk have to be addressed directly and assessed credibly by a neutral whose opinion will be respected by all parties and their counsel.

Parties also use "med/arb" and neutral case evaluation. "Med/Arb" is a technique in which mediators or settlement conferencing is initially utilized to resolve as many issues as possible with the remaining unresolved issues and the case itself being decided by arbitration where mediation ends in an impasse. This technique is usually invoked as a result of a contractual provision or at the suggestion of the parties and counsel to save the costs of litigating or arbitrating all of the issues.

Neutral case evaluation is just what its name suggests—"a process in which the parties, their attorneys or both appear before an impartial evaluator and present in summary fashion the evidence and legal arguments to support their respective positions and the evaluator renders an evaluation of their positions and an opinion as to the likely outcome of the litigation."[3] *Caveat Emptor*—When utilizing the technique of neutral case evaluation be very careful about who is selected to perform the neutral case evaluation. The result can be very different based on the person's background. A judge or retired judge will see a case from a very different perspective than a "neutral expert," defined as an "individual with special expertise to

---

3. Maryland Rule of Procedure 17-102(i) (Definitions); *see also* Arizona Rule of Procedure 17B A.R.S. Rule 66(6); California Rule of Procedure Rule 3.1380; COLO. REV. STAT. ANN. § 13-22-302(7); North Carolina Superior Court of Procedure 11(b)(1); Minnesota General Rules of Procedure 114.02(6); Vermont Rule of Procedure VT. STAT. ANN. tit. 12, § 5713(4).

provide impartial technical background information, an impartial opinion or both in a specific area." Examples of such "neutral experts" include forensic accountants, business evaluators and analysts, or even other litigators whose practices are confined to business tort cases.

Now having concluded our quick survey of ADR techniques, the rest of this chapter focuses on the two ADR techniques most often utilized in business tort disputes—mediation and arbitration.

II. MEDIATION
A. When, and When Not, to Mediate

When should you advise your client to mediate? There are essentially two situations that suggest that mediation might be in order: (1) Do you have a claim or dispute where the parties need a resolution and are currently at an impasse? and/or (2) Do you have a case where the parties need help in structuring a resolution for both short term and long term business and economic purposes? If the answer to both those questions is "yes," then the next question becomes really important in a business tort case. That question is: Are all of the necessary parties in the case and will they be at the table negotiating if mediation goes forward? If the answer to those questions is all affirmative, then mediation has the greatest chance to be successful.

Perhaps a better question or at least an equally important question to ask is when should you *not* mediate a business tort case. The answer to that question is when any of the following factors are present:

1. You and your client lack the information, intelligence, or skills necessary to value your case.
2. Your client is not commercially or economically rational.
3. Your adversary cannot value your case or his own and/or is not commercially or economically rational. Furthermore neither you nor the mediator can educate him or her to the extent necessary to mediate effectively.
4. Necessary parties are not in the case and/or at the negotiating table. Necessary parties may include insurance companies, subcontractors, and others with third-party liability exposure. They may also include parties with insurance coverage issues, indemnification and

contribution issues, and carriers operating under reservations of rights. Simply because these issues are there does not necessarily preclude mediating, but if they produce a refusal to negotiate in good faith the mediation will at best be problematical and at worst pointless.

B. Choosing a Mediator

You have now made a decision to mediate. The most important decision you will now make is choosing the mediator. In fact, this decision is no less important than the decision whether to mediate at all. What are the criteria for selecting the right mediator? The correct answer is the lawyer's classic answer: It depends! The one constant of course is a reputation for intelligence and integrity, which of course at a minimum means a conflicts check. Your selection process also should include personal referrals and references, websites, and organizational listservs of other business tort litigators on both sides of the courtroom and the industry.

You and your client should determine whether including subject-matter expertise as a criterion for your selection process is desirable and, if so, how important is it vis-a-vis a "mediator mind-set." What technique, i.e., analytical, evaluative, facilitative, or transformative, does the prospective mediator employ? Finally, you may wish to interview the prospective mediator and inquire further by examining his/her writing and speaking activities on the subject or issues that may arise during the mediation of your business tort case.

Unfortunately, you and your client may not have the option of participating in choosing the individual who will "mediate" your business tort cases. Since the mid-1990s, various state courts of general jurisdiction, as well as almost all federal district courts, have developed their own "mediation" services or programs. These services or programs vary in structure and personnel from state to state and even county to county or city. Some utilize a combination of retired judges, sitting judges, and practitioners. Others use only retired judges or only practitioners who work at a pre-set rate of compensation for a limited amount of time. The quality of the mediation services rendered and the training and skills of the personnel delivering those services varies dramatically from program to program. There are too many different business models to describe in the space available in this chapter.

23

These programs do, however, have certain policies and procedures in common that have developed for historical, political, and even legal reasons. Most have "opt out" provisions in their program, policies, and procedures. Almost all have "substitution" procedures. These policies and procedures, however, are not readily apparent and never appear on the court order or the notice that "requires" you and your client to "mediate." Competent and attentive counsel should familiarize themselves with each of the policies and procedures governing their participation in these programs in the jurisdictions in which they practice so they can be utilized, when necessary, to save your time and your client's time and money. The information is usually available on the court's website or a brochure where its program or service is described but alas, it may well be buried in the fine print.

The alternative may be your participation in a process that can only be called "mediation" or even a "settlement conference" for charitable reasons because it is conducted by a mediator who is distinguished only by a lack of both knowledge and experience with your business tort case and whose time with your case is programmatically limited in a manner that in effect structures failure. Your client and you deserve better.

C. Preparation for Mediation/Settlement Conference vs. Preparation for Litigation or Arbitration

Effectively preparing for a mediation/settlement conference is not the same process as preparing to litigate or arbitrate. Remember, what you are trying to do is settle your case, not win it. That means you should be preparing to assist the mediator in persuading the opposing party, not a third party, judge, jury, or even arbitrator, to better understand your side of the case and ultimately based thereon to accept your terms for resolving those issues and the case itself. If that is not what you are trying to do, then you and your client should not have agreed to mediate.

That means that value attaches to ideas, not advocacy. It means that your analysis is sound and persuasive enough to dominate the discussion.

It has often been said when training litigators—"Do not play in the other guy's analytical ballpark." Well, in a mediation you do play in the other guy's analytical ballpark, and you prepare your client for that by explaining the process. You are trying to assist the mediator in his/her effort to

24

persuade the adverse party, its lawyer, and/or insurance adjuster, CPA, etc., of the wisdom and leveraged fairness of your position. In doing so, you illustrate the advantages of client control of the outcome of the case versus third-party control, e.g., more measured and nuanced results, business solutions to problems, and the minimization of litigation costs and business opportunities lost. That education should result in the client having a better understanding that what the client is owed is not necessarily the same as what he/she can get because of transaction and litigation costs.

D. Conduct of the Mediation/Settlement Conference

You begin the process by providing the mediator with a confidential pre-mediation statement that includes a candid assessment of the strengths and the weaknesses of your case, as well as suggestions for settlement that create a positive context for negotiators. Once you start the mediation, always remember that effective advocacy in a mediation is not the same as effective advocacy in litigation or even arbitration for the reasons explained earlier.

There are several principles to remember as the negotiations proceed throughout the day. First, unlike in a courtroom—drama is usually not helpful. Economics usually trumps law, and an effective litigation strategy will not necessarily be an effective mediation strategy. In fact, it usually isn't.

Other negotiating lessons learned by this writer are position-based bargaining almost never works with intelligent, experienced negotiators on the other side; the "economics of the case" do not always correspond to the "legal merits of the case." Finally, provide insight to the mediator of "personality issues" if you think they are adversely affecting the mediation and assume opposing counsel is doing the same thing you are, *but you do it better*!

E. Confidentiality and Other Ethical Considerations and Constraints on Counsel and Mediators

In every state, federal courts, and in most foreign countries where mediation is utilized, the mediator and any person present or otherwise participating in a mediation must maintain the confidentiality of all "mediation communications." This usually precludes parties, counsel, and the mediator(s) from disclosing or being compelled to disclose "mediation communications" in any judicial or other proceeding. There are certain almost universal exceptions to this generally accepted rule including when disclosure is necessary to avoid the risk of serious bodily injury or death and when these communications are relevant to assertions of or defenses to allegations of mediator misconduct, negligence, fraud, duress, or misrepresentation.

In addition, no threats of criminal law charges or professional ethics violations by either the parties or their counsel can be ethically raised to leverage negotiations. This ethical constraint can at times butt up against factual or legal reality, particularly where the mediator becomes aware of possible professional misconduct even if not directly related to the merits of the business tort case. This professional misconduct, if reported, could cost one or more of the parties and/or their counsel their license but is best described as "collateral" to the case itself. Nevertheless, this information or allegation in many cases is likely to be discovered and disclosed to law enforcement authorities and/or professional regulators if the case to which it is only peripherally related is litigated rather than mediated successfully and resolved.

This type of situation can arise and does more often than one would suspect. When it does, it presents a dilemma for the mediator and for the parties and counsel. That dilemma has never been satisfactorily resolved in the literature because it involves potentially conflicting ethical considerations. Suffice it to say here, you should recognize it when you see it and proceed with caution.

III. ARBITRATION

Arbitration is an adjudicatory process outside of the court system where one or more arbitrators decide a dispute based upon the submissions of the parties. The decision or award is binding upon the parties by the parties' prior agreement.[4] The process may be formal or relaxed depending

---

4. There are two other forms of arbitration, non-binding and compulsory, which will be considered later in the chapter.

upon the arbitrator or arbitrators and the rules by which the arbitration will be conducted.

Arbitration is for the most part a creature of contract and rules may vary. If a specific arbitration body is specified in the parties' agreement, such as the American Arbitration Association (the "AAA"), its rules will control.[5] If there is flexibility in the arbitration agreement or if the agreement is silent, the parties may select a specific entity or its own set of rules for the process. The arbitration agreement may specify a set of rules that will govern without requiring submission of the dispute to a specific body. For instance, parties may agree that a three-person arbitration panel of their selection will conduct the matter under the rules of the AAA. If the parties do not agree in advance to a specific set of rules, they will need to reach agreement as to the rules to be applied.

As demonstrated in the Federal Arbitration Act[6] (the "FAA") and decisions of the U.S. Supreme Court,[7] federal law has a policy favoring arbitration and the enforcement of arbitral awards. The majority of the states also have some type of arbitration statute, many of which are patterned after the Uniform Arbitration Act or the Revised Uniform Arbitration Act.[8]

Whatever the source of the rules, be sure that costs, procedures, rules of evidence, time and place of the arbitration, type of award, and any other matter that is important to a proper adjudication are set forth, understood, and agreed upon by the parties. These decisions should be made at the outset rather than after arbitration has commenced. It is better to agree in advance to important matters and leave open the possibility of a modification by later agreement of the parties than to never have reached an agreement at all.

Binding arbitration is the most prevalent form of arbitration in the United States. It is also employed internationally. Parties that have agreed to binding arbitration have agreed to adjudication by arbitration and to be bound by the decision. The arbitrator hears the parties' evidence and then renders a

---

5. There are numerous entities that administer arbitrations and most have proprietary rules that are followed.

6. 9 U.S.C. § 1 et seq.

7. *See generally* Prima Pain Corp. v. Flood and Conklin Mfg. Co., 388 U.S. 395 (1967); Southland Corp. v. Keating, 465 U.S. 1 (1984).

8. Please refer to the Appendix for citations.

decision that is legally binding upon the parties and enforceable by a court of proper jurisdiction. As noted above, federal and state courts have statutes for enforcing arbitral awards.

Arbitration is a substitution for the judicial process designed to avoid the time and expense of traditional civil litigation, as well as the perceived biases of judges and juries in certain types of commercial cases. While arbitration is generally successful in shortening the time to resolve the matter and in mitigating perceived biases, it often fails to achieve the goal of reducing expenses.

Legal fees are still the lion's share of arbitration expenses. The lawyers still must review evidence, prepare witnesses, engage experts where appropriate, and otherwise prepare the case as they would for trial. The cost of motions practice is where there is usually a savings. Depending on the governing rules, there is very little motion practice in arbitration. When there is such a procedure, replies and sur-replies can be minimized and often the hearings can be done electronically. Schedules can for the most part be arranged so there is not as much "stop and start" of proceedings as in the court system. It is much easier to control legal fees in an arbitration setting than a trial setting as there are fewer surprises.

The professional fees for the arbitrator are set by the rules of the governing dispute resolution organization such as the AAA. It will specify the costs of the administration of the arbitration itself, which can be tied to the amount in controversy, complexity or type of case, the number of arbitrators, and the number of parties involved. In these instances, most of the administrative costs are equally divided between the parties. The fees for the arbitrator or arbitrators are determined the same way absent fee shifting provisions in the governing contract or rules of a provider organization governing the arbitration.

Parties may be better able to control the costs of arbitration when they structure the administration of the arbitration by agreement as opposed to submitting the dispute to the AAA or another dispute resolution organization. Notwithstanding the greater control over the costs, the parties face more exposure to incurring costs related to the selection of the arbitrator and the individual counsel's legal staff for administrative costs. For example, where the parties self-administer the arbitration and have chosen to have the dispute decided by a three-person panel, each party will generally be responsible to pay the fees of its selected arbitrator and to divide the fees of the third neutral arbitrator selected by the other arbitrators.

Statute-controlled arbitration, be it state or federal, usually has its own specific method of cost allocation. Each party should be aware of that process and research which method is applicable in the venue of the arbitration. In foreign arbitrations, arbitrators' fees are often determined by the amount in controversy, which is determined by the arbitrators themselves rather than the parties. Parties should also be aware that some foreign jurisdictions also have "loser pays" provisions.[9] As noted above, the amount of time lawyers must spend on preparing for arbitration is not unlike the amount of time necessary to prepare for trial. Cost savings may be realized, however, because arbitration procedures generally involve fewer case management conferences and other types of routine appearances as well as more limited motions practice.

The client's resource exposure can be controlled much easier in arbitration. Specifying the issues in a dispute leads to more concise discovery requests. Further, the form of these tasks also can be performed in a way to minimize business disruptions as the parties have a greater flexibility in setting deadlines.

Many jurisdictions do not have compulsory arbitration in the absence of an agreement by the parties. Pennsylvania is an exception. Under Pennsylvania statute, arbitration is required for certain types of cases based upon specific amounts in controversy.[10] Other jurisdictions requiring compulsory arbitration have similar statutes governing the proceedings. In these jurisdictions, no additional costs are assessed to the parties other than the initial filing fees.

Sometimes during the course of conventional litigation, a court may order arbitration and will have specific rules and procedures for it. In most instances, court-ordered arbitration is non-binding or provides a mechanism

---

9. *See, e.g.*, German Institute of Arbitration, DIS–Arbitration Rules 98.
10. *See* 42 PA. CONS. STAT. § 7361.

for trial *de novo*. In court-ordered arbitrations, the arbitrators are hired by the courts and the parties usually are not responsible for their fees.

The factors to be considered to determine whether to arbitrate are often the same factors as those considered to determine whether to mediate. However, the parties may not have a choice regarding arbitration or mediation if their contract contains a compulsory dispute resolution clause resolution by one or more ADR mechanisms. The parties may waive the dispute resolution clause, but waiver is generally the exception rather than the rule. Also, a dispute resolution clause will not be binding upon a party who has not agreed to be bound by it. If this party is indispensable and refuses to participate in the ADR procedures set forth in the dispute resolution clause, then the parties to the dispute resolution clause may be forced to resolve their dispute in court to bind the indispensable party.

A. Choosing an Arbitrator

Choosing an arbitrator or arbitrators is the key to the process. When working within the structure of a dispute resolution organization such as the AAA, the arbitrators must be chosen from a list of arbitrators pre-approved by that organization. Some clients may prefer to have the potential arbitrators chosen this way. However, other clients may prefer not to be limited in their selection of an arbitrator by an organization's pre-approved list. When the parties are selecting an arbitrator from their own resources, the field is much wider.

Regardless of which method of selecting arbitrators is used, the factors for choosing the arbitrator are the same. For the most part, arbitrators in commercial matters will be members of the bar, practicing attorneys, or retired members of the judiciary. In cases involving highly technical issues in manufacturing, pharmaceuticals, or construction, a non-attorney arbitrator with expertise in the relevant field may be employed. This individual ideally should have arbitration experience working with legally trained panels. The person is almost the panel's expert.

In selecting the arbitrators, one should investigate the potential arbitrator as thoroughly as possible. Conflicts are the starting point. Has the individual ever worked for a competitor? Does the individual know any of the parties, lawyers, or witnesses in any way other than professionally?

What has the individual written in the area? Has the individual testified on matters relating to the case? Be sure the arbitrator is experienced and well qualified in the issues of the controversy. A patent attorney will not be of much use in an accounting malpractice case.

Whenever possible and practical, check with colleagues who have had experience with the potential arbitrator. Find out about his or her demeanor, what types of clients he or she has represented, and as much about the individual's career and practice as you can. Be as thorough as possible and discuss the choice with your client so that the client can have as much input as needed.

Often, you are confined by the arbitration agreement as to whether you will have a panel or single arbitrator. A single arbitrator usually has a cost advantage since the parties are dividing the cost of one arbitrator as opposed to paying for three arbitrators. Depending on the length of the arbitration, this can become a significant cost factor, as each hour is three times more expensive.

Generally speaking, a single arbitrator will more likely render an award in favor of one or the other party, whereas a panel may be more likely to be more "Solomonesque" in its award. But if your experience says otherwise, go with your experience. With a single arbitrator, you will need to persuade only one person of the merits of your position whereas with the three-person panel you will need to persuade at least two of them that your position is correct. On the other hand, the other side faces the same challenges and potential benefits. A one-person panel may be more risky, especially if that arbitrator is more likely to be sympathetic to your opponent. With a complicated case that involves issues from different disciplines or types of issues, one is more likely to get the necessary experience and expertise with a panel rather than one arbitrator. Regardless of whether you are dealing with a single arbitrator or a panel, in your selection process you should have discovered the strengths, weaknesses, likes, and dislikes of the arbitrator(s), and you should tailor your presentations, evidence, and witnesses to the strengths, weaknesses, likes, and dislikes discovered during this process.

An important factor to consider before you begin the process of selecting the arbitrator(s) is to be sure there is a mechanism in place in case of a deadlock. The AAA has such a mechanism if the parties cannot agree. A default selection mechanism is necessary but should be avoided if at all possible. In selection you may have to reach out to colleagues or have those colleagues refer you to someone who has experience with an individual to help you make your decision.

If not specified in the arbitration agreement the parties should, in advance, agree upon the procedural rules that will apply to the arbitration. The Federal Rules of Civil Procedure are often used as the default rules. Depending upon the nature of the dispute and the location of the parties, parties should reach an agreement as to the choice of substantive law to be applied. If the parties cannot agree, then the issue must be decided by the arbitrators based on conflicts of laws principles.

The parties should also reach an agreement on the location of the arbitration if it is not set forth in the arbitration agreement. Ideally, the parties should attempt to reach a reasonable agreement that does not overburden one party over another. Enlist the arbitrator if need be.

B. The Type of Award

If the arbitration award is required to be in writing, the award can be as simple as a finding in favor of the plaintiff for "x" dollars or in favor of the defendant and no damages. This will meet most requirements for a written award. In most commercial arbitrations, however, the parties will want the arbitrators to issue a "reasoned award" or written findings of fact and conclusions of law. The form in which the arbitrators issue the written award should be decided before the arbitration commences.

A "reasoned award" is similar to a judicial opinion. The arbitrators, upon receiving closing briefs from the parties, prepare an opinion that sets forth their award and the reasoning, based upon the law and evidence. Findings of fact and conclusions of law are usually prepared after the hearing and after both sides submit their own proposed findings of fact and conclusions of law for the panel's consideration.

While both of these types of written awards add time and expense to the arbitration, they both give the process more credibility. In some scenarios, such awards may give the parties a basis to set aside an award if the requirements for such an action are present, as discussed in greater detail below.

The costs for arbitration with an organization such as the AAA are set forth in its rules. Administrative costs are shared as are those for the arbitrator or arbitrators. The parties bear their own costs for witnesses, discovery, and travel, much like for regular trial. If a neutral site is selected for the arbitration such as a separate facility, those costs are also divided evenly between the parties.

When the parties craft their own procedure costs are also evenly divided or arranged in some other way that they agree upon. Individual case costs are borne by each party.

C. Conduct of the Arbitration

As stated above, the parties should agree in advance on the procedural and evidentiary rules for the arbitration. Authentication procedures can be relaxed for documentary, physical, and electronic evidence as long as the parties have so agreed. Sometimes the arbitrator will decide.

Discovery plays an important part in any type of dispute resolution. The parties should decide in advance whether state or federal rules will be applied. It must be remembered that arbitration is primarily a creature of contract, and the parties can agree to any type of discovery they wish among themselves. When it comes to third-party discovery, the parties must look to local laws.[11] It is not as easy as one would think. Fees and costs as to witnesses are usually determined by rules of the state or federal district in which the arbitration will take place.

Effective arbitrators ask questions and may even want to question witnesses themselves. This should be encouraged. Remember, this is *alternative* dispute resolution and there are alternative procedures within it.

There may be post-arbitration submissions. These are requested by the arbitrators or requested by the parties as an aid to the decision-making

---

11. The Third Circuit addressed the issue in *Hay Group, Inc. v. E.B.S. Acquisitions Corporation*, 360 F.3d 404 (3d Cir. 2004), narrowly interpreting the FAA by limiting the subpoena power of a panel to compelling attendance at the arbitration. The Pennsylvania Arbitration Act is broader providing that arbitrators may issue subpoenas. 42 PA. CONS. STAT. §§ 7301–7320. The power is discretionary, however. Cotterman v. Allstate Ins. Co., 666 A.2d 695 (Pa. Super. Ct. 1995). The Ohio Act grants the subpoena authority to the arbitrators as well. OHIO REV. CODE § 2711.06.

process. The arbitrators often give suggestions as to what they want, which should be heeded.

Binding arbitration is just that, binding. There is no appeal. However, there can be procedures to set aside awards that are usually set forth in a governing statute. Since arbitration is favored by the courts, the reasons for setting aside an award are narrow. The most common reasons are fraud; fundamental discord with the prevailing law; or the arbitrators exceeded their powers.[12] Such a challenge is not an easy undertaking and, frankly, usually fruitless.

D. Preparing the Client for Arbitration

You should make sure that your client understands the procedure. The client should not experience any surprises as to the procedure. While there may be surprises in the evidence or in rulings by the panel, there should not be anything unexpected about procedure.

Prepare the client as you would for a bench trial. Review the case's strengths and weaknesses so that you, the client, and the witnesses can present the case to the panel in the best possible light.

Remember there is nothing preventing settlement negotiations during an arbitration and counsel as well as the client should be prepared if the opportunity presents itself.

---

12. The Supreme Court limited grounds for vacating an arbitration award in *Hall Street Associates, LLC v. Mattel, Inc.*, 552 U.S. 576 (2008). Grounds for overturning an award are very idiosyncratic to the jurisdiction as well as to the type of arbitration and one should research before one attempts to set an award aside.

APPENDIX

STATE ARBITRATION STATUTES

1. Alabama: Ala. Code § 6-6-1 et seq.
2. Alaska: Alaska Stat. § 09.43.010 et seq.
3. Arizona: Ariz. Rev. Stat. Ann. § 12-1501 et seq.
4. Arkansas: Ark. Stat. Ann. § 16-108-101 et seq.
5. California: Cal. Civ. Proc. Code § 1280 et seq.
6. Colorado: Col. Rev. Stat. § 13-22-201 et seq.
7. Connecticut: Conn. Gen. Stat. Ann. § 52-408 et seq.
8. Delaware: Del. Code Ann. tit. 10, § 5701 et seq.
9. District of Columbia: D.C. Code Ann. § 16-4301 et seq.
10. Florida: Fla. Stat. Ann. § 682.01 et seq.
11. Georgia: Ga. Code § 9-9-1 et seq.
12. Hawaii: Haw. Rev. Stat. § 658-1 et seq.
13. Idaho: Idaho Code § 7-901 et seq.
14. Illinois: 710 Ill. Comp. Stat. 5/1 et seq. (formerly Ill. Rev. Stat. ch. 10, § 101 et seq.)
15. Indiana: Ind. Code Ann. § 34-4-2-1 et seq.
16. Iowa: Iowa Code § 679A.1 et seq.
17. Kansas: Kan. Stat. Ann. § 5-401 et seq.
18. Kentucky: Ky. Rev. Stat. Ann. § 417.045 et seq.
19. Louisiana: La. Rev. Stat. Ann. § 9:4201 et seq.
20. Maine: Me. Rev. Stat. Ann. tit. 14, § 5927 et seq.
21. Maryland: Md. Code Ann., Cts. & Jud. Proc. § 3-201 et seq.
22. Massachusetts: Mass. Ann. Laws ch. 251, § 1 et seq.
23. Michigan: Mich. Stat. Ann. § 27A.5001 et seq.; Mich. Comp. Laws § 600.5001 et seq.
24. Minnesota: Minn. Stat. Ann. § 572.08 et seq.

25. Mississippi: Miss. Code Ann. § 11-15-1 et seq.
26. Missouri: Mo. Ann. Stat. § 435.350 et seq.
27. Montana: Mont. Code Ann. § 27-5-111 et seq.
28. Nebraska: Neb. Rev. Stat. § 25-2601 et seq.
29. Nevada: Nev. Rev. Stat. § 38.015 et seq.
30. New Hampshire: N.H. Rev. Stat. Ann. § 542:1 et seq.
31. New Jersey: N.J. Stat. Ann. § 2A:24–1 et seq.
32. New Mexico: N.M. Stat. Ann. § 44-7-1 et seq.
33. New York: N.Y. Civ. Prac. Law § 7501 et seq.
34. North Carolina: N.C. Gen. Stat. § 1-567.1 et seq.
35. North Dakota: N.D. Cent. Code § 32-29.2-01 et seq.
36. Ohio: Ohio Rev. Code Ann. § 2711.01 et seq.
37. Oklahoma: Okla. Stat. Ann. tit. 15, § 801 et seq.
38. Oregon: Or. Rev. Stat. § 36.300 et seq.
39. Pennsylvania: 42 Pa. Stat. Ann. § 7301 et seq.
40. Puerto Rico: P.R. Laws Ann., tit. 32, § 3201 et seq.
41. Rhode Island: R.I. Gen. Laws § 10-3-1 et seq.
42. South Carolina: S.C. Code Ann. § 15-48-10 et seq.
43. South Dakota: S.D. Codified Laws § 21-25A-1 et seq.
44. Tennessee: Tenn. Code Ann. § 29-5-301 et seq.
45. Texas: Tex. Rev. Civ. Stat. Ann. art. 224 et seq.
46. Utah: Utah Code Ann. § 78-31a-1 et seq.
47. Vermont: Vt. Stat. Ann tit. 12, § 5651 et seq.
48. Virginia: Va. Code § 8.01-577 et seq.
49. Washington: Wash. Rev. Code Ann. § 7.04.010 et seq.
50. West Virginia: W. Va. Code § 55–10–1 et seq.
51. Wisconsin: Wis. Stat. Ann. § 788.01 et seq.
52. Wyoming: Wyo. Stat. § 1-36-101 et seq.

CHAPTER 3

The Complaint

Daniel D. Quick

I. DEFINE THE OBJECTIVES OF THE COMPLAINT

The complaint is a tool. There are certain baseline requirements for the tool, spelled out in the rules of civil procedure or court rules, fleshed out by case law. Beyond these required elements, the shape, contours, and tenor of the complaint are determined by strategic considerations. While every now and then lawyers get tripped up on the formalities, the artistry of crafting a complaint to achieve strategic goals presents a career-long arc for refinement and polishing.

Thus, the strategic purpose of the lawsuit must first be defined and considered before one can craft a pleading to fulfill that goal. Within the question of "why are you suing?" lie several distinct questions: (1) What wrong has occurred for which your client seeks redress? (2) Can redress be achieved through litigation? and (3) Is seeking redress through litigation the optimal and desired strategy for your client?

Starting with the harm that has befallen your client often helps clarify strategic goals. Is the harm more to one's ego than to one's true interests? Is the litigation being pursued not so much for harm done but rather ulterior business motives? Of course, consideration of the harm inevitably leads to consideration of the causes of action implicated by the wrongful conduct, but by focusing upon the harm, oftentimes clarity is achieved on all that follows—both what claims are pled as well as how the case is litigated. For example, a jilted minority shareholder will convey his or her reaction to and harm caused by being squeezed out in layman's terms; it is for the lawyer to first understand and then navigate the tricky lines between direct claims, derivative claims, breach of fiduciary duty, and minority shareholder oppression claims.

Focusing first on the harm brings clarity to that thought process. Moreover, focusing first upon the harm aligns the attorney's thinking with that of the client. After all, the clients oftentimes do not conceptualize legal causes of action, but rather first engage with counsel because of some perceived harm that has befallen them. By identifying and focusing upon the harm, the lawyer does not let the litigation become the proverbial tail wagging the dog, but rather aligns the interests of the litigation with that of the client.

The second question—whether redress may be achieved through litigation—is often one overlooked by both client and lawyer. There are really two considerations here: whether there is technically, or legally, redress available for the harm committed; and whether, practically, a good result is possible. The first consideration is the creative lawyer's stock in trade, and the remainder of this book shall help elucidate the right tool for the job. Too often the lawyer, perhaps hoping not to incur costs early in the process, falls back upon old reliable causes of action. While sometimes there is no magic to the process, and the claim is of some standard variety, your creative consideration of claims up front may take the case in an entirely different and more advantageous direction. Or perhaps some preliminary step—such as a shareholder request for books and records before simply filing a lawsuit for breach of fiduciary duty—will help place your client in a superior position.

The second aspect, practical likelihood of success, is more of a judgment borne of experience. There are some aspects of this on which a little investigation would shed light, such as the collectability of the potential defendant, or the particular court's record of granting the relief that your client desires. But you must also make judgment calls as to how much resistance you are likely to encounter from the putative defendants, the amount of time to resolution (and whether, by then, resolution is of a different nature or of lesser value), and a panoply of other factors all going to whether what seems like such a great plan the day you file the complaint turns to ashes by the time you receive your judgment.

The third question—whether the seeking of redress through litigation is the optimal and desired strategy for your client—is a multi-faceted, complex question. Too often lawyers serve as dutiful soldiers, happy to march up a hill with a spear, but shirk their duties as counselors, advising clients when a desired strategy is no longer ideal or achievable. Sometimes this results from inadequate knowledge of the client's overall business and goals or a pushy client, hell-bent on litigation. Yet the lawyer who ignores that little voice whispering ill omens usually only puts off the moment of reckoning with the client. Confident advice early in the process, or even before the lawsuit is filed, is the best client service a lawyer may offer. Sometimes litigation truly is the last, best option. Yet too often clients, either from lack of experience or emotion, forget the apt definition provided by Ambrose Bierce: "Litigation: a machine which you go into as a pig and come out as a sausage." The lawyer's goal is to prevent the client from becoming sausage while aggressively protecting the client's interests and working to achieve the client's goals, all within the proper and practical boundaries of our judicial system. A small list of issues to consider includes:

- Likelihood of success on the merits relative to relief to be achieved;
- Consideration of costs, client time, and distraction relative to the harm committed and likely remedy;
- The potential of counter- or third-party claims, with their attendant additional cost, parties, and risk;
- Indirect fallout from the decision to sue (e.g., burning bridges in a necessary supply arrangement; likelihood of third parties either learning of or being dragged into the litigation; media coverage; the potential impact of a loss or, worse yet, establishing some legal precedent injurious to your client's long term interests); and
- The "message sending" aspect of the litigation—whether to other employees by suing the departed employee on a non-compete agreement, or market actors when you sue an infringer for the violation of intellectual property rights. The issue here really is harmonizing the goals of the litigation with broader, entity-wide goals, as opposed to having the litigation either act at cross-purposes or proceed as someone's personal vendetta.

39

II. FILING THE COMPLAINT WITH PRELIMINARY RELIEF REQUESTED

There are cases where a perfunctory complaint is perfectly serviceable; it need do no more than satisfy the notice pleading requirements, enumerate the parties and causes of action, and omit most narration. However, filing a complaint along with some form of preliminary relief usually changes the nature and tenor of the complaint. Oftentimes a verified complaint will serve double duty as the factual basis for a motion for preliminary injunction or an ex parte seizure order. As a result, the complaint may end up being more narrative than technically required. And even where the facts are set forth outside of the complaint (e.g., a supporting affidavit), the necessity of moving for preliminary relief should still force changes in the pleading.

First, the decision to move for preliminary relief usually means that the case—from its factual predicates to its legal underpinnings—will garner more up-front attention from the plaintiff, defendant, and the court than might otherwise be the case. This presents both opportunity and peril. A well-conceived complaint can set the table for the rest of the litigation; the court will view the case through the rubric you have provided, thus granting you a significant advantage in the tussles to come, regardless of the outcome on the initial motion. In contrast, the pursuit of preliminary relief may expose early in the process any flaws in either the facts or the law supporting the complaint, and deal a near-fatal blow to a plaintiff. This is the case even where the flaw is not spotted immediately. There are often cases where an aggressive plaintiff fires both barrels early in the case, and might even procure some form of injunction or other preliminary relief. By granting that relief, the court relies upon the veracity and legal position advanced by the plaintiff. Should it subsequently turn out that plaintiff's position was not quite as initially presented, the entire process can boomerang, with the judge irked (or worse) at having become complicit in an undertaking that, it turns out, is not well supported.

Second, the fact that some early relief shall be sought from the court requires careful consideration as to the ultimate relief being sought in the complaint. The plaintiff must be prepared to move forward with or without the preliminary relief sought. There are some instances where the preliminary motion may well decide the entire case, either legally or practically

40

(the non-compete case is frequently an example). But with forethought, a plaintiff who loses a preliminary motion can still convey a position of determination and strength. Only the plaintiff who places all of its eggs in the preliminary basket risks the loss of credibility by losing the initial motion.

Here are some additional factors to keep in mind when coupling a complaint with a preliminary motion:

- Develop the complaint with the motion so they are harmonious in tone and factual allegations.
- Take extra pains to plead foundational issues with specificity, such as the basis for subject matter or personal jurisdiction, so the court may tick off those prerequisites before getting to the substance of your motion.
- Do not feel constrained from pleading alternative counts as you normally would, even though those counts may not be featured in your motion. Those counts may take on added import after the parties hash out the issues during the motion practice.
- It is perfectly acceptable to stick with a minimalist complaint and then flesh out details in an affidavit supporting your motion, so long as the tone, claims, and averments remain harmonious. This might even provide added room to pivot based upon what happens with the initial motion.
- After the initial motion hearing, consider amending either to eliminate claims now too peripheral or to add other claims or parties.

III. ARBITRAL DEMAND VS. LITIGATION COMPLAINT

There are few technical differences between the arbitral demand and the litigation complaint. If anything, technical pleading standards are reduced in arbitration. The Commercial Litigation Rules of the American Arbitration Association provide that a demand "shall contain a statement setting forth the nature of the dispute, the names and addresses of all other parties, the amount involved, if any, the remedy sought, and the hearing locale requested." (AAA CAR 4(a)). The real touchstone appears later in the rule: "(d) When filing any statement pursuant to this section, the parties are encouraged to provide descriptions of their claims in sufficient detail to make the circumstances of the dispute clear to the arbitrator."

What this means is that in arbitration you are writing for the arbitrator, not opposing counsel. As a result, arbitration claims are often more narrative than court pleadings; this author recently received a claim that was 104 pages. Similarly, given the perception that equity is a stronger force in arbitration than legalities, oftentimes there is only a minimal pleading of required elements for the causes of action. Whether arbitration truly is more pre-disposed to Solomonic justice is a topic for another book. But regardless of how much truth there is in that conventional wisdom, given that the arbitrator will likely read the claim carefully, it remains a best practice to "tell your story" in the claim. Of course, doing so carries its own peril, as it locks you in to a narrative early in the case. Lastly, one might take greater care to spell out the requested relief in an arbitration claim. A complaint typically includes a vague ad damnum. In arbitration, the arbitrator will want to know up front what it is you want from the process should you prevail.

In some instances, the practitioner should be mindful of practices unique to the arbitral forum. There are certain customs and best practices that have evolved around specialty arbitral bodies, such as FINRA or the ICC, and counsel should consider and incorporate them.

IV. SELECTING THE FORUM
A. State vs. Federal

Like in any litigation, sometimes there are federal claims that will mandate a federal court forum, there is the potential of either an original filing in or removal to federal court based upon diversity, and there are strategic considerations where you have a choice between the state or federal court. All of those traditional considerations and issues apply with full effect to the business torts complaint and will not be repeated here but include the need for out-of-state discovery, the length of the respective dockets, discovery rules, and the method of assigning judges to cases.

In some areas of business torts, there is more room for strategic considerations because of overlap between federal and state law claims. For example, in a case involving palming off, one might plead the case under the Lanham Act or might assert claims under state common law. Depending upon the case law in your particular forum, your client might be best served with moving forward under a state law claim rather than the federal claim if, for example, the mature case law surrounding the Lanham Act might cause you trouble, but the loose definition of "unfair competition" under state law might be broad enough to support your claims.

Finally, it may be relevant to consider the Supreme Court's recent heightened pleading requirements, as set forth in *Bell Atlantic Corp. v. Twombly*[1] and *Ashcroft v. Iqbal*.[2] While application of these cases varies by court and is still being fleshed out, a federal court might hold a complaint to a more exacting initial standard than a state court filing.[3]

B. Geography

While venue and forum rules are generic, there may be certain causes of action that, by statute, dictate a different result. For example, certain shareholder or corporate claims must be filed in the state of incorporation and the county where the entity's principal place of business is located.

The more dominant consideration is choice of law. Jurisdictions can vary dramatically on how they handle business torts claims, from trade secrets to shareholder claims to non-competes. Even where there is a choice of law provision in a contract, some jurisdictions may not apply that law if doing so would conflict with public policy of another relevant state. There may also be substantial differences as to available damages dependent upon controlling law. These issues must be carefully vetted and fleshed out prior to filing.

V. DEFENDANTS

Business tort cases present unique opportunities for strategic decisions as to who to sue. Take, for example, a typical non-compete scenario. The departed employee's new employer is a competitor who (probably, but not definitely) had knowledge of the non-compete. In some jurisdictions,

---

1. 550 U.S. 544 (2007).
2. 556 U.S. 662 (2009).
3. *See, e.g.,* Sedona Corp. v. Ladenburg Thalmann & Co., No. 03-civ-3120, 2009 U.S. Dist. LEXIS 44748 (S.D.N.Y. May 27, 2009) (applying Iqbal to dismiss tortious interference claims).

knowledge might make the new employer liable for tortious interference, conspiracy, or inducement to breach fiduciary duties. Moreover, since leaving, the employee has successfully solicited customers, some of whom have moved either some or all of their business to the employee's new employer. Your client will continue to do business with some of those customers.

Where the departed employee essentially starts his or her own business with your client's trade secrets or in violation of a non-compete, complete relief likely requires that you add that entity as a defendant. But where the entity is an established business, the topic requires more thought. By naming the entity, you place the corporate pocketbook in jeopardy. Perhaps the business will simply fire the employee, or move him or her to a different position, rather than face the hassle of a lawsuit. On the other hand, by naming the business, you now have a defendant with resources opposing you. If you just name the employee, and the employer is not paying for the defense, the employee may simply not be able to litigate the case effectively, thus leading to an early resolution. Moreover, by not naming the new entity, your client faces less risk of having to disclose sensitive business information during the litigation to a direct competitor. Finally, there is the issue of damages—if the purpose of the lawsuit is compensatory damages, then suing the individual may limit your recovery.

There are situations where others might also be named. A customer that is complicit with an employee in misappropriating confidential information and switching jobs might be named, especially when there is no prospect of future business. This is unusual, however, because going after customers is taboo in some industries. Other third parties, including suppliers, parent entities, headhunters, and consultants, occasionally also make proper defendants.

You should approach the topic of naming individuals with much care. In most jurisdictions, business torts provide the opportunity to name both a business entity and those individuals who committed the wrong. Sometimes plaintiffs calculate that by naming someone personally they are "upping the ante" and making sure the other side is fully vested in the litigation. In reality, and except where specifically necessary (for example, in an oppression claim), naming individuals where the business is the true defendant rarely adds anything except expense and complexity. The company may indemnify those individuals, and may defend them, but those individuals

44

may also hire separate counsel, thus pitting you against a cavalcade of lawyers. While there certainly are discretionary situations where naming individuals in addition to the business is appropriate, you should always carefully consider the issue.

VI. ADDITIONAL BUSINESS TORTS PLEADING ISSUES

In addition to the regular considerations as to the level of specificity either required or desired in a complaint, business torts complaints often have various additional required elements that must be specifically pled. These requirements emanate out of the particular torts at issue and must be carefully considered before filing.

The most common and familiar additional requirement is the obligation to plead fraud with specificity under Fed. R. Civ. P. 9(b) and many analogous state law provisions. Especially in light of *Iqbal*,[4] pleadings must be carefully crafted with an eye toward withstanding an initial motion to dismiss.

Other causes of action require that prerequisites be adequately pled. For example, in a derivative shareholder claim, the complaint must normally plead that demand was made and either rejected or sufficient time passed without response (or, in certain jurisdictions, that demand would be futile). Failure to plead these essential gateway issues will bring a swift end to a filing.

VII. PLEADING DAMAGES AND RELIEF REQUESTED

Business torts present additional challenges when it comes to pleading damages. Normally, there is a basic ad damnum that states only damages sufficient to establish jurisdiction. One additional requirement is Fed. R. Civ. P. 9(g), which requires heightened pleading for "special damages." The rule does not define "special damages"; however, the United States Court of Appeals for the Sixth Circuit, for example, explained it as follows: "The distinction between general and special damages is not that one is and the other is not the direct and proximate consequence of the breach complained of, but that general damages are such as naturally and ordinarily follow

---

4. Ashcroft v. Iqbal, 556 U.S. 262 (2009).

the breach, whereas special damages are those that ensue, not necessarily or ordinarily, but because of special circumstances."[5] Federal courts do not uniformly agree as to what constitutes "special damages," so already a trap for the unwary exists. In state courts, there is likely even less law on the topic, so practitioners should at least consider this issue before going with a "vanilla" damages statement.

The very nature of business torts may require additional consideration of how specifically to plead damages. For example, if the plaintiff is attempting to allege breach of contract as well as business torts, thus potentially implicating the economic loss doctrine, how the damages are pled may be very important in either defending the additional tort claims on a motion to dismiss or arguing for their dismissal.[6]

VIII. ATTACHMENTS AND CONFIDENTIALITY

An issue that often arises in business torts litigation is how to handle confidential information. As to the plaintiff's information, usually one can plead around the issue sufficiently to avoid issues and yet satisfy pleading requirements. However, when there is a preliminary injunction along with the complaint, the plaintiff may be forced to first file the complaint, seek an ex parte protective order permitting the filing of confidential information under seal, and then file the preliminary injunction motion. This interim step can interrupt the timing of a "bang-bang" complaint-motion filing, but may be essential if what one is protecting is trade secrets or otherwise confidential information. Where confidentiality is an issue, it must be a factor in every decision that is made with regard to filings. Local procedures will vary and practitioners must be familiar with the procedures employed by the particular court and judge.

---

5. Ruggles v. Buffalo Foundry & Machine Co., 27 F.2d 234, 235 (6th Cir. 1928). *See* Figgins v. Advance Am. Cash Advance Centers of Mich., Inc., 482 F. Supp. 2d 861, 869 (E.D. Mich. 2007) (stating that "special damages are those that are unusual for a type of claim").

6. It is beyond the scope of this chapter to discuss substantively the damages issues involved in business torts, including the issue of contract versus tort damages remedies, but *see, e.g.,* Amy G. Doehring, *Blurring the Distinction between Contract and Tort: Courts Permitting Business Plaintiffs to Recover Tort Damages for Breach of Contract,* A.B.A. BUS. TORTS J., Winter 2005.

CHAPTER 4

Emergency Relief

Peter J. Glennon

Businesses know well that time and cash flow are two critical ingredients to success. When a dispute arises between businesses that could affect these issues or their core business, their business reputation and goodwill, or their client base, the business's survival and future is often determined by the ability to maintain the status quo. Failing in that goal could have untold or unimagined financial consequences. As a result, it is critical that business litigators possess a degree of "legal nimbleness" that can be exercised at a moment's notice in the defense of their clients' business interests, particularly through the use of emergency relief. This chapter provides litigators an overview of obtaining emergency relief, specifically preliminary injunctions and temporary restraining orders in federal court.

Federal Rule of Civil Procedure 65 is the main basis for seeking emergency relief in federal courts. It provides a mechanism for parties to maintain the "status quo" until a controversy is resolved. The focus of this discussion is based primarily on the Federal Rules of Civil Procedure and federal case law. It is always necessary, and a good practice, to review all local rules and procedures, including court rules and specific judge rules, prior to seeking emergency relief.

I. WHAT IS EMERGENCY RELIEF
AND WHEN IS IT NECESSARY?

Advocating for emergency relief on a client's behalf may be the only opportunity to defend a client's position and to maintain the status quo before the business is seriously affected. In some situations, failing to obtain a preliminary injunction to maintain the status quo could mean the difference between continuing or failing in the marketplace.

The purpose of a preliminary injunction is to maintain the "status quo" until the court renders a final decision on the merits of a legal dispute. The status quo has been defined as "the last peaceable uncontested status" before the controversy arose.[1] Occasionally, courts grant preliminary injunctions to alter the status quo when it is necessary to require a party to perform an action to avoid harm to the moving party. However, such an injunction is only granted when an "unusual circumstance" exists and the merits of a case overwhelmingly favor one side.[2] A permanent injunction is not considered until the case concludes.

In comparison, a temporary restraining order (TRO) maintains the status quo, but is enforceable only for a short period of time. A temporary restraining order may only be in place until a full hearing can be held on a motion for a preliminary injunction or for a maximum of "just a fleeting fourteen days."[3] Significantly, it can be ordered ex parte without notice and can be based on an incomplete record. However, federal courts are reluctant to grant temporary restraining orders ex parte.[4]

In the context of business torts, there are several common scenarios that precipitate a preliminary injunction or a TRO. They are often considered as a means to prevent misappropriation of trade secrets and unfair competition, including disclosure of confidential information, and to enforce non-compete agreements in suits by a company against former employees and their new employers to protect legitimate interests.

---

1. Stemple v. Board of Educ. of Prince's County, 523 F.2d 893, 898 (4th Cir. 1980), *cert. denied*, 450 U.S. 911 (1981).
2. *See* Dominion Video Satellite, Inc. v. EchoStar Satellite Corp., 269 F.3d 1149, 1154–55 (10th Cir. 2001).
3. Clearone Commus. v. Bowers, No. 11-4136, 2013 U.S. App. LEXIS 2489, at *6 (10th Cir. Feb. 5, 2013). *See generally* FED. R. CIV. P. 65(b).
4. *See generally* Granny Goose Foods, Inc. v. Brotherhood of Teamsters, Local No. 70, 415 U.S. 423 (1976).

II. PRELIMINARY INJUNCTIONS

A. Overview

A preliminary injunction is a court order that enjoins or prohibits a party from performing or not performing a certain act *preliminarily*, meaning until the matter has been resolved. An injunction may be one of two types: prohibitory or mandatory. Simply stated, a prohibitory injunction is one that prohibits a party from performing a particular act, such as selling a branded product. A mandatory injunction is one that requires a party to perform a particular act, such as continuing to supply a retail business with inventory. A preliminary injunction is an important procedural tool that may avoid what is considered to be *irreparable harm* to a party.

Irreparable harm, the hallmark concern requiring emergency relief, is generally a harm for which no monetary damages would sufficiently compensate the injured party. Examples of cases in which irreparable harm is alleged include brand tarnishment; misappropriation of confidential information, intellectual property, or trade secrets; and the provision of personal services by unique employees to a competitor. Where a party can convince a court that it would otherwise likely suffer irreparable harm in these situations, courts may issue a preliminary injunction to preserve the status quo until the parties' dispute is resolved.

B. Federal Rules of Civil Procedure 65

Rule 65 of the Federal Rules of Civil Procedure governs the process of seeking a preliminary injunction. It sets forth the procedure for seeking a preliminary injunction and the scope for which it may be sought.

Rule 65(a)(1) authorizes a court to issue a preliminary injunction on notice to the non-moving party. Therefore, unlike with temporary restraining orders, the court is prevented from issuing a preliminary injunction ex parte. Rule 65(a)(2) enables the court in its discretion to consolidate the preliminary injunction hearing with the trial on the merits, meaning that evidence presented at the preliminary injunction hearing that would be admissible at trial becomes part of the trial record.

Rule 65(a)(2) also authorizes the judge "before or after beginning the hearing on a motion for a preliminary injunction [to] . . . advance the trial on the merits and consolidate it with the hearing." The Supreme Court ruled that consolidation is proper if both parties understand this procedural adjustment.[5] In addition, as noted earlier, "even when consolidation is not ordered, evidence that is received on the motion and that would be admissible at trial becomes part of the trial record, and need not be repeated at trial."[6]

The scope of a preliminary injunction may extend to third parties and other nonparties. Rule 65(d)(2) constrains "(A) the parties; (B) the parties' officers, agents, servants, employees, and attorneys; and (C) other persons who are in active concert or participation with anyone [described in this rule]."[7] Additionally, as a practice note, having a relationship with an enjoined party of the sort set forth in Rule 65(d) "exposes a non-party to liability for contempt for assisting the party to violate the injunction, but does not justify granting injunctive relief against the non-party in its separate capacity."[8]

This broad determination of which parties are bound by the injunction is highly fact specific and not subject to a set formula.[9] Parties seeking to expand the scope of a preliminary injunction's enforceability should be specific in explaining to the court the direct relationship each person has to the underlying litigation.[10] This rule provides counsel in complex litigation cases insurance that all threats of irreparable injury are mitigated whether the enjoined party is a competing business and its subsidiaries or a former employee now competing.

C. Standard to Obtain a Preliminary Injunction?

Generally, a preliminary injunction will be granted when a party demonstrates:

1. threat of irreparable injury if the preliminary injunction is not granted;
2. a likelihood of success on the merits of the underlying case;

---

5. *See* University of Texas v. Camenisch, 451 U.S. 390, 395 (1981).
6. *See* FED. R. CIV. P. 65(a)(2).
7. *Id.* 65(d)(2)(A)–(C).
8. Addictive Controls and Measurement Sys., Inc. v. Flowdata, Inc., 96 F.3d 1390, 1395–96 (Fed. Cir. 1996).
9. *See* United States v. Int'l Brotherhood of Teamsters, 964 F.2d 180, 184 (2d Cir. 1992).
10. *Id.*

3. that a balance of harms between the parties is favorable to the moving party; and

4. that the public interest will be served by granting the preliminary injunction.[11]

Notably, this is the standard for the typical prohibitory injunction, which is most common and is sought where a party seeks to prevent irreparable harm, the traditional purpose of "seeking only to maintain the status quo."[12] In contrast, a mandatory injunction "commands action rather than merely prohibiting it," which requires the moving party to satisfy the higher burden of showing "a clear or substantial likelihood of success."[13] Even though several courts have made a distinction between prohibitory and mandatory injunctions this distinction is not universal. For example, the Second Circuit acknowledged that "the distinction between mandatory and prohibitory injunctions is not without ambiguities or critics, and that in a close case an injunction can be framed in mandatory or prohibitory terms."[14]

1. Irreparable Harm

Irreparable harm is the "lynchpin factor" in the court's decision to issue a preliminary injunction.[15] The court defines irreparable harm as "an injury that is not remote or speculative but actual and imminent, and for which a monetary award cannot be adequate consideration."[16]

Irreparable harm is a realistic and probable harm for which there is no remedy at law. Having no remedy at law means that it is impossible or very challenging to calculate monetary damages or that the subject of

---

11. University of Texas v. Camenisch, 451 U.S. 390, 392 (1981) (citing Canal Auth. of Fla. v. Callaway, 489 F.2d 567 (5th Cir. 1974)). *See also* Jackson Dairy, Inc. v. H.P. Hood & Sons, Inc., 596 F.2d 70, 72 (2d Cir. 1979).

12. Cacchillo v. Insmed. Inc., 638 F.3d 401, 406 (2d Cir. 2011).

13. Ligon v. City of New York, 12 Civ. 2274, 2013 U.S. Dist. LEXIS 2871, at *11 (S.D.N.Y. Jan. 8, 2013).

14. Jolly v. Coughlin, 76 F.3d 468, 474 (2d Cir. 1996).

15. *See* Boston Laser, Inc. v. Qinzin Zu, 07-cv-0791, 2007 U.S. Dist. LEXIS 78021, at *27 (N.D.N.Y. Sept. 21, 2007) (citing Ticor Title Ins. Co. v. Cohen, 173 F.3d 63, 68 (2d Cir. 1999)).

16. *See* Tom Doherty Assocs. v. Saban Entm't, Inc., 60 F.3d 27, 37 (2d Cir. 1995).

the injunction is unique, such as real estate or other personal property or heirlooms. The harm must also be probable, not a hypothetical harm or a harm based on apprehension or fear.

A simple test to determine if a probable harm is irreparable is whether you can calculate money damages and the opposing party is able to pay those damages. If yes, then an injunction is unlikely; but if no, then an injunction is possible.

Typical examples of irreparable harm include:

- loss of or damage to real property that is considered unique and cannot be replaced;
- damage to business's reputation or goodwill;
- improper crediting for designs or creations;
- misappropriation of trade secrets;
- infringements on patents, copyrights, or trademarks;
- violations of restrictive covenants and other forms of unfair competition;[17] and
- threat of bankruptcy.

Examples of harm that is not irreparable include interference with contract, customers, or prospective customers and the loss of income producing property. Money damages are typically available in these situations. Notably, hypothetical injuries are not irreparable harm because a party cannot obtain a preliminary injunction based on the speculation of future injuries. Finally, injuries from the past and "trifling" injuries are not considered irreparable harm.

2. A Likelihood of Success on the Merits

Determining whether the element of "a likelihood of success" exists is a fact specific test subject to the court's discretion. This prong is typically demonstrated by the presentation of evidence either on submission or at a

---

17. McNeil Lab v. Am. Home Prods., 848 F.2d 34 (2d Cir. 1988) (affirming District Court's finding of presumed harm from a finding of false or misleading advertising).

hearing. As discussed earlier, evidence presented at this hearing may become part of the trial record.

Proving a likelihood of success has challenges, albeit not overwhelming ones. Courts understand that typically discovery has not occurred prior to a motion for a preliminary injunction. The facts or averments made, however, will aid the court in determining if a real issue is present.

Courts typically expect a moving party to establish a 51 percent or greater probability of success. Where a "mandatory" injunction is sought, the court might apply a heightened standard of a more substantial likelihood of success. Courts consider an injunction as mandatory if the requested relief "affirmatively requires the nonmovant to act in a particular way, and as a result . . . places the issuing court in a position where it may have to provide ongoing supervision to assure the nonmovant is abiding by the injunction."[18] Accordingly, because of this additional burden on the non-moving party and the court, courts apply a heightened standard. In fact, some courts have gone so far as to rule that there is a presumption against granting a mandatory injunction. "When a mandatory preliminary injunction is requested, the district court should deny such relief 'unless the facts and law clearly favor the moving party.'"[19] Other courts have held that in the event the "clear showing" standard is not met, a mandatory injunction will only be granted "where extreme or very serious damage will result from a denial of preliminary relief."[20]

It should be noted that courts in different areas may approach the analysis in different manners. Some courts require that what is called the "sequential test" be established, meaning that each element in order must be satisfied.[21]

---

18. Schrier v. University of Colo., 427 F.3d 1253, 1261 (10th Cir. 2005).
19. Stanley v. Univ. of S. Cal., 13 F.3d 1313, 1320 (9th Cir. 1994) (quoting Anderson v. United States, 612 F.2d 1112, 1114 (9th Cir. 1979); and Martinez v. Mathews, 544 F.2d 1233, 1243 (5th Cir. 1976)).
20. Tom Doherty Assocs. v. Saban Entm't, Inc., 60 F.3d 27, 34 (2d Cir. 1995) (internal quotations and citations omitted).
21. See, e.g., Opulent Life Church v. City of Holly Springs, Miss., 697 F.3d 279, 288 (5th Cir. 2012).

Others look more closely at the irreparable harm and likelihood of success elements.[22] Still others consider either a two- or three-part balancing test.[23]

Regardless of the analysis used by the court, the party seeking the relief must establish a reasonable relationship between the likely success and the preliminary relief sought. For example, even if the court determines the movant is likely to succeed on a multi-million-dollar claim, the court will not freeze the respondent's assets.

Examples of where the court has found a likelihood of success on the merits in business tort matters include

- Court granted an injunction ordering dispossession as such was an appropriate remedy in the franchise agreement between the parties.[24]
- After finding that "[respondent's] alleged breach and misappropriation would impair [movant's drug's] chances at FDA approval for medical use and make it difficult for [movant] to secure research funding for the drug," the court granted an injunction enjoining respondent from disseminating any information it obtained from movant.[25]
- The court found plaintiff's misappropriation-of-trade-secrets claim was based on archetypal trade secrets, and therefore plaintiff demonstrated a likelihood of success on the merits, and that plaintiff would suffer irreparable injury (loss of goodwill, competitive advantage, and research incentives) absent an injunction.[26]
- The court enjoined respondent from taking employment with movant's competitor because movant established the likelihood of success on the merits of its underlying breach of contract claim because it provided clear and convincing evidence that the noncompete agreement was reasonable.[27]

---

22. *See, e.g.,* Ohio ex rel. Celebrezze v. Nuclear Regulatory Com., 812 F.2d 288 (6th Cir. 1987).

23. *See, e.g.,* Random House v. Rosetta Books LLC, 283 F.3d 490 (2d Cir. 2002).

24. SOL P.R., Ltd. v. Morales-Collazo, 2009 U.S. Dist. LEXIS 53008 (D.P.R. June 22, 2009) ("After examining the arguments and evidence presented, the Court finds that Plaintiff has demonstrated a high likelihood of success on the merits of its [claims].").

25. Daniels Health Scis., LLC v. Vascular Health Scis., LLC, 710 F.3d 579 (5th Cir. 2013).

26. Brake Parts, Inc. v. Lewis, 443 F. App'x 27 (6th Cir. 2011).

27. Firstenergy Solutions Corp. v. Flerick, No. 12-4558, 2013 U.S. App. LEXIS 7520 (6th Cir. Apr.15, 2013).

Notably, even if a likelihood of success on the merits is not proven, a preliminary injunction may still be possible. Some courts have found that a preliminary injunction is permissible where the moving party establishes "sufficiently serious questions going to merits to make them a fair ground for litigation, and a balance of hardships tipping decidedly in its favor."[28]

3. Balance of Harms

The next element considered by the courts is a balance of harms, meaning the effect on both parties if the preliminary injunction is granted. Where the moving party may have established irreparable harm to it, the non-moving party may be harmed if the preliminary injunction is granted. For example, if a company is enjoined from shipping goods to a third party, that company may be harmed due to the loss of business. These two (or more) harms must be weighed and balanced against each other. Where both parties face harm, any injunction tends to be narrowly tailored to reduce the respective harms.[29]

Weighing the competing harms is done within the court's discretion.[30] This means that the greater likelihood of success by the moving party will likely tip the scale in its favor. A lesser likelihood of success will tip it in the respondent's favor.[31] Each situation's unique facts and circumstances need to be considered.

---

28. Centeno-Bernuy v. Perry, 302 F. Supp. 2d 128, 137 (W.D.N.Y. 2003).

29. *See, e.g.,* Mohr v. Bank of N.Y. Mellon Corp., 393 F. App'x 639, 645 (11th Cir. 2010) (limiting the number of cities where restrictive covenant is effective); Ikon Office Solutions v. Dale, 22 F. App'x 647, 648 (8th Cir. 2001) (shortening the term of the restrictive covenant and altering the definition of the competitive activity it enjoined).

30. *See, e.g.,* Roland Machinery Co. v. Dresser Indus., 749 F.2d 380 (7th Cir. 1984) ("[S]ince the defendant may suffer irreparable harm from the entry of a preliminary injunction, the court must not only determine that the plaintiff will suffer irreparable harm if the preliminary injunction is denied—a threshold requirement for granting a preliminary injunction—but also weigh that harm against any irreparable harm that the defendant can show he will suffer if the injunction is granted.").

31. *See* Friendship Materials, Inc. v. Michigan Brick, Inc., 679 F.2d 100, 105 (6th Cir. 1982) ("[T]he likelihood of success that need be shown (for a preliminary injunction) will vary inversely with the degree of injury the plaintiff will suffer absent an injunction." (internal quotations and citations omitted)).

4. Public Interest

This element is not always considered. Regardless of whether it is part of the standard, any detrimental effect to the public may be considered, even informally, in a court's decision. In situations that might affect the public, when weighing or balancing the harms, the court may consider the effect an injunction would have on the public.

Examples of public interests include public welfare, health, or safety; consumer interests; and environmental or conservation issues.

D. What Is the Process and Procedure for Obtaining a Preliminary Injunction?

Emergency relief is called as much because time is usually of the essence in obtaining preliminary or temporary relief. But wise litigators know that it is better to get it right and to move swiftly than it is to rush to the courthouse.

The process and procedure for obtaining a preliminary injunction and TRO is the same, with a few variations. The variations are generally mentioned below, but are more specifically discussed in Section III.

The first step is to determine (i) whether an actual irreparable harm is likely and (ii) whether the moving party is likely to succeed on the merits. To do so, relevant facts must be identified and investigated. Start by interviewing the clients and relevant witnesses. Make sure to research and understand the legal issues involved so that a correct analysis is made after applying the facts—seeking a preliminary injunction is not wise until the litigator is confident that the moving party has a realistic chance of success.

Determining a realistic chance of success is important so that the client does not expend legal fees unnecessarily. Seeking emergency relief is costly. Litigators and their staff must get to work right away researching the legal issues, investigating the claims, obtaining the facts, preparing the relevant papers, and attending court appearances. Indeed, as with any litigation, a cost-benefit analysis should be conducted by the litigator and client to determine that the time and expense associated with emergency relief is worth the effort.

If the client decides that it must seek emergency relief, then the following papers must be prepared and actions must be taken:

1. Prepare the complaint (or counterclaim).
2. Prepare the motion (or notice of motion) seeking a preliminary injunction, including:
    a. a supporting memorandum of law;
    b. supporting affidavits with exhibits; and
    c. a proposed order.
3. Obtain appropriate bond, security, or undertaking.
4. File and serve the pleadings and motions.
5. Subpoena any nonparty witnesses for a preliminary-injunction hearing.

1. Complaint or Counterclaim

Claims should include specific facts and details to establish irreparable harm and likelihood of success on the merits. Verifying the pleading is always a good idea as well, for evidentiary purposes.

2. Notice

Notice to the non-moving party is required. Unlike temporary restraining orders, Rule 65(a)(1) prohibits the courts from granting a preliminary injunction ex parte without notice to the adverse party.[32] There is no established rule on what constitutes adequate notice. The Supreme Court has held that same-day notice is insufficient.[33] However, beyond that, federal courts are split on what constitutes proper notice—some abide by the notice rule of Federal Rule of Civil Procedure 6 and others apply a deferential standard to the decision of the trial court.[34] On the state level, certain state statutes specifically define the required notice, but many do not.[35] Because of these disparities, it is wise to practice diligence.

---

32. *See* Western Water Mgt. Inc. v. Brown, 40 F.3d 105, 109 (5th Cir. 1994) (vacating a modification of injunction made without notice to defendant).
33. Granny Goose Foods, Inc. v. Brotherhood of Teamsters & Auto Truck Drivers Local No. 70, 415 U.S. 423, 433 n.7 (1974).
34. *See, e.g.*, Marshall Durbin Farms, Inc. v. National Farmers Org., 446 F.2d 353 (5th Cir. 1971); Four Seasons Hotels & Resorts, B.V. v. Consorcio Barr, S.A., 320 F.3d 1205 (11th Cir. 2003) (ruling that sufficiency of notice is left to the trial court's discretion).
35. *Compare* N.Y. C.P.L.R. § 6311 (2013) ("A preliminary injunction may be granted only upon notice to the defendant."), *with* Or. R. Civ. P. 79(C)(1) ("No preliminary injunction

A typical "Notice of Motion" format is sufficient, but local practice provides the best guidance as to what notice documents need to be served.[36]

3. Bonds/Security

Rule 65(c) is applicable to both preliminary injunctions and temporary restraining orders and requires that a movant provide "security in an amount that the court considers proper to pay the costs and damages sustained by any party found to have been wrongfully enjoined or restrained."

The proper amount of security is dependent on the specific circumstances of each case and subject to the court's discretion.[37] The court will usually set an amount that "covers the potential incidental and consequential costs as well as either the losses the unjustly enjoined or restrained party will suffer during the period he is prohibited from engaging in certain activities or the complainant's unjust enrichment caused by his adversary being improperly enjoined or restrained."[38]

To post this security, an attorney may (1) post such directly with the court or (2) obtain a bond and file the proof of such with the court. Again, please note that different jurisdictions have different rules regarding posting a bond, so best practice is always to check the rules in the jurisdiction. To post directly with the court, the client must produce the amount of the bond in cash. Conversely, a bond may be obtained from a fidelity company or a surety or a letter of credit may be issued by the client's bank. Once either the bond or letter of credit has been obtained, proof of the bond must be filed with the court. Again, check local rules to determine the proper procedure.

In a trade secret case, the court required an employer accusing a former employee of the misappropriation of trade secrets to provide a $100,000 bond. The $100,000 amount was the amount of the plaintiff's annual salary with his new employer plus the estimated amount of annual bonuses he

---

shall be issued without notice to the adverse party at least five days before the time specified for the hearing, unless a different period is fixed by order of the court.").

36. *See* Wyandotte Nation v. Sebelius, 443 F.3d 1247, 1253 (10th Cir. 2006).

37. *See* Elite Licensing, Inc. v. Thomas Plastics, Inc., 250 F. Supp. 2d 372, 391 (S.D.N.Y. 2003).

38. Hoechst Diafoil Co. v. Nan Ya Plastics Corp., 174 F.3d 411, 421 n.3 (4th Cir. 1999).

would receive.[39] Therefore, counsel seeking a preliminary injunction should account for the possibility of a substantial bond in determining whether to pursue a preliminary injunction.

If a party is unsatisfied with the posted bond, it has an obligation to present evidence that a bond in a particular amount is needed.[40] A trial court's decision of the amount of a bond can be appealed; however, the standard of review can be high. One court stated, "Although we allow the district court much discretion in setting bond, we will reverse its order if it abuses that discretion due to some improper purpose, or otherwise fails to require an adequate bond or to make the necessary findings in support of its determinations."[41]

If it is determined a party was wrongfully enjoined, his damages are limited to the posted bond.[42] But adversely affected parties can file a separate action for malicious prosecution if the bond amount is unsatisfactory.[43] As stated earlier, federal courts are reluctant to grant preliminary injunctions and counsel should prepare for the possibility of being required to post a higher bond than expected.

4. Motion Papers

It has been said that a successful motion for a preliminary injunction consists of language intended for a non-legal audience. In fact, the Seventh Circuit held that Rule 65(d), which governs the drafting of motions for preliminary injunctions and TROs, requires language "such that a reasonable person could understand what conduct is proscribed."[44]

Rule 65(d) provides the requirements litigants must follow in drafting both preliminary injunctions and temporary restraining orders. Every

---

39.   Innovant v. Morganstern, 390 F. Supp. 2d 179, 195 (N.D.N.Y. 2005).
40.   Connecticut General Life Ins. Co. v. New Images of Beverly Hills, 321 F.3d 878, 883 (9th Cir. 2003).
41.   Hill v. Xyquad, Inc., 939 F.2d 627, 632 (8th Cir. 1991); Gateway E. Ry. v. Terminal R.R. Ass'n, 35 F.3d 1134 (7th Cir. 1994) (applying an abuse of discretion standard in reviewing bond amounts, specifically whether it is "within the range of options from which one could expect a reasonable trial judge to select" a bond amount).
42.   See W.R. Grace & Co. v. Local Union 759, 461 U.S. 757, 770 n.14 (1983).
43.   See Meyers v. Block, 120 U.S. 206, 211 (1887).
44.   See Medtronic, Inc. v. Benda, 689 F.2d 645 (7th Cir. 1982).

injunction is required to (i) state the reasons why the preliminary injunction should be issued; (ii) state the preliminary injunction's terms specifically; and (iii) describe in reasonable detail—and not by referring to the complaint or other document—the act(s) to be restrained or required. Fed. R. Civ. P. 65(d)(1)(A)–(C). The drafters of the rule recognized the risk that an injunction could be misunderstood by a non-lawyer thereby rendering it ineffective.[45] Accordingly, litigants must ensure that their motions and proposed orders are clear and concise.

It should also be noted that the motion cannot make reference to other documents or pleadings in describing the acts that are being prohibited or required. Rather, these must be included directly in the motion.[46] Drafters of motions for preliminary injunctions who place themselves in the position of a non-lawyer and reduce the language to the simplest terms will therefore increase their chances of a favorable outcome.

5. Supporting Evidence

All forms of evidence, including oral testimony and affidavits, may be presented at a preliminary injunction hearing because strict evidentiary rules are generally not enforced. A preliminary injunction hearing is not a trial, but a mechanism to prevent irreparable harm, and a party "is not required to prove his case in full."[47] As a result, "affidavits and other hearsay materials are often received in preliminary injunction proceedings" and may be examined by the court.[48] The relaxation of evidentiary standards provides litigators with an opportunity to be aggressive in their pursuit of emergency relief; however, most of this evidence will not be admitted during trial and should not be relied on as the basis of a claim, but used only for proving irreparable harm.

---

45. *See* Reno Air Racing Association, Inc. v. McCord, 452 F.3d 1126, 1134 (9th Cir. 2006).

46. *See* Advent Elecs., Inc. v. Buckman, 112 F.3d 267 (7th Cir. 1997).

47. FSLIC v. Dixon, 835 F.2d 554, 558 (5th Cir. 1987) (quoting Univ. of Texas v. Comenisch, 451 U.S. 390, 395 (1981)).

48. *Id.* at 558 (quoting Asseo v. Pan American Grain Co., 805 F.2d 23 (1st Cir. 1986)). *See also* Sierra Club v. FDIC, 992 F.2d 545, 551 (5th Cir. 1993).

E. Defending Against a Motion for Preliminary Injunction

The party facing a motion for emergency relief should perform the same analysis and consider the same issues presented with the prior section. Of particular consideration should be the investigation into possible counterclaims, which need to be included in the answer to the complaint alleging the underlying claim. A motion to dismiss should be prepared for the motion seeking emergency relief and, if necessary, for the complaint. Of course, after consulting with the client and relevant witnesses, facts and evidence refuting the claims and undermining the movant's irreparable harm and likelihood of success arguments should be gathered and presented to the court.

In addition to refuting the allegations and claims of irreparable harm and likely success, respondents may also assert equitable defenses. First and foremost, the responding party needs to consider articulating how the respondent would be overly and unfairly burdened by any emergency relief, thereby tipping the balance of harms analysis in its favor.

1. Bad Faith

The lion's share of commercial litigation involves contract disputes, and the equitable defense of bad faith is frequently set forth by parties defending against a preliminary injunction. Contract law "imposes a duty, not to 'be reasonable,' but to avoid taking advantage of gaps in a contract in order to exploit the vulnerabilities that arise when contractual performance is sequential rather than simultaneous."[49] The purpose of raising a bad faith defense is to prevent a party from "exploiting the vulnerabilities" in a contract, and accordingly, bad faith may be employed as a defense in nearly every dispute. It seeks not to defend against specific terms of a contract that may be deemed "unreasonable," but rather against terms "invoked dishonestly to achieve a purpose contrary to that for which the contract had been made."[50] The validity of a contract is consistently an issue in commercial litigation cases and clients will be well served if counsel sets forth this defense.

---

49.   Original Great Am. Chocolate Chip Cookie Co. v. River Valley Cookies, Ltd., 970 F.2d 273, 280 (7th Cir. 1992).
50.   *Id.*

2. Unclean Hands

Justice would not be served if the plaintiffs themselves were to blame for their own irreparable injury. "The maxim of unclean hands mandates that he who comes into equity must come with clean hands. Specifically, the plaintiff must be frank and fair with the court, nothing about the case under consideration should be guarded, but everything that tends to a full and fair determination of the matters in controversy should be placed before the court."[51] The defense of unclean hands posits that a defendant should not be held accountable for damaging results for which the plaintiff is also responsible. In asserting this defense, litigators should be aware that there have been instances of courts requiring a "close relationship" between the alleged misconduct and the underlying claim.[52]

Furthermore, defendants should not be discouraged from asserting the defense of unclean hands in a preliminary injunction hearing. There is "no requirement . . . that those asserting equitable defenses have led blameless lives, it is [only] necessary that they shall have acted fairly and without fraud or deceit as to the controversy in issue."[53] If a respondent can portray the movant as the main reason for the irreparable harm, the movant will find it difficult to argue that preventing the actions of another will prevent injury.

3. Laches

The equitable defense of laches does not concern the merits of a motion for a preliminary injunction, but instead prevents a movant from waiting for a more beneficial moment to bring a claim. Specifically, laches is "an equitable time limitation on a party's right to bring suit, resting on the maxim that one who seeks the help of a court of equity must not sleep on his rights."[54]

Note that this defense should be distinguished from a statute of limitations defense as it does not concern a set deadline for a suit, but focuses on the specific facts of the case. If a party seeking a preliminary injunction only

51. Medpointe Healthcare Inc. v. Hi-Tech Pharmacal Co., 380 F. Supp. 2d 457, 463 (D.N.J. 2005).
52. See In re New Valley Corp., 181 F.3d 517, 525 (3d Cir. 1999).
53. Aeroplate Corp. v. United States, 71 Fed. Cl. 568, 569 (2006).
54. Jarrow Formulas, Inc. v. Nutrition Now, Inc., 304 F.3d 829, 835 (9th Cir. 2002).

pursues it at his convenience, it undermines the emergency relief's purpose. A plaintiff cannot prove immediate irreparable harm when the action he seeks to stop has been occurring for a substantial period of time. In the context of preliminary injunctions, laches may provide an effective defense against the movant's argument that the current controversy requires emergency relief.

4. Waiver

The defense of waiver penalizes a party for not asserting its right at the proper time. A successful waiver defense is not the result of the plaintiff's intentionally failing to enforce a claimed right, but his failure for not pursing all claims at once. By allowing defendant's reliance on the plaintiff's original assertion of claims, waiver seeks to prevent inequity against the defendant.

F. Appealing a Preliminary Injunction

In the event that a preliminary injunction is ordered, it is immediately appealable by the burdened party.[55] The standard to reverse a preliminary injunction is whether the burdened party demonstrates that the "court made a clear error of judgment in weighing relevant factors or exercised its discretion based upon an error of law or clearly erroneous factual findings."[56]

III. TEMPORARY RESTRAINING ORDERS
A. Overview

A temporary restraining order is the quickest form of emergency relief to protect a business from immediate injury. Rule 65(b) authorizes the court to issue a temporary restraining order ex parte without providing notice to the opposing party. However, the moving party must demonstrate in his affidavit or complaint that providing notice to the opposing party was not possible given the "immediate and irreparable injury, loss, or damage [that would] . . . result to the movant before the adverse party can be heard in

---

55. *See* 28 U.S.C. § 1292(a)(1) (2013); *see also* Nutrasweet Co. v. Vit-Mar Enters., Inc., 112 F.3d 689 (3d Cir. 1997).

56. Momenta Pharms., Inc. v. Amphastar Pharms., Inc., 686 F.3d 1348, 1352 (Fed. Cir. 2012); *see also* FED. R. CIV. P. 62(c).

opposition."[57] Notably, because of the TRO's emergency nature, a court typically does not have time to complete a hearing. Therefore, specific facts need to be pled in the complaint or supporting motion.

Temporary restraining orders are similar to preliminary injunctions because their purpose is to maintain the status quo; but, in contrast, a TRO may only be in place until a preliminary injunction hearing. Further, as with preliminary injunctions, the court may modify or dissolve a temporary restraining order if it establishes the circumstances so dictate.[58]

B. What Is the Difference Between a TRO and a Preliminary Injunction?

As noted earlier, temporary restraining orders and preliminary injunctions maintain the status quo; however, their differences are important and should be readily understood by litigators.

1. Notice

The notice requirements governing temporary restraining orders are the main difference from a preliminary injunction. Rule 65(b)(1) authorizes the court to issue a temporary restraining order ex parte without providing notice to the opposing party.[59] However, movants must certify "in writing any efforts made to give notice [to the opposing party] and the reasons why it should not be required."[60]

Courts disfavor ordering temporary restraining orders ex parte because they "often [facilitate] manifest injustices."[61] The requirements of Rule 65 reflect this reluctance, and litigators should craft their motions accordingly. The more measures a movant takes to notify the opposing party, even if unsuccessful, the more likely a court will rule in the movant's favor. The

---

57. FED. R. CIV. P. 65(b)(1)(A).
58. *See* Favia v. Ind. Univ. of Pa., 7 F.3d 332, 337 (3d Cir. 1993); *see also* FED. R. CIV. P. 62(c).
59. FED. R. CIV. P. 65(b)(1).
60. *Id.*
61. Redken Labs., Inc. v. Levin, 843 F.2d 226, 228 (6th Cir. 1988).

most preferred method is by written notice but courts are authorized to approve other methods, such as oral notice, if deemed reasonable.[62]

2. Duration

Another significant difference between TROs and preliminary injunctions is the duration of the injunction. If a TRO is granted without providing notice to the opposing party it cannot be in place for more than 14-days.[63] The date the temporary restraining order was stamped and endorsed signifies the official start of the TRO's 14-day duration. Once a movant obtains a temporary restraining order he must file it with the federal clerk promptly.[64]

The court may in its discretion, "for good cause, extend [a temporary restraining order] . . . for a like period or if the adverse party consents to a longer extension."[65] A movant must seek an extension before the TRO expires and show good cause for the extension. The determination of good cause is fact specific, but a movant may argue successfully for an extension to provide the court additional time to consider whether a preliminary injunction should be issued.[66] Even if notice is successfully provided by the movant, it does not automatically result in an indefinite TRO and the movant must still seek to evolve the TRO into a preliminary injunction.[67]

A temporary restraining order is similar to a preliminary injunction in that it is not intended to be the final outcome and its existence is contingent upon a proactive movant. Rule 65(b) requires that a preliminary injunction hearing be scheduled "at the earliest possible time, taking precedence over all other matters except hearings on older matters of the same character."[68] If the movant does not pursue a preliminary injunction, the temporary restraining order is terminated immediately.

---

62. *See* People of State of Ill. *ex rel.* Hartigan v. Peters, 871 F.2d 1336, 1340 (7th Cir. 1989).

63. *See* FED. R. CIV. P. 65(b)(2).

64. *See* Women's Med. Prof'l Corp. v. Taft, 199 F.R.D. 597 (S.D. Ohio 2000) (citing Maine v. Fri, 483 F.2d 439, 441 (1st Cir. 1973)).

65. FED. R. CIV. P. 65(b)(2).

66. *See* Women's Med. Prof'l Corp., 199 F.R.D. 597 (citing *Maine*, 483 F.2d at 441).

67. *See In re* Criminal Contempt Proceedings Against Gerald Crawford, 329 F.3d 131, 137 (2d Cir. 2003).

68. FED. R. CIV. P. 65(b)(3).

3. Security

The provision requiring movants to post a security applies to both preliminary injunctions and temporary restraining orders. Rule 65(c) requires a movant to give "security in an amount that the court considers proper to pay the costs and damages sustained by any party found to have been wrongfully enjoined or restrained." As stated earlier, it is within the court's discretion to determine the appropriate amount of security.[69]

C. What Is the Standard and Procedure for Obtaining a TRO?

The standard for a temporary restraining order is similar to that for a preliminary injunction. In fact, a TRO and preliminary injunction may be sought at the same time; indeed, a preliminary injunction must be sought once a TRO is granted. Rule 65(b) provides that a court may issue a TRO if "specific facts in an affidavit or a verified complaint clearly show that immediate and irreparable injury, loss, or damage will result to the movant before the adverse party can be heard in opposition."[70] The court conducts the same four-part test used in granting a preliminary injunction, that is,

(1) whether there is a likelihood that the movant will succeed on the merits; (2) whether the movant will suffer irreparable harm without the injunction; (3) the probability that granting the injunction will cause substantial harm to others; and (4) whether the public interest will be advanced by issuing the injunction.[71]

The court makes a final determination by balancing these factors against each other as they are not considered "prerequisites."[72]

The greatest difference between a TRO and a preliminary injunction is the imminence of the possible irreparable harm. Demonstrating an immediate, irreparable injury goes to the primary purpose of a TRO—to protect a

---

69. *See supra* Section II.D.3 for further discussion.
70. FED. R. CIV. P. 65(b).
71. Six Clinics Holding Corp., II v. Cafcomp Sys., Inc., 119 F.3d 393, 399 (6th Cir. 1997).
72. *See* Jones v. Caruso, 569 F.3d 258, 265 (6th Cir. 2009).

party from imminent harm by preserving the status quo. Therefore, courts look closely at the movant's argument of immediate, irreparable harm.

For example, in trade secret cases, the court considers "the loss of customers and good will . . . [as] an irreparable injury."[73] Temporary restraining orders are often appropriate in trade secret cases because "when damages that might be suffered are speculative—as in the case of misappropriated trade secrets—the harm is properly characterized as irreparable because an inadequate remedy at law is presumed."[74] However, it should be noted even if damages are speculative "other than simply alleging damage to its business reputation, [a movant must] demonstrate how it will suffer such damage."[75] Therefore, a movant should submit all available evidence in his possession when setting forth an argument.

The procedure for seeking a TRO is virtually the same as discussed above for a preliminary injunction. The key differences are that the moving party must plead an immediate, irreparable harm and any specific concerns regarding the motion being filed ex parte and must understand that a hearing for a TRO is not permitted.

Moreover, the available defenses for a respondent against a temporary restraining order are the same as those against preliminary injunctions and are also based in equity.

IV. CHECKLISTS
A. Preliminary Injunction Checklist (Review of Considerations and Procedure)

1. Review the four-part standard in determining whether a preliminary injunction is appropriate.
2. Draft a pleading in support of your motion.
3. Follow the Federal Rules of Evidence as closely as possible even if precedent dictates they are relaxed under a specific set of facts. The

---

73. Ferrero v. Associated Materials Inc., 923 F.2d 1441, 1449 (11th Cir. 1991).
74. All Leisure Holidays Ltd. v. Novello, 2012 U.S. Dist. LEXIS 168744, at *14–15 (S.D. Fla. Nov. 27, 2012).
75. Allure Jewelers, Inc. v. Mustafa Ulu, 2012 U.S. Dist. LEXIS 13361, at *12 (S.D. Ohio Feb. 3, 2012).

evidence will officially become part of the trial record if it complies with the Federal Rules of Evidence.

4. Provide notice to the opposing party.
5. Prepare for the possibility that the court will consolidate the hearing on the motion for the preliminary injunction with a hearing on the merits.
6. Post a security. Expect the amount to be substantial if the amount in controversy is high.

B. TRO Checklist (Review of Considerations and Procedure)

1. Determine if the situation requires a temporary restraining order or preliminary injunction.
2. Become familiar with local procedures on obtaining a temporary restraining order.
3. Review the four-part test when considering if a temporary restraining order is achievable.
4. Determine whether the situation requires moving for a TRO ex parte. Be prepared to explain in detail to the court your efforts to notify the opposing party. Take into account the court's reluctance when drafting pleadings. TROs granted without notice may only be in place for a maximum of 14 days.
5. When requesting a temporary restraining order, provide specific and narrow facts in your motions. Maintaining a balance between detail and "non-legalese" language is encouraged. Avoid overbroad language.
6. If possible, provide witnesses to verify the complaint or an affidavit in support.
7. Determine if a writ of injunction is required in your jurisdiction.
8. Submit the required filing fees.
9. Post a security. Expect the court to require a substantial amount in cases with a high amount in controversy.
10. Once your TRO is granted, prepare and file a motion for a preliminary injunction. A TRO is only effective for a limited time and will be terminated if the movant does not seek a subsequent preliminary injunction.

CHAPTER 5

Motions Directed to the Complaint

Heath Szymczak

You just received a call from a brand new client. His company has been served with a complaint. He is in the process of having it scanned and will email it to you shortly. The complaint contains various business tort claims accusing your client of a myriad of nefarious acts, all of which have supposedly caused irreparable harm to the plaintiff.[1] He says that the plaintiff is coming after him personally by trying to "pierce the corporate veil" of his company. He is anxious and has turned to you for guidance. He wants to know what this means to him and his company, and what will happen next. The conflicts check has cleared. The sound of the clock ticks loudly and your mind begins to race. Now what?

There are many issues to consider. How long has your client had the complaint? Was service proper? What about jurisdiction and venue? Are the correct parties named? What are the claims? Should you answer or make a motion? You recall something about waiving certain defenses if you are not careful, but which ones? The allegations against your client are scandalous. Fueled by your client's sense of outrage, you feel compelled to charge to his defense and jump right in to the details of the merits. Resist

---

1. The analysis to be considered when emergency relief is also sought against your client is discussed in Chapter 4.

this temptation. Step back and slow down. There are many threshold considerations to look at before you get bogged down in the minutiae of the merits—issues that may be simpler to address and could give your client a quicker, more cost-effective strategic advantage.

Keep in mind that your opponent has been methodically planning and investigating his case for weeks, even months. He has carefully selected his forum, interviewed his witnesses, framed his facts, and researched and honed his legal theories. You, however, do not have the luxury of time— you must move fast. In this chapter we consider the most common types of motions that may be directed at a complaint in a business torts case.[2] You can achieve various strategic and substantive objectives depending upon the motion you use. In fact, the selection of the right type of motion is akin to selecting a golf club: each has a unique function and must be sized up and selected depending on the specific circumstances presented. This chapter is intended to assist you in picking out the right motion for the job (or in making the decision to pass on a motion altogether) so that you can get the best possible result for your client (or at least stay out of the rough).

I. MOTION TO DISMISS: OVERVIEW

A motion to dismiss can be a devastating tactical weapon, which, if not handled carefully, may backfire on its wielder.[3] This chapter gives you a practical overview of the considerations involved in formulating and bringing your motion to dismiss, along with some other related motions. The emphasis is on the Federal Rules of Civil Procedure since many state civil practice rules generally follow federal practice (with some deviations that may vary significantly from state to state). If you are in state court, be sure to consult the corresponding state practice rules as there may be additional bases for dismissal not listed in the Federal Rules.

---

2. The answer, affirmative defenses, and counterclaims are discussed in Chapter 6.

3. *See* Heath J. Szymczak, *Motions to Dismiss in New York: A Primer on a Procedural Gatekeeper*, New York State Bar Association's Business Torts and Employment Litigation Blog, http://nysbar.com/blogs/nybusinesslitigation/2011/07/motions_to_dismiss_in_new_york.html (July 29, 2011).

As an initial matter, the practical impact of a motion directed at the complaint is that it has the effect of slowing down your opponent's momentum. Not only does your opponent have the upper hand by ambushing your unsuspecting client with the lawsuit, but the procedural rules at the start of the case are also slanted decidedly in his favor. A defendant has only a few short weeks to make a motion or serve an answer or face the risk of a default judgment being taken against him. This is true whether the plaintiff is seeking tens of thousands or tens of millions in monetary damages. There is one paramount consideration at the outset: stopping that clock. A response to a complaint is generally due within 21 days after service of the summons and complaint.[4] Under Federal Rule of Civil Procedure 6(a), the response time begins the day following receipt of the complaint and *includes* Saturdays, Sundays, and legal holidays. If, however, the last day of the period falls on a Saturday, Sunday, or legal holiday, the due date is the next regular business day.

You must immediately figure out when your client received service. This is not always as easy as it sounds because a complaint has a way of being shuffled around (or left sitting on a desk, a fax machine, or in an email inbox) before it finds its way to you. Several critical days may have been lost in the process. As a rule of thumb, there is one thing you should *always* do upon getting your hands on the complaint: pick up the phone. You should immediately call the counsel listed to ascertain the date of service and discuss an agreed-to responsive date. This also opens the door to collegial dialogue with opposing counsel, which by itself can result in significant cost savings for your client down the road. Be aware, however, that extensions granted by a plaintiff are often conditioned upon some *quid pro quo*, such as waiver of objection to venue or personal jurisdiction.[5] If an extension is coupled with an unacceptable condition, or if opposing counsel refuses altogether (or time is simply running out), immediately give thought to making a simple motion to extend time to answer or move, which the courts are

---

4. *See* Fed. R. Civ. P. 12(a)(1)(A); *see also* 1 Robert L. Haig et al., Business & Commercial Litigation in Federal Courts § 8:11 (3d ed. 2011).
5. *See infra* Section II.B.1–3.

often quick to grant (particularly where a reasonable request was already made to plaintiff and refused).

Once you manage to take the specter of a default judgment out of the equation, the mood and tenor of the case changes significantly. You and your client can breathe a sigh of relief, at least for the moment. A motion directed at the complaint may also give you an opportunity to put the plaintiff on the defensive, diffuse the allegations against your client, educate the court about the true nature of the case, narrow the issues in the litigation, and possibly result in a complete and total victory. Other times, the best thing that you can do is serve an answer, preserve your defenses, and go on the offensive with your client's own counterclaims and discovery demands, all the while waiting patiently to build your case so you can later spring your attack with a motion for summary judgment.

Federal Rule of Civil Procedure 12(b) is amply loaded with the implements that you may need to craft your motion to dismiss the complaint. It puts seven specific defenses at your disposal: (1) lack of subject matter jurisdiction, (2) lack of personal jurisdiction, (3) improper venue, (4) insufficient process, (5) insufficient service of process, (6) failure to state a claim upon which relief can be granted, and (7) failure to join a party. When you approach your motion to dismiss, you must carefully consider the relative strengths and tactical advantages of each defense, as well as the time and expense that will be incurred in the process. More often than not a court's analysis of a motion to dismiss will be limited to review of questions of law, which typically involve application of a statutory rule or case authority to the factual allegations. On such motions the plaintiff's allegations are generally taken as true, though in some instances a court will permit limited discovery and even hold a hearing on a narrow factual issue critical to resolution of the motion.[6]

If a motion is not properly analyzed and supported, a plaintiff may take shelter within the liberal and generous pleading standards afforded to a non-movant to easily defeat the motion.[7] A motion directed at only one

---

6. See, e.g., Kerns v. United States, 585 F.3d 187 (4th Cir. 2009) (remanded for discovery on jurisdictional issue).
7. See Szymczak, supra note 3.

cause of action, however, will also generally automatically stay the time to answer the entire complaint.[8] As you only get one shot at a motion to dismiss under the "single motion rule," you have to make it count.[9] Be careful not to leave out certain Rule 12(b) defenses in your motion (or answer) or you may waive them altogether.[10] Rule 12(h)(1) expressly states that a party waives any defense listed in Rule 12(b)(2) through (b)(5) if not raised in a motion or answer (including lack of personal jurisdiction, improper venue, insufficient process, and insufficient service of process).

II. DISRUPTION OF PLAINTIFF'S SELECTED FORUM

From a practical perspective, your best strategic advantage may lie in trying to use a motion to dictate where the litigation will take place (assuming another forum is more advantageous for your client). One of the oldest maxims in combat (whether military or legal) is to "seize the high ground." It is often said that good generals have always sought to fight on terrain that is either familiar or provides the best tactical advantage. This difference has been determinative in countless conflicts, even in the face of an opponent with overwhelming numbers and resources. Instead of steep slopes, narrow canyons, or the sun at our back, we are looking for favorable legal precedent, statutory rules, and sympathetic jury pools. Given that complete and final dismissals on a motion to dismiss are somewhat rare, a procedural attack on the plaintiff's selected forum may give your client the biggest bang for the buck. Dictating where the litigation will take place (particularly where it results in application of law more favorable to your client) takes the wind out of the plaintiff's sails, may deflate his willingness to pursue the case, or may lead to settlement talks. A substantive attack, on the other hand, may not only cost more, but it may simply educate your opponent and (even if your motion is granted) merely result in a fine-tuned amended pleading (with additional causes of action thrown in for good measure).

As such, this chapter places particular emphasis upon motions targeted at disrupting the plaintiff's selected forum. The first part of this chapter deals

---

8. *See* FED. R. CIV. P. 12(a)(4).
9. *See id.* 12(g)(2) (with respect to waivable defenses).
10. *See* HAIG ET AL., *supra* note 4, § 8:17.

with the *type* of jurisdictional forum (e.g., state, federal, or arbitration) with consideration of a motion to dismiss for lack of subject matter jurisdiction, including lack of justiciable claim, federal question, diversity jurisdiction, and supplemental jurisdiction. It also considers motions to compel arbitration as well as to remove litigation from state court to federal court. The second part of the chapter deals with the geographic *location* of the forum selected, with a review of motions to dismiss for lack of personal jurisdiction, as well as improper process, service, and venue. Finally, this chapter reviews motions directed at the substance of the legal claims and factual allegations contained within the complaint, including motions to dismiss for failure to state a claim, failure to join a party, for a more definite statement, and to strike.

A. Disruption of the *Type* of Jurisdictional Forum Selected by the Plaintiff

One of the first things that you should look at in a new business torts complaint is the type of forum that has been selected by the plaintiff. By "type" we mean the nature of the legal jurisdiction, as opposed to its simple geographic location. This generally refers to federal court or state court, but it may also apply to an extra-judicial forum such as arbitration. Approach the analysis as if you were "reverse engineering" plaintiff's forum selection determination. Put yourself in his shoes. Why do you think the plaintiff has selected the given type of forum? Does the forum selected give the plaintiff any particular advantage? Would your client be better served by trying to have the case moved to another type of forum?

Generally speaking, as between state and federal court, you should consider that federal district judges generally have more experience in handling complex commercial litigation. They are also less likely to be subject to local political considerations since they do not have to run for re-election. Federal jury pools are also more likely to be drawn from a wider geographic area (typically encompassing several counties), whereas a state trial court may only be drawn from a small area (often a single county). As a result, federal juries tend to be less demographically concentrated. This could be particularly important if the plaintiff is a local business that employs a significant number of citizens in that location.

With respect to state courts, it is important to note that approximately one-half of all states now have specialized business courts (sometimes referred to as "commercial divisions") for resolving business tort cases and other commercial disputes. These state business courts have many of the advantages previously thought to be found only in federal court or in arbitration.[11] State courts also tend to be more informal in nature, more hands on, and have quicker and broader provisional remedies. You may also be able to have more direct participation in jury voir dire in state court than you will in federal court. In addition, take a look at the relative velocity of the local state and federal dockets to see how quickly lawsuits are moving through the systems. You can often find this information on the web, but real-time anecdotal reports from your local contacts may be the most precise barometer. Other considerations include the types of discovery rules that apply (particularly with regard to e-discovery, which are generally more robust in federal court), stays of proceedings pending dispositive motions (generally not applicable in federal court), and availability of appellate procedures (such as interlocutory appeals, which are also generally not available in federal court).[12]

One of the most significant factors to consider in a business torts case is your ability to depose the plaintiff's expert. Your ability to gain access to your opponent's expert is often a function of the type of forum selected. In many business torts cases the lynchpin to the dispute may be the measure of damages, if any. This often requires a battle of experts. In some state courts, however, a pre-trial examination of the plaintiff's expert is often only permitted after a motion is made establishing "special circumstances," with an actual examination being the exception rather than the rule. In federal court, on the other hand, examination of the plaintiff's expert is not only permitted,

---

11. *See* Szymczak, *Standardizing Efficiencies in Business Litigation*, A.B.A. BUS. TORTS LITIG. J., Spring 2013.

12. *See* HAIG ET AL., *supra* note 4, § 11:2; *see also* Report of the Faster-Cheaper-Smarter Working Group of the Commercial and Federal Litigation Section of the New York State Bar Association (June 12, 2012); Report of New York Court of Appeals Chief Judge Jonathan Lippman's Task Force on Commercial Litigation in the 21st Century.

but is a matter of routine.[13] Many times a plaintiff will specifically seek to have his case heard in state court rather than federal court simply to insulate his expert from pretrial examination, and thus maximize the impact of his expert's testimony (and minimize the effect of your cross-examination) at trial.

Finally, if an arbitration clause exists in the agreement at the center of the dispute, then consider whether you want to seek enforcement of that provision and have the case removed from the courts altogether.[14] As discussed below, there are many factors that also go into consideration of selecting of arbitration as the adjudicative forum. If an arbitration clause does exist, think about why the plaintiff is seeking to avoid it. Is his case weak on the legal merits? Is he trying to leverage a settlement by airing his potentially embarrassing and scandalous allegations publicly? Is he banking upon winning over jury sympathies with a "David and Goliath" story? Also consider that the procedural and evidentiary rules are more relaxed in arbitration. Is he trying to avoid exposure to a piece of evidence that might be considered inadmissible by a judge, but might be considered by an arbitrator? Similarly, the scope and extent of discovery in arbitration is often more restricted than in the courts. Would forcing the case into arbitration truncate your ability to seek full discovery, including expert depositions, to flush out the plaintiff's case?

1. Motion to Dismiss for Lack of Subject Matter Jurisdiction—Rule 12(b)(1)

If you find yourself in federal court and, for the reasons noted above, you believe that your client would fare better in state court, you should consider a motion to dismiss for lack of subject matter jurisdiction. As business tort cases are generally creatures of state law, an attack on federal subject matter jurisdiction is often a likely candidate in a defense counsel's arsenal. The plaintiff may have chosen the federal forum in the hope of minimizing the

---

13. Rule 26(b)(4)(a) provides that "a party may depose any person who has been identified as an expert whose opinions may be presented at trial. If Rule 26(a)(2)(B) requires a report from the expert, the deposition may be conducted only after the report is provided." FED. R. CIV. P. 26(b)(4)(a).

14. *See* discussion *infra* Section II.A.3.

impact of sympathies that state court judges and juries may have for your client (particularly if it is a respected local company). The plaintiff may also have jerry-rigged a federal cause of action (such as a civil RICO or antitrust claim) to try to bring the parade of state law business tort claims in through the federal courthouse door. Plaintiff may have also undertaken some artful pleading in an attempt to manufacture diversity of citizenship.[15] You should analyze whether the federal claim is insubstantial or meritless, and whether you can also obtain dismissal of the supplemental state law claims.[16]

The analysis starts with understanding that federal courts are courts of limited jurisdiction. Unlike state courts (which generally have broad subject matter jurisdiction) a federal court may only exercise jurisdiction if it is authorized to do so by the United States Constitution or by federal statute.[17] An attack on subject matter jurisdiction questions the ability of the federal court to produce a judgment that can even be enforced. Thus, a motion to dismiss for lack of subject matter jurisdiction will be considered first, cannot be waived (or even agreed to by the parties), may be raised sua sponte by the court, and can be raised at any time (even on appeal).[18]

(a) Dismissal for Lack of Justiciable Claim

A threshold consideration as to whether a court has subject matter jurisdiction (federal or otherwise) is whether a claim is "justiciable." This concept has more to do with the separation of powers (between the legislative and judicial branches of government) than any distinction as between state and federal jurisdiction. Simply put, the legislative branch is in the business of governing future behavior, whereas the judicial branch is relegated to resolving actual disputes as between presently aggrieved parties. This restriction derives from Article III of the Constitution, which specifically limits the scope of the federal judicial power to the adjudication of actual

---

15. *See* discussion *infra* Section II.A.1.c.
16. *See* discussion *infra* Section II.A.1.d.
17. Adam v. Jacobs, 950 F.2d 89, 92 (2d Cir. 1991); *see also* Caterpillar Inc. v. Lewis, 519 U.S. 61 (1996).
18. *See* Steel Co. v. Citizens for a Better Environment, 523 U.S. 83, 89–90 (1998); Sosna v. Iowa, 419 U.S. 393, 398 (1975) (agreement or stipulation of parties cannot provide subject matter jurisdiction); Szymczak, *supra* note 3.

"cases" or "controversies."[19] The courts may not issue "advisory opinions" on past disputes or hypothetical potential disputes as that would be an improper invasion of the legislative prerogative.

The triad of analytical principles that underpin the justiciability framework are standing, ripeness, and mootness. "Standing" focuses on *who* is entitled to bring a lawsuit—whether the plaintiff has suffered an "injury-in-fact" and has a personal stake in the outcome of the controversy so as to warrant exercise of federal court jurisdiction.[20] "Ripeness" and "mootness" focus on *when* judicial review is appropriate. The ripeness doctrine relates to whether a dispute is ready for adjudication, and requires the court to evaluate "the fitness of the issues for judicial decision and the hardship to the parties of withholding court consideration."[21] Mootness is merely the flip side of ripeness: it prohibits adjudication of lawsuits in which there is no longer an actual dispute.

(b) Dismissal for Lack of Federal Question

Section 1331 of Title 28 is the "federal question" statute. It allows federal question jurisdiction in cases "arising under the Constitution, laws, or treaties of the United States."[22] As you might guess, federal question jurisdiction simply applies to claims touching upon material issues of federal law. Although it is rare for a business torts case to present a pure question of federal law, you may encounter the occasional antitrust[23] or civil RICO[24] causes of action. Nevertheless, the federal claim or issue, if present, must be substantial to sustain the invocation and application of federal jurisdiction.

(c) Dismissal for Lack of Diversity Jurisdiction

There is, however, a somewhat gaping exception to the tight restrictions imposed upon the availability of federal jurisdiction: "diversity jurisdiction."

---

19. U.S. CONST. art. III, § 2.
20. Toll Bros., Inc. v. Twp. of Readington, 555 F.3d 131, 138 (3d Cir. 2009); *see also* HAIG ET AL., *supra* note 4, § 1:60.
21. Abbott Labs. v. Gardner, 387 U.S. 136, 149 (1967).
22. 28 U.S.C. § 1331.
23. *Id.* § 1337, et seq.
24. 18 U.S.C. § 1964, et seq.

In contrast to federal question jurisdiction, which is based upon an issue of federal law, diversity jurisdiction is merely based upon the locations or "citizenships" of the parties. Section 1332 of Title 28 grants federal courts the authority to hear cases between citizens of different states and foreign countries, *irrespective* of whether a federal claim is asserted.[25] The only real catch is that it is limited to "civil actions where the matter in controversy exceeds the sum or value of $75,000, exclusive of interest and costs."[26] Diversity must also be complete across the "v" (as in "plaintiffs '*v.*' defendants") and must exist at the time the complaint is filed.[27] That is, if any plaintiff and any defendant share a common citizenship, then diversity jurisdiction dissolves. Your Rule 12(b)(1) motion can challenge diversity jurisdiction by undermining the supporting allegations relating to citizenship and the claimed jurisdictional amount.[28]

An individual's "citizenship" is based upon his or her "domicile," which is generally the location to which the party has the greatest physical or economic connection. An individual may have multiple residences, but only one "domicile" for purposes of diversity jurisdiction analysis. Certain indicia of an individual's domicile may include where he works, where his family is located, where he votes, and where he registers his vehicles. Significantly, corporations are deemed to have "dual citizenship," and are considered to be citizens both of the state of their incorporation as well as where they have their principal place of business. Where a corporation is incorporated in more than one state, it is considered to be a citizen of *every* state (domestic and foreign) in which it is incorporated *and* where it maintains its principal place of business.[29] You should also keep an eye out for the potential that plaintiff has purposefully avoided joining a necessary party to create diversity (or fraudulent joinder of a non-diverse party to

---

25. 28 U.S.C. § 1332.
26. *Id.*
27. If a case is removed to federal court, you have to show diversity jurisdiction both at the time of filing and removal, and a joined party, if indispensable, may defeat preexisting diversity.
28. 28 U.S.C. § 1332.
29. The Federal Courts Jurisdiction and Venue Clarification Act of 2011, Pub. L. No. 112-63 (Dec. 7, 2011), 125 Stat. 758, amended and clarified 28 U.S.C. § 1332(c) to apply the same citizenship status to both domestic and foreign corporations.

purposefully defeat diversity and the risk of removal by the defendants if the plaintiff prefers state court).

A defendant may be able to slow down a plaintiff, and begin to build his defense, by pursuing discovery on threshold jurisdictional issues, such as ascertaining actual domicile of the parties, fraudulent joinder (or non-joinder) of parties, and the nature of the amount claimed to be in controversy. As the burden of showing fraudulent joinder is high, however, a good faith basis must exist to challenge these jurisdictional elements, and consideration should be given to the time and cost that will be expended in the process. If the jurisdictional challenge is weak and unfocused, you will not only waste time and money, but you will also make a very bad first impression with the court (and even possibly face sanctions). As such, the strategic benefits involved and the possible negative impacts must be deliberately considered.

(d) Dismissal for Lack of Supplemental Jurisdiction

If the basis for federal jurisdiction is weak or attenuated, you may seek not only dismissal of the federal claims, but also dismissal of the pendant state law business tort claims contained in the complaint. Section 1367 of Title 28 provides for "supplemental jurisdiction" over state law claims so long as they are related to the existing federal claims.[30] The underlying purpose of this requirement is to avoid the waste of time and expense imposed upon the parties by having to litigate federal and related state law claims in separate jurisdictional forums. Federal courts, however, do not want to adjudicate state law claims that were merely bootstrapped to an artificial federal claim that never should have been brought in federal court in the first place. In addition, supplemental jurisdiction may not be exercised by a federal court in the absence of complete diversity of citizenship as required by Section 1332. It also may not be exercised, even in the presence of complete diversity, to determine questions of state law that are a matter of first impression or are unique in nature. A federal court will decline supplemental jurisdiction under those circumstances and defer to the state

---

30.   28 U.S.C. § 1367(a).

court.[31] It should also be noted that a dismissal for lack of subject matter jurisdiction is not a resolution on the merits, and has no binding effect on the substantive issues.

2. Motion to Compel Arbitration

Because a contractual provision providing for arbitration may be considered to deprive the court of subject matter jurisdiction, a motion may be made to dismiss under Rule 12(b)(1) for lack of subject matter jurisdiction or 12(b)(6) for failure to state a claim for which relief may be granted.[32] That is, if arbitration is the proper type of jurisdictional forum that applies, other courts will defer to that forum. If, however, you seek not only dismissal, but also an affirmative grant of power by the federal district court to *compel* the plaintiff to proceed to arbitration, you must bring a petition to compel arbitration.[33] In that case, you must demonstrate that the federal court has subject matter jurisdiction over the dispute itself, and that the dispute falls within the ambit of the arbitration clause at issue. State courts often have their own independent statutory mechanisms that allow for enforcement of arbitration clauses. If such a clause exists, you should not wait to seek its enforcement, but should act promptly, as delay (or participation in the litigation) may result in waiver.

Of course, before pursuing this route, you should consider the pros and cons of arbitration itself, and whether or not a public forum (with a right to appeal) may be more advantageous for your client. There is a growing perception that many of the advantages of arbitration, particularly in terms of cost savings, have eroded, with arbitration often ending up costing just as much as, or more than, litigation.[34] This is due in part to up-front fees (which are a function of the amount in controversy) and the fact that dispositive motions are almost nonexistent.[35] There is also a belief that arbitrators are more inclined to "split the baby" rather than make a difficult decision. There

---

31. *See id.* § 1367(c)(1), (2), (4).
32. Discussed at Sections 11.A.1, *supra*, and III.A, *infra*.
33. *See* 9 U.S.C. § 4.
34. *See* Szymczak, *supra* note 11; *see also* Christopher R. Drahozal, *Business Courts and the Future of Arbitration*, 10 CARDOZO J. CONFLICT RESOL. 491 (2009).
35. *See* Szymczak, *supra* note 11.

are still many reasons to choose arbitration over litigation (e.g., privacy and jury avoidance), but it appears that those reasons increasingly have less to do with saving money.[36] As noted above, many states have their own specialized business courts that borrow much from the arbitration model, and may be preferable to your client depending upon the specific circumstances.

3. Removal to Federal Court

Much of the above discussion has been presented from the perspective of a defendant that finds itself in federal court. To close out this part of the chapter, we consider briefly the defendant who is in state court and seeks to remove the case to federal court. Section 1441 of Title 28 governs the removal of cases from state court to federal court.[37] It provides that a case may only be removed if the plaintiff could have brought it in federal court in the first place. As such, all of the questions discussed above (justiciability, federal question, diversity, and supplemental jurisdiction) may come into play and should be considered. Given its wide applicability, diversity jurisdiction is by far the most common basis upon which a defendant may seek to invoke federal jurisdiction for purposes of removal. A strategically awkward situation may arise, however, where a defendant is seeking removal based upon diversity and is forced to argue that the plaintiff's potential damages are likely to be in excess of the jurisdictional amount of $75,000 (something that you might want to avoid). However, if the weight of factors tips strongly in favor of federal court, then that may be a bitter pill that you may just have to swallow.

To remove a case to federal court, you must first file your notice of removal containing a short and plain statement of the grounds for removal (together with a copy of all process, pleadings, and orders served upon your client) in federal court within 30 days after *receipt* (through service or otherwise) of a copy of the initial pleading.[38] You must also file a copy of the

---

36. *Id.; see also* Steven Badger, *To Arbitrate or Litigate, That Is the Question*, IND. LAW., Jan. 2, 2013.
37. 28 U.S.C. § 1441 et seq.
38. *Id.* § 1446(a)–(b).

MOTIONS DIRECTED TO THE COMPLAINT

notice with the state court clerk's office.[39] Do not forget to page through the relevant local rules of practice for the particular federal district court involved (as well as any individual judge's rules) as they may contain additional requirements. If there are multiple defendants, all defendants (with the exception of certain limited circumstances such as fraudulent joinder) must consent to removal or the attempt will fail.[40]

Once again, if you fail to move quickly you may lose your ability to remove the state court action to federal court. If the case was not removable at the time it was filed, but later becomes removable, you will have 30 days after receipt of a copy of the document that creates federal jurisdiction to remove, so long as it is not based solely on diversity and more than one year has not passed since the original filing.[41] Under no circumstances, however, will you be able to remove a case based upon your client's own counterclaims.[42] Please note that the mere act of removing the case does not impact your right to make a motion to dismiss under Rule 12(b) (with the exception of federal jurisdiction that you just worked to establish).

B. Disruption of the Geographic *Location* of the Forum Selected by the Plaintiff

1. Motion to Dismiss for Lack of Personal Jurisdiction—Rule 12(b)(2)

Unlike subject matter jurisdiction, which relates to the type of forum, personal jurisdiction relates to the geographic location of the particular forum, and sounds in principles of due process and fairness, rather than the boundaries of judicial authority. As such, unlike subject matter jurisdiction, attempts to challenge personal jurisdiction *can* be waived if not raised by motion or ensuing answer to the complaint.[43] While somewhat similar

---

39. *Id.* § 1446(d).
40. *See* Lewis v. Rego Co., 757 F.2d 66, 68 (3d Cir. 1985); Blazik v. County of Dauphin, 44 F.3d 209, 213 n.4 (3d Cir. 1995).
41. 28 U.S.C. § 1446(b). The Federal Courts Jurisdiction and Venue Clarification Act of 2011, however, now provides that the one-year time period *may* be extended if the court concludes that a plaintiff acted in bad faith to prevent removal. *See* 28 U.S.C.A. § 1446(c)(1); *see also* Thomas A. Gilson, *Updating Federal Procedures for Removal and Venue*, A.B.A. BUS. TORTS LITIG. J., Spring 2012.
42. *See* HAIG ET AL., *supra* note 4, § 11:70.
43. *See* FED. R. CIV. P. 12(g)–(h)(1).

to diversity jurisdiction analysis, personal jurisdiction analysis goes a step further and looks to the nexus of contacts between the court, the claim, and the defendant involved. That is, for personal jurisdiction to exist the location of the court must generally be one where the defendant may have anticipated being sued as a result of its physical presence in, or the benefits it derives from, the forum's location.

Thus, assuming proper service,[44] personal jurisdiction may be established by showing a relationship between the defendant and the forum, which is typically referred to as "minimum contacts" analysis.[45] Personal jurisdiction can be characterized either as specific or general. Specific jurisdiction (which is more limited) applies where a defendant has *purposefully* directed its activities at the forum state and the "litigation results from alleged injuries that 'arise out of or relate to' those activities."[46] There must be a direct link between the defendant's actions and the claim. General jurisdiction (which is much broader) applies where a defendant's contacts with the forum are "continuous and systematic," *irrespective* of any nexus to plaintiff's claims.[47] For this reason, a plaintiff has a high burden to show the existence of general jurisdiction.

The nature of this analysis naturally lends itself to an intensive factual investigation. As such, it is imperative that you perform your due diligence to establish the contacts (or lack thereof) that your client has to the particular geographic forum involved. Take the time to sit down with your client and develop a sound evidentiary basis for challenging personal jurisdiction before making the motion. If a question of fact is shown, the court may permit limited discovery or hold an evidentiary hearing. As a plaintiff need only make a prima facie showing, however, you should be circumspect about the time and energy devoted to this exercise unless the question is close or the law of another jurisdiction is much more favorable to your client or is potentially dispositive (such as a shorter statute of limitations period).

---

44. *See* discussion *infra* Section II.B.2.

45. Fed. R. Civ. P. 4 governs service of process. Contacts analysis has developed through case law. *See, e.g.,* International Shoe Co. v. State of Washington, 326 U.S. 310, 316 (1945).

46. Burger King Corp. v. Rudzewicz, 471 U.S. 462, 472 (1985) (quoting Helicopteros Nacionales de Colombia, S.A. v. Hall, 466 U.S. 408, 414 (1984)).

47. Helicopteros, 466 U.S. at 415–16.

Because a personal jurisdiction determination may render other defenses moot, a court may address this question first before proceeding to other defenses. It also makes sense to couple your Rule 12(b)(2) motion with a motion to transfer venue.[48] As it does not deal with the merits, a dismissal for want of personal jurisdiction is also not binding on the substantive claims as a bar to future litigation in another forum.

2. Motion to Dismiss for Improper Process or Service—Rules 12(b)(4) & (5)

Case authority dealing with the application of Rules 12(b)(4) and 12(b)(5) tend to blur the line between the two. Generally, Rule 12(b)(4) involves objections to the form of *what* was served under Rule 4 (misspelled names, incorrect wording, wrong caption or index number, wrong entity); Rule 12(b)(5) involves *how* the process was served. Rule 4(m) also requires that the summons and complaint be served within 120 days after its filing. If this does not happen, a court will dismiss the action without prejudice or direct that service be completed by a date certain (assuming plaintiff can show a good reason for the failure). Do not be too quick to exalt form over substance here unless you are able to articulate prejudice or the statute of limitations is about to run out. At the same time, you should recognize that objections under these rules can be easily waived. Not surprisingly, a court will usually deny a motion to dismiss for minor deviations from these rules and simply direct plaintiff to reserve. The fundamental purpose of these rules is to provide adequate notice and an opportunity to be heard, i.e., basic due process protection. The success of a motion made under these rules will basically be a function of the severity with which the defendant's due process rights were cut short through no fault of its own.

3. Motion to Dismiss for Improper Venue—Rule 12(b)(3)

Like personal jurisdiction and service of process analysis, a motion directed at the venue of the litigation under Rule 12(b)(3) is also founded upon principles of fairness and judicial economy. It may also be waived. A motion to

---

48. *See* 28 U.S.C. § 1404(a), or *id.* § 1406(a).

dismiss under Rule 12(b)(3) may lie where a contractual forum selection clause specifies a different venue, where the selected venue is disproportionately inconvenient, or where another action involving the same facts and parties was previously filed in another venue under the "first-filed rule." As with personal jurisdiction under Rule 12(b)(2), a court under Rule 12(b)(3) may also permit consideration of evidentiary materials and hold a hearing to ascertain the proper venue. In considering the convenience of the forum, a court may consider the location of the witnesses and physical evidence, availability of compulsory process, the relative means of the parties involved, and the degree of congestion in the respective venues at issue.[49] As a practical matter, an outright dismissal under Rule 12(b)(3) is also unlikely. Rather than dismiss the action, the court is much more likely to transfer venue.[50]

III. MOTIONS AIMED AT THE SUBSTANCE OF THE COMPLAINT

A. Motion to Dismiss for Failure to State a Claim—Rule 12(b)(6)

Last, but certainly not least, we come to motions directed at the merits of the complaint. A grant of a motion to dismiss on the merits, and with prejudice, is the "holy grail" of defense practice. It is a quick, complete, and relatively inexpensive victory. Even if you are not able to obtain a complete dismissal, a dismissal of some of the claims may derail the plaintiff's case, significantly narrow the scope of discovery, or package the case for settlement talks and mediation. You may also have the opportunity to take control of the narrative of the case to the benefit of your client and to undermine the plaintiff's credibility. It is important to note that, unlike motions seeking dismissal for lack of personal jurisdiction, improper venue, or insufficiency of process or service, a motion to dismiss for failure to state a claim *cannot* be waived. You may make such a motion at any stage of the litigation,

---

49. Gulf Oil Corp. v. Gilbert, 330 U.S. 501, 508, 509 (1947); *see also* HAIG ET AL., *supra* note 4, § 3:49.
50. *See* 28 U.S.C. § 1404(a), or *id.* § 1406(a).

86

although it may be more properly clothed as a motion for summary judgment at a later phase of the case.[51]

A motion to dismiss for failure to state a claim under Rule 12(b)(6) is akin to a scientific forensic examination. You are essentially placing the plaintiff's complaint under the analytical microscope and systematically dissecting each cause of action for technical deficiencies by severing and measuring the factual allegations against the applicable legal standards. You should always begin your review by looking for the lowest hanging fruit. For example, if the factual allegations seem somewhat stale, look to see if you can obtain dismissal due to the expiration of an applicable statute of limitations as to some or all of the claims. Once you determine the applicable statute of limitations as to each claim, it is a matter of using plaintiff's own allegations to establish that the date of accrual dispositively establishes that the claim or claims are time-barred. Similarly, if the legal dispute has already been adjudicated (whether in court or in arbitration), determine if you can assert a motion based upon res judicata as a complete bar to the present litigation.[52] Remember that although the plaintiff's factual allegations (as opposed to legal assertions) will be taken as true, and limited to the four corners of the complaint, you may often still use the exhibits attached to the complaint to your advantage as if they were set forth in the complaint in full.

After you review the complaint for a statute of limitations or a res judicata attack, you should next look to claims that have some degree of heightened pleading requirements that require sufficiency in factual detail to survive dismissal. In the business torts context, such claims may include fraud, piercing the corporate veil, breach of fiduciary duty, and tortious interference with actual or prospective contractual relations. The best place to start the process is with the relevant pattern jury instructions in hand. Use the jury instructions as a litmus test to challenge the sufficiency of the allegations

---

51. *See* HAIG ET AL., *supra* note 4, § 8:22.
52. As noted above, if a related matter is still pending, but not yet adjudicated, you may seek to dismiss under Rule 12(b)(3). You may also look to see whether abstention principles may dictate that the federal court defer to state court proceedings relative to unique or significant matters of state law under Rule 12(b)(1).

leveled at your client. As the instructions are the last thing the jury will hear, it makes sense to start there.

Significantly, two recent Supreme Court cases, *Atlantic v. Twombly* and *Ashcroft v. Iqbal*, have altered the analytical framework for a facial sufficiency challenge on a motion to dismiss, and have increased the likelihood that your motion may be granted.[53] Under *Twombly* and *Iqbal*, a court must "tak[e] note of the elements a plaintiff must plead to state a claim," identify allegations that are mere conclusions, and sort through the factual allegations to determine whether they plausibly give rise to an entitlement for relief.[54] Thus, plaintiffs are now required to do *more* than merely restate the bare legal elements of a cause of action to suggest the "possibility" of a claim; they must now set forth sufficient factual detail to demonstrate that the claim is "plausible." Although the plausibility standard does not impose a "probability requirement," it does require "more than a sheer possibility that a defendant has acted unlawfully."[55] The lower courts are still working to find a balance for the application of these principles, but you should advocate for the most robust interpretation for your client in seeking dismissal of all claims asserted in the lawsuit.

B. Motion to Dismiss for Failure to Join a Party—Rule 12(b)(7)

In addition to the claims that have been asserted, look also at the parties that have been named in the suit and, more significantly, consider if anyone has been left out. As noted above in discussion of diversity jurisdiction, at times a plaintiff will purposefully omit a defendant to maintain diversity of the parties.[56] Rule 19 addresses the omission of parties and Rule 12(b)(7) provides the mechanism for its enforcement by allowing for dismissal of actions in the face of Rule 19 violations. To get to Rule 12(b)(7) via Rule 19,

---

53. Bell Atl. Corp. v. Twombly, 550 U.S. 544 (2007); Ashcroft v. Iqbal, 556 U.S. 662 (2009).
54. Santiago v. Warminster Twp., 629 F.3d 121, 130 (3d Cir. 2010) (quoting *Iqbal*, 556 U.S. at 667–78).
55. *Iqbal*, 556 U.S. at 678 (citing *Twombly*, 550 U.S. at 556).
56. Rule 21 governs improperly joined (rather than omitted) parties who may have been added solely to defeat diversity. Under such circumstances you should promptly move to drop or sever, not to dismiss under Rule 12. See Haig et al., *supra* note 4, § 13:38.

however, requires a complicated series of analytical machinations as there are numerous equitable and prudential factors that the court will consider relative to unnamed defendants and the impact of proceeding without them. The overarching policy objective is to avoid piecemeal claim adjudication (as well as possible inconsistent judgments) and to conserve judicial resources by avoiding duplicative litigation in the future.[57]

Determining whether a party is "required" under Rule 19 involves a multi-step analysis.[58] Initially, Rule 19(a) requires that the party must be subject to service of process *and* that joinder of the party will not deprive the court of subject matter jurisdiction if it is joined. If that is the case, Rule 19(a)(1) requires that the court will look to (1) whether it will still be able to provide complete relief among existing parties without that party and (2) whether that party has a claim relating to the subject of the action such that adjudication without them may prejudice their claim or whether an existing party may have to re-litigate the same issues in the future with that party. If the prospective party meets one of these two standards, it must be joined "if feasible" under Rule 19(a)(2).

If joinder is *not* feasible, "the court must determine whether, in equity and good conscience, the action should proceed among the existing parties or should be dismissed" under Rule 19(b). Rule 19(b) sets forth a number of additional equitable factors that a court will systematically weigh to determine if the case should be allowed to proceed or be dismissed under Rule 12(b)(7). Under Rule 19(b)(1) through (b)(4), the court will consider, among other things, whether a judgment rendered in the person's absence would be adequate or might prejudice that person or other existing parties. If there is prejudice, the court will see if it can be mitigated or avoided by crafting a carve-out in the judgment or otherwise shaping the relief in some way to protect the existing and absent parties. The Rule 19(b) factors, however, are neither exclusive nor dispositive.[59] Given the discretionary nature of the analysis, and the potential harm to a plaintiff in the event of dismissal,

---

57. *See* Republic of the Philippines v. Pimentel, 553 U.S. 851, 862–63 (2008).
58. Center for Biological Diversity v. Pizarchik, 858 F. Supp. 2d 1221, 1229 (D. Colo. 2012).
59. *Id.*

more often than not a court may err on the side of proceeding without a party inasmuch as Rule 19 does not necessarily negate the ability of the court to adjudicate the dispute among the parties that have been joined.[60]

C. Motion for Judgment on the Pleadings—Rule 12(c)

Rule 12(c) provides that "[a]fter the pleadings are closed—but early enough not to delay trial—a party may move for judgment on the pleadings." A motion for judgment on the pleadings, however, is something of a vestigial motion: it exists but does not serve much purpose. It is uncommon in commercial litigation. It is essentially just a Rule 12(b)(6) motion made later in the procedural posture of the case (after the pleadings are closed). Just as with a Rule 12(b)(6) motion, the same standards (including application of the *Twombly* and *Iqbal* standards) will apply and the court is still constrained by the four corners of the complaint. Of course, if a motion to dismiss under Rule 12(b)(6) is warranted, then it makes more sense to just bring that motion at the outset rather than incurring the costs of litigation, wasting time, and possibly waiving some defenses in the process.[61] Loosely speaking, Rule 12(c) is nothing more than a "safety net" to permit you to bring a post-answer motion to dismiss (assuming you have not already made a motion under 12(b)(6)) in a particularly complicated or vexing matter that did not lend itself to a straightforward pre-answer 12(b)(6) motion. As a practical matter, if you are able to make a Rule 12(b)(6) motion, then do so. If not, you may just be better off bringing a motion for summary judgment. In any event, if you plan on bringing a Rule 12(c) motion, it is better not to wait too long after serving your answer to make your motion.

D. Motion for More Definite Statement—Rule 12(e)

Rule 12(e) motions also do not serve much purpose in commercial litigation. Rule 12(e) provides in part that a "party may move for a more definite statement of a pleading to which a responsive pleading is allowed but which is so vague or ambiguous that the party cannot reasonably prepare

---

60. *See* FED. R. CIV. P. 19 advisory committee's note.
61. *See generally* HAIG ET AL., *supra* note 4, § 8:38.

a response." As you might expect, the "cannot be responded to" standard is pretty high. Although some commercial litigators can be overly verbose, they are rarely completely unintelligible. If the complaint is so bad that you cannot remotely decipher what claims it contains, then you may be better off bringing a motion to dismiss for failure to state a claim under Rule 12(b),[62] or simply answering, preserving your defenses, and seeking amplification of the pleading through discovery. On the other hand, if it is clear to you that the litigation is brought without foundation or is frivolous in nature, it may be worthwhile to bring a Rule 12(c) motion to call out your opponent's credibility and possibly couple it with other Rule 12 objections (as well as a Rule 11 motion for sanctions). Otherwise, the courts are rarely receptive to Rule 12(e) motions.

E. Motion to Strike—Rule 12(f)

Rule 12(f) provides that a "court may strike from a pleading an insufficient defense or any redundant, immaterial, impertinent, or scandalous matter . . . (1) on its own; or (2) on motion made by a party either before responding to the pleading or, if a response is not allowed, within 21 days after being served with the pleading." As with Rule 12(e) motions, courts are not eager to deal with Rule 12(f) motions either. They also rarely appear in commercial litigation. For a court to strike allegations from a complaint as "scandalous" they must be extremely offensive and prejudicial to your client. This standard is even harder to meet than Rule 12(e)'s "unintelligible" standard because you are asking the court to wade out into the perilous waters of the First Amendment, which most courts are reluctant to do. In the rare case that a complaint does contain such vitriolic and irrelevant allegations to warrant a Rule 12(f) motion, a court would also likely entertain a Rule 11 motion for sanctions while it is at it.

IV. CONCLUSION

From the technical aspects of the manner of service and the form of the complaint, to the place of the litigation, and the substance of the allegations,

---

62. Along with any other possible Rule 12(b) defenses to avoid possible waiver.

you can approach the lawsuit with confidence. Before getting bogged down in the factual allegations, step back and take a practical approach to the analysis to find the best motion for the job—one that will give your client the greatest strategic advantage at the lowest possible cost. A finely crafted motion may allow you to turn the tables on the opposition, or even obtain a complete dismissal of the case.

CHAPTER 6

Answer, Affirmative Defenses, and Counterclaims

Chadwick A. McTighe

Few clients like answers (if they can be said to like any pleading). They prefer not to have been sued in the first place. When avoiding litigation is impossible, however, the next best thing is to have the suit dismissed at the outset. Therefore, the first instruction from many clients upon hiring counsel to defend against the complaint is to find a way to get rid of it (perhaps even an express instruction to file a motion to dismiss). Many litigators similarly seem to have a default assumption that a motion to dismiss will be filed almost before they read the complaint. For some, filing an answer thus may seem like a sign of defeat, the result of a failed attempt to escape the case before having to engage in prolonged and expensive discovery, motion practice, and the many other undesirable components of a lawsuit.

Of course, as any litigator knows, motions to dismiss do not always succeed and sometimes cannot be filed at all. Even in federal court, where *Bell Atlantic Corp. v. Twombly*[1] and *Ashcroft v. Iqbal*[2] establish a plausibility pleading standard seemingly higher than the standards imposed by many

---

1. Bell Atlantic Corp. v. Twombly, 550 U.S. 544 (2007).
2. Ashcroft v. Iqbal, 556 U.S. 662 (2009).

state courts, motions to dismiss often are denied. In some cases, a good faith motion to dismiss will not even be possible. In others, the grounds for a motion to dismiss may be so tenuous that prudence counsels forgoing the opportunity to file a document that will do little more than undermine the credibility of the defendant and its counsel.

Business torts, in particular, can be difficult to dispose of through a motion to dismiss. Fiduciary duty claims, for example, frequently can survive a motion to dismiss because of the factual and legal analysis required to determine whether such a duty exists (even before considering any other elements of the claim).[3] Tortious interference claims (in their various forms) also can be difficult to dismiss because the elements of such claims, such as proof of "improper" interference, can require consideration of fact-intensive factors not likely to be subject to resolution on a motion to dismiss.[4] Because it can be especially difficult to obtain outright dismissal of many business tort claims, knowing how to draft a proper answer is especially important for attorneys litigating such claims.

Given the critical nature of the answer, attorneys often pay surprisingly little attention to it. Many unfortunately tend to treat the answer as a procedural necessity that can be thrown together quickly, filed, and forgotten—after all, no one reads them anyway, right? Too many answers filed by different attorneys in different cases look like carbon copies—a series of generic denials followed by a list of boilerplate affirmative defenses stated in conclusory terms. Admittedly, answers are somewhat formulaic by nature, and the provisions of Rule 8 provide few opportunities for creative pleading (nor would it necessarily be useful, or advisable, to stray from the Rule). That said, following a basic formula is a far cry from simply cobbling together generic denials and boilerplate affirmative defenses. The answer is important, and it is unwise to give it too little thought.

---

3. *See, e.g., In re* Cardinal Health ERISA Litig., 424 F. Supp. 2d 1002, 1030 (S.D. Ohio 2006); *In re* Electronic Data Sys. Corp., 305 F. Supp. 2d 658, 665 (E.D. Tex. 2004).

4. *See* RESTATEMENT (SECOND) OF TORTS ch. 37, introductory note (1979); *id.* §§ 766–67; Prime Contr., Inc. v. Wal-Mart Stores, Inc., No. 06-383-JBC, 2008 U.S. Dist. LEXIS 56449, at *19 (E.D. Ky. July 22, 2008) (holding that questions of good faith, improper purpose, and motive are questions of fact).

This chapter addresses some basic issues regarding answers and, because the two often will be filed together, counterclaims. Part I discusses answers generally. Part II discusses affirmative defenses, which present their own set of considerations, including potential pleading requirements in light of *Twombly* and *Iqbal*. Part III discusses counterclaims. Part IV briefly addresses the amendment of pleadings.

I. ANSWERS

Pleadings serve four basic purposes: (1) providing notice of the nature of a claim or defense; (2) identifying facts that the parties believe to exist; (3) narrowing the issues to be litigated; and (4) enabling the "speedy disposition of sham claims and insubstantial defenses."[5] The answer "should apprise the opponent of those allegations in the complaint that stand admitted and will not be in issue at trial and those that are contested and will require proof to be established to enable the plaintiff to prevail."[6] With these purposes in mind, it is helpful to look first to the Federal Rule[7] setting forth the requirements for an answer, and then to build from the requirements of the Rule to consider effective means of setting forth the answer to the complaint.

A. Rule 8(b)

Rule 8(b) of the Federal Rules of Civil Procedure sets forth the requirements for an answer. First, "in responding to a pleading, a party must: (A) state in short and plain terms its defenses to each claim asserted against it; and (B) admit or deny the allegations asserted against it by an opposing party."[8] Rule 8 adds several qualifiers to this basic requirement. "A denial must fairly respond to the substance of the allegation."[9] The Rule allows a general

---

5. CHARLES ALAN WRIGHT & ARTHUR R. MILLER, FEDERAL PRACTICE AND PROCEDURE § 1202, at 88 (3d ed.) (2004).
6. *Id.* § 1261, at 526.
7. Due to the nature of this book, citations are made to the Federal Rules of Civil Procedure and case law interpreting them. Obviously, it is prudent to consult any local rules as well, and litigants in state court likewise should review the rules of civil procedure (or their equivalent) for the relevant jurisdiction.
8. FED. R. CIV. P. 8(b)(1).
9. *Id.* 8(b)(2).

denial of all allegations, if made in good faith.[10] The likelihood of being able simply to deny every allegation can be slim if the complaint is well-drafted. Thus, the Rule provides that in the absence of a general denial, the party "must either specifically deny designated allegations or generally deny all except those specifically admitted."[11] To a degree, the Rule also requires a defendant to parse the allegations against it, as the party must admit any part of an allegation that is true when denying only part of an allegation.[12]

There are times when a defendant can neither admit nor deny an allegation against it. Pleading a lack of knowledge or information sufficient to form a belief as to the truth of an allegation thus is permissible, and this has the effect of a denial.[13] One should not invoke this provision as a means of avoiding the need to conduct basic due diligence to determine whether an allegation is true, however. Courts reject "sham" assertions that the defendant lacks knowledge or information regarding matters that it reasonably should know, and, as a result, these courts deem the facts admitted.[14] A defendant also cannot simply rely on a lack of top-of-mind knowledge, and it has a duty to exercise reasonable efforts to educate itself in answering allegations against it.[15] In light of these obligations, answers can be especially burdensome on corporate defendants—and many business torts litigators have corporate clients—as the company may know (or should know) more than the individuals assisting counsel with the litigation. Attorneys litigating business torts thus should be cognizant of the potential need to conduct interviews and otherwise investigate matters before pleading a lack of knowledge or information.

Failing to deny any allegation other than one relating to the amount of damages constitutes an admission (unless the pleading is one to which no responsive pleading is required, in which case the allegation is deemed

---

10. *Id.* 8(b)(3).
11. *Id.*
12. *Id.* 8(b)(4).
13. *Id.* 8(b)(5).
14. *See, e.g.,* Harvey Aluminum (Inc.) v. NLRB, 335 F.2d 749, 758 (9th Cir. 1964).
15. *See, e.g.,* Djourabchi v. Self, 240 F.R.D. 5, 12 (D.D.C. 2006); Porto Transp., Inc. v. Consol. Diesel Elec. Corp., 20 F.R.D. 1, 2 (S.D.N.Y. 1956) (holding that defendant may not deny knowledge or information regarding matters of public record); *see also* Fed. R. Civ. P. 11(b) (requiring a reasonable inquiry before signing a pleading).

denied or avoided).[16] One should therefore take care to respond to all allegations. Special care is warranted when addressing complex allegations and responding with partial admissions, denials, and qualifications to avoid missing a portion of an allegation and giving rise to an argument that the allegation is admitted.

1. Straying from the Rule Carries Risk

Based on the simplicity of Rule 8(b), one would think that drafting an answer would be a simple matter. Maybe it should be, and often it can be. It takes little effort to respond to a factual allegation that the defendant believes to be completely untrue. It is more difficult to respond to a complex allegation containing some matters that are true, others that are not (at least according to the defendant), and others that the defendant has no way of knowing either way. Still, with attention to detail, such allegations can be addressed with a modest amount of effort.

There are many times, though, when answering a complaint is a more difficult matter, especially when litigating business torts. Business torts often involve complex allegations and may implicate the actions of numerous individuals in different jurisdictions (along with the laws of those various jurisdictions). The plaintiff filing the complaint has the luxury of time to investigate and craft its complaint, with the main constraints being only the applicable statutes of limitations and the need for basic diligence. The defendant, by contrast, has a short time to investigate the complaint, conduct any necessary research, and file its answer. As discussed above, pleading a lack of knowledge or information may not be an option even if the allegations are complex and require investigation. A flat denial also carries risk if made simply as a means of getting an answer filed regardless of whether the allegation might be true.[17] While one can always seek additional time to answer, it is never certain that any additional time given will be sufficient. It is unsurprising, then, that there is a temptation to try to find a way to avoid admitting, denying, or pleading a lack of knowledge.

---

16. FED. R. CIV. P. 8(b)(6).
17. *See, e.g., id.* 11.

BUSINESS TORTS: A PRACTICAL GUIDE TO LITIGATION

An even worse situation exists when an allegation is actually true—and damaging to one's defense. There is no shame in not wanting to admit an opponent's allegations. Each allegation admitted is one less thing for the plaintiff to prove. One naturally wants to be cautious before making an admission. Although both the Rules and the case law reflect a liberal policy toward amended pleadings and a preference to resolve cases on the merits rather than procedural technicalities, there is always the risk that an inadvertent admission will haunt the pleader in the future. An erroneous denial carries its own risks as well.[18] Thus, the temptation once more exists to find a way to plead something else.

Whether because of concerns such as those above, a desire for creativity, or something else, many litigators likely have seen (and perhaps drafted) answers that do not necessarily follow the precise formula set forth in Rule 8. Depending on the reasons for and manner of the departure, there may be good reasons to do so. Nevertheless, one should proceed cautiously in such an endeavor.

One type of allegation that seems to spawn an inherent desire not to respond is one that states a legal conclusion. Such matters seem ill-suited for pleadings—better left for briefs in which the parties can cite to the mountains of precedent in their favor after hours of exhaustive research and analysis. And, why should one be expected to address a legal conclusion before discovery reveals the full measure of facts to which the law will apply? Perhaps unsurprisingly, many attorneys seek to avoid the legal conclusions alleged in the complaint. Thus, many reading this chapter will have seen (and may have drafted) a response along the lines of the following: "Paragraph 3 of the complaint states a legal conclusion to which no response is required."

At first blush, stating that no response is required to a legal conclusion appears logical. The court ultimately decides the law, not the parties.[19] Con-

---

18. *Id.*
19. *See, e.g.,* Roysdon v. R.J. Reynolds Tobacco Co., 849 F.2d 230, 235 (6th Cir. 1988) ("Regardless of whether the parties agree upon an interpretation of the law, the district court has an independent duty to determine if that interpretation is correct."); Andrews v. St. Louis Joint Stock Land Bank, 107 F.2d 462, 470 (8th Cir. 1939).

clusions of law are not accepted as true even on a motion to dismiss.[20] At least one court has expressed "wonder" as to whether an admission of an allegation even extends to legal conclusions in the allegation.[21] And, finally, one might consider an analogy to Rule 36, which courts generally hold not to permit requests to admit pure conclusions of law.[22]

Whether the above reasoning is logical or not, prudent counsel should be aware that many courts disagree with it. Numerous cases hold that it is impermissible to make such a departure from the plain language of Rule 8, which requires a defendant to admit or deny all allegations. As held in *State Farm Mutual Automobile Insurance Company v. Riley*, declining to respond to an allegation on the basis that it states a legal conclusion "violates the express Rule 8(b) requirement that *all* allegations must be responded to."[23] Other courts have been more lenient in addressing efforts to dodge legal conclusions in the answer, but they have hardly endorsed the practice.[24] Pleading that a legal conclusion requires no response is a risky proposition.

Legal conclusions are not the only category of allegations that seem to prompt a desire to respond in some way other than admitting, denying, or denying knowledge. Sometimes, admitting an allegation simply seems damaging to one's case. Since the plaintiff is supposed to prove his case anyway, one might wish to respond with something like: "In response to

---

20. Ashcroft v. Iqbal, 556 U.S. 662, 678 (2009); Papasan v. Allain, 478 U.S. 265, 286 (1986).

21. *See* Almand v. DeKalb County, 103 F.3d 1510, 1514 (11th Cir. 1997).

22. *See, e.g.*, Disability Rights Council of Greater Washington v. Washington Metro. Area Trans. Auth., 234 F.R.D. 1, 3 (D.D.C. 2006).

23. State Farm Mutual Automobile Insurance Company v. Riley, 199 F.R.D. 276, 278 (N.D. Ill. 2001); *see also, e.g.*, Farrell v. Pike, 342 F. Supp. 2d 433, 440–41 (M.D.N.C. 2004) (same); CapitalSource Fin., LLC v. Pittsfield Weaving Co., Inc., 571 F. Supp. 2d 668, 674–75 (D. Md. 2006) (declining to deem allegations admitted based on the technical violation of Rule 8, instead giving leave to amend to fix the error). *State Farm* is a particularly useful reference, as the court not only struck the offending answer sua sponte (with leave to refile at defense counsel's expense, to be confirmed by a letter from counsel to the client explaining this), but published an appendix of common pleading errors to facilitate the resolution of future pleading disputes.

24. *See, e.g.*, The New Hampshire Ins. Co. v. MarineMax of Ohio, Inc., 408 F. Supp. 2d 526, 530 (N.D. Ohio 2006) (construing the response that a legal conclusion need not be responded to as a denial); Barnes v. AT&T Pension Benefit Plan—Nonbargained Program, 718 F. Supp. 2d 1167, 1175 (N.D. Cal. 2010) (holding same in light of defendant's denials of related factual allegations).

paragraph 6 of the complaint, the defendant neither admits nor denies the allegation, but holds the plaintiff to his burden of proof." Other times, the complaint may be sprinkled with surplus language and allegations that do not appear critical to the complaint, leading some to respond: "Paragraph 4 of the complaint contains immaterial allegations to which no response is required." And, as a final example, when the plaintiff quotes from or, worse, paraphrases a contract, statute, or some other item, a common response seems to be along the lines of: "The document [or statute, regulation, or anything else that exists outside of the complaint itself] referenced in paragraph 7 of the complaint speaks for itself." Are any of these common departures from the literal language of Rule 8 any more acceptable than disclaiming a need to respond to legal conclusions?

The answer to the above question is "no." As held in *State Farm*, Rule 8(b) sets forth an "unambiguous path" that must be followed if the defendant can neither admit nor deny an allegation, and the Federal Rules contain no authority simply to demand proof.[25] Similarly, the Rules do not allow for a response that a particular allegation requires no response, even if the allegation is "immaterial."[26] *State Farm* is especially harsh in addressing the response that a document speaks for itself, calling it an "unacceptable device, used by lawyers who would prefer not to admit something that is alleged about a document in a complaint (or who may perhaps be too lazy to craft an appropriate response to such an allegation)."[27] Of course, there is no harm in referring to a document for its terms in otherwise pleading a proper response.[28]

Again, there may be fair arguments against the reasoning in *State Farm* and other cases rejecting the use of answers that do not comport with Rule 8. But, when the risk of non-compliance is that the answer may be

---

25. 199 F.R.D. at 278.

26. *See id.* at 279; *see also* FED. R. CIV. P. 8(b) advisory committee's note 2007 amendments (noting the change in the Rule to avoid any implication that a pleader may deny something believed to be true that the pleader claims is immaterial).

27. 199 F.R.D. at 279. *See also New Hampshire*, 408 F. Supp. 2d at 530 (deeming responses to be admissions that the documents said what the plaintiff asserted they said).

28. *See Barnes*, 718 F. Supp. 2d at 1175 (holding that bare statements that documents speak for themselves would be improper, but accepting defendant's use of the phrase when coupled with responses amounting to admissions and denials making clear the intent to admit factual allegations actually supported by the documents and to deny all others).

stricken or other penalties imposed, the wisdom of taking that road certainly is subject to question.

2. Read and Plead Carefully

If departing from Rule 8 is not an option, a defendant is hardly helpless in responding to a well-crafted complaint. While there will be times when a defendant will have no choice but to admit an allegation against it, by paying close attention both to what Rule 8 requires *and* what it allows, and by carefully evaluating the specific allegations in the complaint, a defendant can craft an effective answer that does not run afoul of the Rule.

Consider a complaint alleging breaches of fiduciary duty by a corporate officer. It should be easy enough for the defendant to deny an allegation along the lines of "Jones breached his fiduciary duties to Alpha Corporation." If such an allegation cannot be denied, the answer is the least of the defendant's worries. But, the plaintiff can put the same defendant in a far more difficult position by making a series of carefully crafted allegations that build toward the conclusion that Jones breached his fiduciary duties to Alpha (e.g., identifying Jones's position with the company, his responsibilities, the actions that he took, etc.). In such a situation, the defendant may indeed be forced to make a series of admissions, but carefully reviewing the allegations in the complaint, as a whole and individually, and understanding what they do—and do not—say can be critical in preparing an effective answer.

For example, with respect to factual allegations, it may seem difficult to respond to an allegation that "Jones was the president of Alpha" with anything other than an admission if Jones was, in fact, the president of Alpha. But, what if the remaining allegations of the complaint reveal that the matters at issue occurred after Jones resigned as president and became an independent consultant? Responding with a bare admission to the allegation regarding Jones's presidency not only might be damaging to Jones's defense, but may inadvertently give an inaccurate impression of the situation (perhaps the very one that the plaintiff intended to create). Would it violate Rule 8 to answer the presidency allegation by an answer along the lines of "Jones admits that he was the president of Alpha from 2010–2011, but he resigned from that position effective December 31, 2011"? In light

101

of the defendant's duties to state his defenses in short and plain terms and to fairly respond to the substance of an allegation,[29] an argument can be made that such an answer better conforms to the letter and spirit of Rule 8 than a bare admission that, literally speaking, is all that seems to be required by the Rule. A careful review of the allegations would prevent a needless, and ultimately misleading, admission.

A defendant also is far from helpless in responding to conclusions of law. One might think that if asserting that no response is required is not an option, the better route is simply to deny any conclusions of law. Denying an allegation that simply states a well-established legal principle can damage credibility, to say the least. But, even if the complaint appears to make an accurate statement of the law, it may be possible to deny the allegation. Has the plaintiff invoked the correct law? The law of one state may impose duties that the law of another does not. If the plaintiff has correctly stated the law of Kentucky, but that law does not apply, and the applicable law imposes a different standard, denying the allegation is simple. Given the fact that business torts often involve companies operating in multiple states and interaction between individuals and entities in multiple states, the potential need for a choice of law analysis is always something to bear in mind.

It also is important to consider factual and legal allegations together and the complaint as a whole. Perhaps the complaint accurately describes the statutory duties of a particular corporate officer and asserts that the defendant owed those duties. Is there a legitimate argument that the defendant did not owe those duties for some reason (e.g., he did not truly occupy the alleged position with the company, but merely performed some of the roles traditionally performed by a particular type of officer)? If so, the facts at issue might provide the basis to deny an allegation of law that, on its face, appears to be accurate. Careful review of what is alleged followed by a thoughtful drafting of the answer can accomplish much better results than scrambling to find a way around Rule 8.

---

29.   FED. R. CIV. P. 8(b)(1)–(2).

3. Addressing Complex Allegations—Nuance Matters

The above examples are overly simplified for purposes of illustrating a point. More often in the real world, allegations (even when stated in short and plain terms) can be quite complex. Allegations regarding a breach of fiduciary duty can implicate a wide range of both factual and legal issues that will determine whether a duty exists and, if so, whether a breach has occurred. Tortious interference and unfair competition claims similarly can involve complicated fact patterns and allegations implicating both factual and legal matters. A litigator should review such allegations with particular care, keeping in mind that even a slight nuance in the words chosen by the plaintiff can make a substantial difference in the outcome of the litigation, and, more importantly for present purposes, what the defendant can plead in its answer. And, defense counsel should remember the importance of consulting with the client in evaluating the allegations.

For example, whether a defendant was an officer of a company may determine whether his conduct is governed by statutory standards, common law principles, or both. Building upon an earlier example, the complaint may accurately set forth the law regarding an officer's duties and responsibilities to the company—which, as discussed above, cannot simply be disregarded as "legal conclusions" without some measure of risk. But, is the defendant truly an officer of the company, or does he simply have some responsibilities comparable to those expected to be held by a particular officer? The only way to know this is by speaking with the client (and possibly conducting an independent investigation as well) and going over the allegations carefully. An attorney may feel that his time could be better spent planning a summary judgment motion, and the client will seldom relish diverting time and attention from its business to preparing an answer. But, especially in complex cases—and business tort cases often are—taking extra time to ensure that both the defendant and counsel truly understand what is being alleged and to develop an answer that accounts for the complexities inherent in the situation is a prudent investment if it prevents the need to try to amend or otherwise address an admission that could have been avoided at the outset by paying proper attention to the answer.

B. Strategic and General Considerations

Obviously, a principal objective in preparing an answer is to file a responsive pleading that complies with Rule 8 (as well as any other relevant Rules or requirements, depending on the circumstances, not the least of which is Rule 11). Good strategy thus would include drafting an answer that complies with Rule 8, accurately responds to the allegations made in the complaint, and sets forth one's defenses. It is important to plead carefully, as there is no guarantee that an erroneous admission, denial, or other statement can be corrected (especially if left uncorrected until later in the case). Even when an amendment is allowed, the amendment will take time and expense that could have been avoided, especially if the plaintiff decides to challenge the attempt to amend.

It also is important to consider what the answer can accomplish (aside from avoiding a default judgment, of course). The complaint is the plaintiff's first chance to state its case—to inform the defendant and the court of what is being claimed. The answer can serve a similar purpose for the defendant, albeit in a different way. Assuming that no one will ever really read the answer and treating it as a formality not only is inaccurate, but deprives the defendant of an opportunity to make its position known. There also are other strategic considerations in filing an answer. Has the plaintiff filed suit in a forum that the defendant believes to be favorable to the defendant? If so, filing an answer, instead of a motion to dismiss, can limit the plaintiff's ability to escape a poorly chosen forum.[30] Especially if a motion to dismiss appears unlikely to succeed, or perhaps if the defendant has a counterclaim to assert, filing an answer to better anchor the case to the chosen forum may be preferable to moving to dismiss and giving the plaintiff a chance to preview the defenses and then voluntarily dismiss to file in a more favorable jurisdiction.

Simply stated, answers are important. A motion to dismiss can be an effective tool that disposes of the case (and further time and expense for the defendant) if successful and can have beneficial purposes even if unsuccessful (e.g., by framing the issues to the court at an early stage). There are

---

30. *See* FED. R. CIV. P. 41(a)(1)(A)(i), (a)(2).

times, though, when the benefits of filing an answer are greater. A prudent attorney should consider the circumstances presented in each case before advising and making a final decision with the client. And, in pleading the answer, the attorney should be sure to do so carefully and with due regard for the requirements of Rule 8.

II. AFFIRMATIVE DEFENSES

Affirmative defenses are a critical component of most answers. Oftentimes, defenses to a complaint arise outside of the context of the plaintiff's prima facie case. The complaint may set forth allegations that would entitle the plaintiff to recover, but the claim may be barred by the relevant statute of limitations, the plaintiff may have released the claims, or any of a number of other scenarios may exist to bar recovery. There may be other matters beyond the scope of the allegations that the court or jury should consider before reaching an outcome. Fortunately, the Rules provide the defendant with an express means of apprising the court and the plaintiff of such matters—and require the defendant to do so.

A. Rule 8(c)

"In responding to a pleading, a party must affirmatively state any avoidance or affirmative defense. . . ."[31] The Rule identifies a non-exclusive list of common avoidances or affirmative defenses. This provision raises two basic questions: (1) what is an avoidance or affirmative defense (other than the ones enumerated in the Rule); and (2) how should one plead an avoidance or affirmative defense?

1. What Constitutes an "Avoidance or Affirmative Defense"?
Because the list set forth in Rule 8 is non-exclusive, there is room for debate as to what must be pleaded as an "avoidance or affirmative defense." This is especially true when dealing with business torts, as there are many instances in which the lines between a prima facie case and a defense, and

---

31. *Id.* 8(c).

the associated burdens of proof, tend to blur.[32] Making the determination of whether something is a defense that needs to be asserted is not a mere academic exercise. The failure to plead can have serious consequences, perhaps the most significant of which is that the defense or avoidance may be waived.[33] Of course, there are many means of avoiding waiver (for example, raising the defense in a pre-answer motion, trying the defense by express or implied consent of the parties, or moving to amend the pleading). At least one court has noted that, as a practical matter, waiver may be rare.[34] As that same court aptly observed, however, "the very possibility of waiver makes it important (and certainly prudent) to plead all appropriate affirmative defenses."[35] And, it takes little effort in searching the case law to find cases in which courts have deemed defenses waived for the failure to assert them in the proper manner.

Generally speaking, an affirmative defense is a matter that will bar the claim even if the defendant more or less admits to the allegations in the complaint.[36] Affirmative defenses either provide some reason why the plaintiff should not recover even if his allegations are true or relate to matters otherwise beyond the scope of the plaintiff's prima facie case that cannot be addressed through a simple denial.[37] Whether something must be asserted as an affirmative defense also can rest on principles of fairness and avoidance of surprise, and a defendant may be required to raise the matter as an affirmative defense if all or most of the relevant information regarding the issue is in his control or if the defendant has a "unique nexus" with the issue.[38] Such descriptions, while helpful, still lack precision. At the end of the day, the "cautious pleader is fully justified in setting up as affirmative

---

32. See, e.g., RESTATEMENT (SECOND) OF TORTS Ch. 37 Introductory Note (1979).
33. See, e.g., 2 MOORE'S FEDERAL PRACTICE § 8.08[3] (3d ed.) [hereinafter MOORE'S].
34. Bobbitt v. Victorian House, Inc., 532 F. Supp. 734, 736 (N.D. Ill. 1982).
35. Id.
36. Siegemund v. Shapland, 324 F. Supp. 2d 176, 183 (D. Me. 2004).
37. WRIGHT & MILLER, supra note 5, § 1271, at 585; see also MOORE'S, supra note 33, § 8.08[1] (stating that an affirmative defense, if established, "will defeat an otherwise legitimate claim for relief").
38. Zimmer v. United Dominion Indus., Inc., 193 F.R.D. 616, 619–29 (W.D. Ark. 2000) (refusing to allow defendant to argue that it was not the proper defendant because the defendant failed to plead the issue as an affirmative defense, and the plaintiff had made a good faith effort to identify the correct defendant).

defenses anything that might possibly fall into that category, even though that approach may lead to pleading matters as affirmative defenses that could have been set forth in simple denials."[39]

While a cautious defendant may well want to assert anything that possibly qualifies as an affirmative defense or other avoidance, there are dangers in pleading too much. "A defense which demonstrates that plaintiff has not met its burden of proof is not an affirmative defense."[40] If something is an element of the plaintiff's prima facie case or otherwise falls upon the plaintiff to prove, it should not be necessary to assert, as an affirmative defense or avoidance, the plaintiff's anticipated inability to prove that element.[41] Asserting such matters as affirmative defenses can create confusion and even carry the unintended implication that the defendant bears the burden of proof on an issue that the plaintiff actually must prove.[42] While it may be wise to err on the side of asserting a possible defense, one who asserts too much may fare no better.

2. Considerations Regarding How to Plead

Even when one determines *what* to plead as an affirmative defense or other avoidance, the question remains *how* to plead it. Again, it must be remembered that a chief purpose of the answer is to provide fair notice of issues that will need to be litigated. Traditionally, relatively little has been required of defendants to provide such notice. As one leading treatise has commented (and many courts have held): "[A]n affirmative defense may be pleaded in general terms and will be held to be sufficient, and therefore invulnerable to

---

39. Bobbitt, 532 F. Supp. at 736.

40. Zivkovic v. S. Cal. Edison Co., 302 F.3d 1080, 1088 (9th Cir. 2002).

41. *See* Nat. Mkt. Share, Inc. v. Sterling Nat. Bank, 392 F.3d 520, 526–28 (2d Cir. 2004) (holding that an argument regarding intervening cause was not waived by the defendant's failure to plead it, and that the district court thus did not err in considering it sua sponte, because causation was an element of plaintiff's prima facie claim).

42. *See* Barnes v. AT&T Pension Benefit Plan—Nonbargained Program, 718 F. Supp. 2d 1167, 1174 (N.D. Cal. 2010) (describing the assertion of matters on which the defendant does not bear the burden of proof as affirmative defenses as "curious" and striking defenses that were merely negations of elements of the plaintiff's case); *see also* Gwin v. Curry, 161 F.R.D. 70, 72 n.1 (N.D. Ill. 1995) (holding that a defendant "is not justified in inserting a putative [affirmative defense] out of some superabundance of caution" when the matter is clearly put into issue by the existing pleadings).

a motion to strike, as long as it gives the plaintiff fair notice of the nature of the defense."[43] Thus, a general assertion that the claim is barred by res judicata,[44] or that the complaint is barred by the statute of limitations,[45] should be sufficient.

Unfortunately, just as *Twombly* and *Iqbal* changed the landscape for pleading a complaint, a number of courts have drawn upon these cases to alter the standards for pleading affirmative defenses. These courts have raised the bar for pleading affirmative defenses to more closely correspond to the "plausibility" requirement in *Twombly* and *Iqbal*.[46]

Courts have offered several reasons for requiring something more than a bare bones invocation of an affirmative defense. For example, some courts have noted the similarity between the relevant provisions of Rule 8.[47] Courts also have held that fairness requires a defendant to meet the same plausibility standards to which the plaintiff is held.[48]

Notwithstanding what some courts have called the "majority" approach, a sizeable number of courts have declined to apply *Twombly* and *Iqbal* to affirmative defenses and have instead applied the more traditional view of determining whether the affirmative defense is stated in a way that provides fair notice.[49] Courts following this approach, in addition to citing the

43. WRIGHT & MILLER, *supra* note 5, § 1274, at 616–17.

44. Davis v. Sun Oil Co., 148 F.3d 606, 612 (6th Cir. 1998).

45. Montgomery v. Wyeth, 580 F.3d 455, 467–68 (6th Cir. 2009).

46. *See, e.g., Barnes*, 718 F. Supp. 2d at 1171 ("While neither the Ninth Circuit nor any other Circuit Courts of Appeals has ruled on this issue, the vast majority of courts presented with the issue have extended *Twombly*'s heightened pleading standard to affirmative defenses."); McLemore v. Regions Bank, No. 3:08-cv-21 & 3:08-cv-1003, 2010 U.S. Dist. LEXIS 25785, at *45–46 (M.D. Tenn. March 18, 2010) (collecting cases demonstrating a split of authority on the subject); MOORE'S, *supra* note 33, § 8.08[1], at 8-57.

47. *See, e.g.,* Bradshaw v. Hilco Receivables, LLC, 725 F. Supp. 2d 532, 536 (D. Md. 2010) (comparing Rule 8(b)'s requirement to "state in short and plain terms its defenses to each claim asserted against it" to Rule 8(a)'s requirement for a complaint to provide a "short and plain statement of the claim showing that the pleader is entitled to relief"); HCRI TRS Acquirer, LLC v. Iwer, 708 F. Supp. 2d 687, 691 (N.D. Ohio 2010) ("[T]he shared use of the 'short and plain' language—the essence of the pleading standard—indicates the pleading requirements for affirmative defenses are the same as for claims of relief.").

48. *See, e.g., Bradshaw*, 725 F. Supp. 2d at 536; *HCRI*, 708 F. Supp. 2d at 691.

49. *See, e.g.,* Tyco Fire Prods., LP v. Victaulic Co., 777 F. Supp. 2d 893, 900 (E.D. Pa. 2011) ("An affirmative defense need not be plausible to survive; it must merely provide fair notice of the issue involved."); *McLemore*, 2010 U.S. Dist. LEXIS 25785, at *48 ("The Sixth

obvious fact that neither *Twombly* nor *Iqbal* expressly discussed affirmative defenses, have compared the relevant provisions of Rule 8 and noted the differences between them (i.e., a plaintiff must make allegations "showing" that he is entitled to relief, whereas a defendant need only "state" an affirmative defense).[50] There are other reasonable arguments as well; for example, that it is unfair to require a defendant forced to answer allegations within a relatively short time to carry the same burden as a plaintiff who has the "luxury of prefiling investigation."[51]

Given the deep divide among district courts and the lack of appellate guidance, a defendant may find itself in a difficult position in determining how to assert an affirmative defense. Pleading that "the complaint is barred by the applicable statute of limitations" might suffice under a fair notice standard, but it may not be enough in a jurisdiction that requires the defendant to plead facts establishing a plausible defense. The dilemma is exacerbated in situations involving other defenses. Fraud, for example, must be identified with the specificity required by Rule 9 when raised as a defense even under a pre-*Twombly/Iqbal* analysis. There may be other defenses that could require something more than a general invocation under either a fair notice or a plausibility standard. Does the plaintiff have fair notice of why its claim would be barred if the defendant provides only a bare reference to the defense of release? Would fair notice require the defendant to explain why it believes that the claim was released (e.g., identifying a settlement), just as it likely would need to do under a plausibility standard? The defense of res judicata similarly could require a defendant to identify, for example, the prior case, regardless of which standard is applied. And, considering the fact that there are many possible affirmative defenses or other avoidances not described in Rule 8, especially in the business torts context where the lines between an element of a claim and an affirmative defense

---

Circuit has consistently used 'fair notice' as the standard for whether a defendant has sufficiently pleaded an affirmative defense. *Twombly* and *Iqbal* did not change this.").

50. *See Tyco*, 777 F. Supp. 2d at 899–900 (quotations omitted).

51. Moore's, *supra* note 33, § 8.08[1], at 8-58; Tyco, 777 F. Supp. 2d at 901. But see Bradshaw, 725 F. Supp. 2d at 536–37 (noting that a defendant is always free to seek leave to amend its answer to plead defenses revealed by discovery, which is liberally given absent substantial prejudice to the opposing party).

are not always clear, an argument can be made that it is even more important to provide additional detail regarding such matters. One thus should give careful thought to how to plead the defenses that one wishes to assert.

B. General Considerations

Determining whether and how to assert affirmative defenses is important in any case. Sometimes, an affirmative defense is the only possible means of avoiding liability, making it especially important to plead the defense carefully and avoid any potential waiver issues. Still, one should be cautious of over-pleading. Rule 8 does not require every possible legal argument to be set forth as an affirmative defense, particularly when dealing with matters that are elements of the plaintiff's prima facie case. For example, a claim for tortious interference with a contractual relationship typically requires proof, among other things, of an existing contract. Pleading that "there is no contract" not only should be unnecessary in most jurisdictions, but can inadvertently imply that the defendant bears some burden of proof on this issue.

One also should be cautious of using boilerplate affirmative defenses and listing (literally) everything in the book without giving due consideration to their applicability to the case at hand. Although motions to strike are not favored, courts can strike defenses that are not facially supportable or otherwise bolstered by factual allegations.[52] Of course, courts are not always gracious even when they strike such defenses: "There is nothing dumber than a motion to strike boilerplate affirmative defenses; it wastes the client's money and the court's time."[53]

---

52. *See, e.g.*, Gessele v. Jack in the Box, Inc., No. 3:10-cv-960-ST, 2011 U.S. Dist. LEXIS 99419, at *5–6 (D. Or. Sept. 2, 2011) (encouraging defendants to "eschew the all too common practice of alleging a litany of boilerplate affirmative defenses with the view of dropping them later if discovery fails to support them," urging them instead to "only plead affirmative defenses that they believe in good faith to have sufficient factual and/or legal support" (emphasis added)); Safeco Ins. Co. of Am. v. O'Hara Corp., No. 08-cv-105-15, 2008 U.S. Dist. LEXIS 48399, at *2–4 (E.D. Mich. June 25, 2008) (expressing distaste for boilerplate affirmative defenses and striking defenses, noting that the defendant would be free to seek leave to amend at a later time).

53. Raymond Weil, S.A. v. Theron, 585 F. Supp. 2d 473, 489–90 (S.D.N.Y. 2008) (nevertheless striking several boilerplate affirmative defenses).

Aside from the danger of having a defense stricken, one should be wary of more substantial sanctions for pleading inapplicable affirmative defenses. Although sanctions for asserting inapplicable affirmative defenses appear to be rare, gentle reminders of the need to comply with Rule 11 in asserting affirmative defenses are more common.[54]

At the end of the day, it may be helpful to determine what affirmative defenses to plead by considering them under a plausibility standard, regardless of whether one ultimately will need to plead them in a way that comports with that standard. Considering how one would support a particular defense if required to state it in a way that makes its application appear plausible can be a good means of ensuring that the defenses asserted are worth asserting. It also can help to avoid having carelessly asserted defenses stricken or sanctions imposed.

III. COUNTERCLAIMS

When preparing an answer, a defendant always should consider whether there is a potential counterclaim to assert. Sometimes, a defendant may want to answer the complaint because it enables him to assert a counterclaim. For example, the defendant may perceive the chosen forum as a favorable one. The defendant may have been planning to sue anyway, but the plaintiff filed a declaratory judgment action or otherwise won a race to the courthouse. In determining whether to assert a counterclaim, a key threshold consideration is whether the counterclaim is compulsory or permissive, as this can have a significant impact on whether to assert it. When asserting a counterclaim, it is important to remember that it is functionally the same as a complaint in many respects and thus is subject to the pleading requirements for complaints. Finally, it may be necessary to choose whether to add additional parties, and a defendant should consider the potential need for joinder in considering whether to assert a counterclaim.

---

54. *See, e.g.*, CapitalSource Fin., LLC v. Pittsfield Weaving Co., Inc., 571 F. Supp. 2d 668, 674 (D. Md. 2006) (striking insufficiently pleaded affirmative defenses with leave to amend, but reminding the defendants that any amendment should comply with Rule 11); Lemanik, S.A. v. McKinley Allsopp, Inc., 125 F.R.D. 602, 610 (S.D.N.Y. 1989) (referring to the assertion of factually baseless affirmative defenses as being discouraged by the 1983 amendments to Rules 11 and 26).

A. Rule 13

Counterclaims are governed by Rule 13 of the Federal Rules of Civil Procedure. If a counterclaim is compulsory, the choice is fairly simple: assert the claim or lose the right to do so. Permissive counterclaims present a more difficult question, especially if asserting the claim may require joinder of additional parties. In either situation, careful thought must be given to whether to assert a counterclaim.

1. Compulsory Counterclaims

The first type of counterclaim is the compulsory counterclaim. "A pleading must state as a counterclaim any claim that—at the time of its service—the pleader has against an opposing party if the claim: (A) arises out of the transaction or occurrence that is the subject matter of the opposing party's claim; and (B) does not require adding another party over whom the court cannot acquire jurisdiction."[55] There are two circumstances in which an otherwise compulsory counterclaim need not be asserted: (1) the claim was the subject of another pending action at the time the current action was commenced; or (2) the opposing party sued by attachment or other process that did not establish personal jurisdiction over the pleader on that claim, and the pleader does not assert any other counterclaim.[56]

Determining whether a counterclaim is compulsory in many cases will turn on the first prong of Rule 13(a)(1)—whether the counterclaim arises out of the same transaction or occurrence that is the subject matter of the complaint. Drawing upon the reasoning in the Supreme Court's pre-Rules decision in *Moore v. New York Cotton Exchange*,[57] courts typically analyze whether a counterclaim is compulsory using some form of the "logical relationship" test.[58] Deciding whether there is a logical relationship can vary slightly among the different jurisdictions. Some courts focus on whether the issues of law and fact are largely the same for both claims, and whether

---

55. FED. R. CIV. P. 13(a)(1).
56. *Id.* 13(a)(2).
57. Moore v. New York Cotton Exchange, 270 U.S. 593 (1926).
58. *See, e.g.,* Mattel, Inc. v. MGA Entm't, Inc., 705 F.3d 1108, 1110 (9th Cir. 2013); Sanders v. First Nat'l Bank & Trust Co. in Great Bend, 936 F.2d 273, 277 (6th Cir. 1991).

the same evidence would support or refute both claims.[59] Some consider similar factors, but also analyze whether res judicata would bar the claim from being asserted in a subsequent proceeding.[60] Others describe the logical relationship in terms of whether the claims arise from the same "aggregate set of operative facts."[61] Although the variations in the test may not appear substantial, even subtle differences can matter.[62]

If a defendant fails to assert a compulsory counterclaim, that claim is barred.[63] Additionally, even if a counterclaim is not compulsory, principles of res judicata or collateral estoppel can affect a future effort to assert a claim that could be asserted as a counterclaim.[64] Thus, unless a defendant is willing to risk waiver of a potential claim—and there may be reasons to do so in a particular case—the prudent course is to assert a counterclaim if one exists and there is any basis to conclude that it may be compulsory.

2. Permissive Counterclaims

Rule 13(b) broadly permits a party to state as a counterclaim any claim that is not compulsory. Of course, there are a range of potential legal impediments to asserting a permissive counterclaim. For example, a federal court having original jurisdiction over a matter may exercise jurisdiction over other claims

---

59. *See, e.g.,* Sanders, 936 F.2d at 277.

60. *See, e.g.,* FDIC v. Hulsey, 22 F.3d 1472, 1487 (10th Cir. 1994).

61. *See, e.g., Mattel,* 705 F.3d at 1110; *see also* 3 MOORE'S, *supra* note 33, § 13.10 (discussing the logical relationship test in depth, including variations among the Circuits in applying the test).

62. *See* 3 MOORE'S, *supra* note 33, § 13.10[2]–[3] (including discussion that courts applying an "aggregate set of facts" standard may find a broader range of counterclaims to be compulsory than courts referring to a need for the "same evidence").

63. Baker v. Gold Seal Liquors, Inc., 417 U.S. 467, 469 n.1 (1974); Polymer Indus. Prods. Co. v. Bridgestone/Firestone, Inc., 347 F.3d 935, 938 (Fed. Cir. 2003). *Cf.* Southern Constr. Co., Inc. v. Pickard, 371 U.S. 57, 60 (1962) (discussing the goal of preventing multiple actions, especially those in which a defendant fails to assert a counterclaim that he then uses as the basis of a second action).

64. *See* Allen v. McCurry, 449 U.S. 90, 94 (1980) ("Under res judicata, a final judgment on the merits of an action precludes the parties or their privies from relitigating issues that were or could have been raised in that action. . . . Under collateral estoppel, once a court has decided an issue of fact or law necessary to its judgment, that decision may preclude relitigation of the issue in a suit on a different cause of action involving a party to the first case.") (citations omitted).

forming part of the same Article III case or controversy.[65] Prior to the enactment of 28 U.S.C. § 1367, several courts held that jurisdiction existed over compulsory counterclaims, but that permissive counterclaims required an independent jurisdictional basis.[66] Several courts now have held that jurisdiction exists over any counterclaims forming some of the same case or controversy (a standard broader in scope than the compulsory counterclaim standard).[67] But, there is no guarantee that every court will apply a broader standard in evaluating its jurisdiction. Even if a federal court would have subject matter jurisdiction over the counterclaim, there may be other legal issues to navigate as well (e.g., if the counterclaim would require joinder of a party over whom the court lacks personal jurisdiction).

Determining that one *can* assert a counterclaim does not always mean that one *should* assert a counterclaim. As noted, if the counterclaim is compulsory, the party should assert the claim unless it is willing to waive its ability to pursue the claim. There may be times when strategic or business considerations counsel that result. If the counterclaim is permissive, even assuming that there would be no jurisdictional or other legal impediment to asserting the claim, there are many other factors to consider before simply asserting the counterclaim. Business torts can be very complicated to resolve. One should consider whether it is worth attempting to assert an unrelated counterclaim that could cause delay, confusion, and additional expense. Whether the forum chosen by the plaintiff appears to be favorable or unfavorable is another factor to consider. In sum, a litigator should work with the client and consider the full range of ramifications when considering whether to assert a counterclaim.

B. Joining Additional Parties

It is worth briefly addressing the joinder of additional parties through counterclaims. Although counterclaims obviously are directed to claims that the

---

65. 28 U.S.C. § 1367.

66. *See* Global Naps, Inc. v. Verizon New Eng., Inc., 603 F.3d 71, 85–87 (1st Cir. 2010) (discussing pre- and post-28 U.S.C. § 1367 jurisprudence).

67. *Id.* at 87–88; Jones v. Ford Motor Credit Co., 358 F.3d 205, 210–14 (2d Cir. 2004); Channell v. Citicorp Nat'l Servs., Inc., 89 F.3d 379, 384–87 (7th Cir. 1996).

pleader has against an existing party, as with an original complaint, there are occasions when a counterclaim involves allegations and claims that pertain to multiple parties. Rule 13(h) contemplates such a situation, providing that Rules 19 and 20 (concerning joinder) "govern the addition of a person as a party to a counterclaim or crossclaim." Occasionally, one will see a defendant assert a counterclaim against the plaintiff and attempt to use a third-party complaint to make the same allegations against a new party. A fundamental flaw in such an approach is that a third-party complaint is designed to join a party who may be liable to the defendant (including a counterclaim defendant) for all or part of the claim against the defendant.[68] Thus, to avoid dismissal or striking of the counterclaim, a defendant should file the counterclaim and seek leave to join any additional parties under Rule 19 and/or 20.

C. Pleading Requirements and Considerations

A party asserting a counterclaim must plead the counterclaim in a manner that satisfies the same requirements imposed on pleading a complaint.[69] A defendant thus should follow the same practices discussed in this book concerning complaints in asserting a counterclaim.

IV. AMENDING ANSWERS, AFFIRMATIVE DEFENSES, AND COUNTERCLAIMS

Discovery or other developments frequently will reveal matters not necessarily encompassed by the parties' initial pleadings. A party asserting a tortious interference claim may discover that another, previously unknown party was involved in the interference. The deposition of the plaintiff's key manager may reveal a defense of waiver that was not evident from the complaint alone and is based on matters outside of the defendant's knowledge. Occasionally (hopefully rarely), a party may discover an error or omission

---

68.   Fed. R. Civ. P. 14(a), (b); *see also* FDIC v. Bathgate, 27 F.3d 850, 873 (3d Cir. 1994) (holding that the pleading at issue was not a third-party complaint because it was not derivative of the defendants' liability on the notes at issue in the original complaint).

69.   E.I. Du Pont De Nemours and Co. v. Kolon Indus., Inc., 637 F.3d 435, 440 (4th Cir. 2011).

in a pleading. To address these types of situations, and consistent with the oft-invoked preference to resolve matters on the merits, rather than on technicalities in pleading, Rule 15 allows parties to amend or supplement their pleadings for a wide range of reasons and at many points in the litigation (including during or after trial in certain circumstances).

The ability to amend a pleading is especially important because failing to plead certain matters typically results in a waiver. As noted earlier, waiver is not likely as a practical matter in most cases because leave to amend is often given, and there are other ways to avoid waiver as well. Still, one should not simply use an anticipated avoidance of waiver as license to avoid careful pleading. There are many situations in which the court, in its discretion, can deny leave to amend, and the defense or other matter will be waived.

Even under the liberal standards of Rule 15, leave to amend is not a matter of right, except in the limited circumstances set forth in Rule 15(a)(1). While there is a virtual presumption in favor of allowing leave to amend under Rule 15, there are numerous reasons why leave can be denied. Among the recognized grounds for denying leave to amend are "undue delay, bad faith or dilatory motive on the part of the movant, repeated failure to cure deficiencies by amendments previously allowed, undue prejudice to the opposing party by virtue of allowance of the amendment, [and] futility of amendment."[70]

Given the longstanding liberal policy toward allowing amendments, a litigant seeking to amend its pleading may be surprised to find that Rule 15 may not actually determine whether the party can amend. Rule 16 typically requires a court to enter a scheduling order after receiving the parties' Rule 26(f) report or after a scheduling conference.[71] The court must issue the order "as soon as practicable, but in any event within the earlier of 120 days after any defendant has been served with the complaint or 90 days after any defendant has appeared."[72] The order "*must* limit the time to join other parties, *amend the pleadings*, complete discovery, and file motions."[73] The

---

70. *See* Foman v. Davis, 371 U.S. 178, 182 (1962).
71. FED. R. CIV. P. 16(b)(1).
72. *Id.* 16(b)(2).
73. *Id.* 16(b)(3)(A) (emphasis added).

Rule further provides: "A schedule may be modified only for good cause and with the judge's consent."[74] The Rule ensures that "at some point both the parties and the pleadings will be fixed."[75]

There is a tension between the strict requirements set forth in Rule 16 and the liberal amendment policies underlying Rule 15. A number of courts have recognized this conflict and concluded that a party seeking to amend its pleading after the time set forth in the scheduling order must satisfy Rule 16's "good cause" requirement to modify the scheduling order before the court will consider whether Rule 15's liberal policies permit an amendment.[76] As explained by one court, "If we considered only Rule 15(a) without regard to Rule 16(b), we would render scheduling orders meaningless and effectively would read Rule 16(b) and its good cause requirement out of the Federal Rules of Civil Procedure."[77] Thus, even before a court considers whether there is undue delay, bad faith, or some other reason to deny leave to amend under Rule 15, the movant must show that it could not meet the existing deadline despite the party's diligence, and the court may consider whether the opponent will be prejudiced by the amendment.[78]

There are other circumstances in which Rule 15's generous treatment of amendments may not apply. Although post-trial or post-judgment amendments technically are allowed in certain circumstances,[79] courts often look with disfavor on such efforts.[80] Given the discretion afforded to the district court even under Rule 15, there are many circumstances in which a court might deny leave to amend.

The best means of avoiding denial of leave to amend is avoiding the need to seek leave in the first place. This does not mean that a defendant should come up with every defense imaginable and throw it into the answer. As

---

74. *Id.* 16(b)(4).
75. *Id.* 16 advisory committee's note (1983).
76. *See, e.g.,* Leary v. Daeschner, 349 F.3d 888, 905–07 (6th Cir. 2003) (citing to cases from the Second, Ninth, and Eleventh Circuits).
77. Sosa v. Airprint Sys., Inc., 133 F.3d 1417, 1419 (11th Cir. 1998).
78. *See Leary,* 349 F.3d at 907, 909.
79. *See, e.g.,* FED. R. CIV. P. 15(b).
80. Leisure Caviar, LLC v. United States Fish and Wildlife Service, 616 F.3d 612, 615–16 (6th Cir. 2010); James v. Watt, 716 F.2d 71, 77–78 (1st Cir. 1983) (citing to cases from the Seventh, Ninth, and Tenth Circuits).

discussed above, one should be hesitant to employ such a strategy. But, one should give careful thought to whether there are defenses that can apply and, if so, probably should assert them. If there is a close call as to whether something is an avoidance or affirmative defense, there likely is little harm in asserting the matter to be cautious. If the court concludes that the asserted defense is not really a defense or otherwise does not apply, as long as the defendant offers a reasonable basis for asserting it, most courts would probably hesitate to impose sanctions or otherwise punish the defendant.

V. CONCLUSION

If the reader takes nothing else from this chapter, hopefully, the foregoing discussion will encourage more careful thought in drafting answers and considering counterclaims and show that giving short shrift to the answer is unwise, to say the least. Pleading an effective answer—which includes ensuring that the answer complies with Rule 8—is an important part of litigating a business tort case (or any other case, really). A poor answer may not cost the defendant the case, but it certainly will not help, and it may lead to undesired results, not the least of which is the increased expense caused by litigating the sufficiency of the answer. Hopefully, this chapter also provides some food for thought in asserting counterclaims. Litigating a business tort case is hard enough. The attorney defending it should not make it harder by paying too little attention to the defendant's initial pleading.

CHAPTER 7

Discovery and Depositions

Deborah Edney

I. INTRODUCTION

Business torts tend to travel in packs, with a variety of legal and factual issues all competing for time and attention during the discovery process. A typical business tort case will contain overlapping, and sometimes competing, claims: fraud, misrepresentation, tortious interference, libel, unfair competition, civil RICO, and breach of contract all fighting for attention during a limited discovery window. This often results in discovery that, though similar to any other civil litigation, must be managed and coordinated in a more thoughtful, precise manner. While you will ask for documents, propound requests for admission and interrogatories, and take depositions as in any other case, the differences appear in the scope of the discovery—more documents, more depositions (certainly more 30(b)(6) depositions), and more complexity.

Because business tort discovery is not vastly different than other discovery, this chapter will necessarily cover the basics of written discovery and depositions that would apply in any case, but with a more specific focus on how the business tort practitioner can navigate aspects of business tort discovery that are different from other cases and emerge on the other side of discovery more prepared for trial.

II. HAVE A PLAN: DISCOVERY PLANNING IN BUSINESS TORTS

In litigation one side of the equation is always somewhat obscured; you don't know what the opposing counsel is thinking, or planning, in terms of its approach to discovery, other than through a short meeting required by Rule 26.[1] Because of this "unknown" it is sometimes difficult to follow a predetermined plan in discovery. But, as Dwight D. Eisenhower pointed out, "[i]n preparing for battle I have always found that plans are useless, but planning is indispensable."

Planning for discovery from the earliest moments of your case is not only wise, but invaluable when you are in the thick of depositions and written discovery. The amount of time dedicated to discovery is enormous, and often more so in business tort cases with the variety of claims and facts that need to be "discovered" and with monetary stakes that are often much higher than in an average case.

Preparing a litigation discovery plan in advance is the best way to help define the scope and timing of discovery up front. A good discovery plan will help ensure the most efficient and effective use of your time, and your clients' money, and will help to direct your efforts at the discovery most likely to support your case.

Ultimately, a discovery plan is a living document that evolves over time as you learn more about your case, the facts, and the claims and law at issue. There is no right or wrong way to prepare a discovery plan and it should be tailored to your specific case. The general steps for most business tort cases will be similar, however, and are generally best determined by preparing a document or binder that gives an outline of the main aspects of the case, including:

1. A summary of the facts;
2. A chronology;
3. A list of the key players and potential witnesses;

---

1. The discussions in this chapter will be limited to the Federal Rules of Civil Procedure as it is beyond the scope of this chapter to address the variety of rules that are encountered in state courts throughout the country.

4. Each claim (or counterclaim) to be, or already, pled and its elements;
5. Each actual or potential defense and its elements;
6. A summary of damages and relief sought;
7. An outline of documentary evidence, including "hot" documents; and
8. A continually evolving list of written discovery that needs to be served, and key witnesses and parties that need to be deposed.

Once this information has been assembled it allows you to identify the discovery methods that will be most effective in supporting or defending the claims and defenses listed, and it gives you a general scope of the number of potential depositions, the types of information/documents you may need to seek, and how much third-party discovery may be warranted.

Federal cases will necessarily have a court-imposed "timeline" for discovery, including dates for expert disclosures and the end of discovery. However, it is within these limitations that you must then create your own schedule to determine the scope of discovery, the order in which you will want to conduct your discovery, and a timetable for conducting each element of the discovery plan. Using the guidance of Rule 26(f)(3) can also aid in the first steps of creating a discovery plan since identifying the "subjects on which discovery may be needed" and the limitations that may or may not be required in your particular case will be necessary to start fleshing out the details that you will need to proceed under your case-specific plan.

Many business tort cases involve corporate entities on one or both sides. Thus, many of the "party" depositions will likely be 30(b)(6) depositions. This provides an excellent opportunity to schedule depositions of individuals like the president of a company early, while saving the 30(b)(6) deposition of the party entity for the end of discovery when written discovery has been completed, and you have an arsenal of information to use from multiple individual depositions, as well as third-party discovery.

Preparing a chart of each claim (or defense) and its requisite elements, along with where support can be found for those elements within your evidence, is also a wise move in preparing a discovery plan. Having one place where you can, at a glance, see that you have many documents supporting one element of your claim, but have no support for another element, allows the business tort practitioner to be focused on what is necessary to

121

support (or defend) that element—whether it be testimony from a deposition or a document. A well-prepared discovery plan with pointed focus on what specific information is needed to support your claims or defenses can also reduce costs by avoiding unnecessary depositions or written discovery.

III. ADMITTING (AND GIVING UP) WHAT YOU'VE GOT—REQUIRED DISCLOSURES

For most business tort lawyers discovery is as much about keeping your cards close to your vest as it is about getting your adversary to reveal the hand she has in her pocket. However, as early as 1983, the Notes of Advisory Committee on Rules noted that "the spirit of the rules is violated when advocates attempt to use discovery tools as tactical weapons rather than to expose the facts and illuminate the issues by overuse of discovery or unnecessary use of defensive weapons or evasive responses. All of this results in excessively costly and time-consuming activities that are disproportionate to the nature of the case, the amount involved, or the issues or values at stake."[2] Thus, ten years later, and following the lead of courts in the United Kingdom and Canada, Rule 26(a) was revised to impose on parties the duty to disclose important information to each other without waiting for a specific discovery request.

While initial disclosures do require the dissemination of certain information, the 1993 Advisory Committee Notes make clear that disclosures are limited to "disputed facts" rather than allegations that are admitted.[3] The rule requires the disclosure, within 14 days of the Rule 26(f) conference, of information regarding (1) potential witnesses (other than for impeachment purposes); (2) documentary evidence; (3) damages; and (4) insurance coverage. These serve as the "functional equivalent of court-ordered interrogatories" and are intended to "eliminate certain discovery, help focus the discovery that is needed, and facilitate preparation for trial or settlement."[4]

---

2. FED. R. CIV. P. 26 advisory committee's note (1983 amendments, introduction).
3. *Id.* 26 advisory committee's note (1993 amendments to subdivision (a)(1)(B)).
4. *Id.* 26 advisory committee's note (1993 amendments to subdivision (a)(1)).

A. Witnesses

The first disclosure required by Rule 26(a) is the identification of individuals likely to have discoverable information that might be used by the disclosing party to support its claims and defenses, as well as a description of what discoverable information those individuals may have. The idea is that the description should inform opposing counsel as to whether they will need to take that individual's deposition, as well as what potential documents that person might have. This is particularly important with respect to nonparty witnesses, and practitioners will want to ensure that they take note of what documents may need to be subpoenaed from third parties to flesh out the discoverable information attributed to that person. While it is not necessary to disclose witnesses that will only be used for impeachment purposes, as a practical matter, it is rare to have a witness whose only function in a business tort case will be to impeach.

Rule 26(a) disclosures are intended to be based on "the investigation conducted thus far" in the case, so to that extent are not intended to be all-inclusive.[5] An important amendment to this rule in 2000 also narrowed the disclosure to witnesses that would be used to support the disclosing party's position, rather than, as originally written, any witness regardless of whether their testimony would be supportive of the position of the disclosing party.[6] Nor do parties have to disclose the identity of witnesses they do not intend to "use." As the Advisory Committee Notes make clear, however, "use" encompasses "use at a pretrial conference, to support a motion, . . . at trial . . . [or] intended use in discovery including to respond to a discovery request or to question a witness during a deposition."[7] Given this breadth, the safe course of action is to disclose all witnesses that you may consider using, as a failure to meet your obligations under Rule 26(a)(1) can result in having a witness prohibited from testifying at trial.[8]

---

5. *Id.*
6. *Id.* 26 advisory committee's note (2000 amendments to subdivision (a)(1)).
7. *Id.*
8. Gen-Probe, Inc. v. Becton Dickson & Co., Case 3:09-cv-02319-BEN-NLS (S.D. Cal. Nov. 26, 2012) (Order on Daubert Motions and Motions in Limine) (granting motion in limine to exclude a witness not identified in Rule 26(a)(1) disclosures and noting that "Federal Rule of Civil Procedure 37(c)(1) states that '[i]f a party fails to . . . identify a witness as required by Rule 26(a) . . . the party is not allowed to use that . . . witness to supply evidence . . . at a trial, unless the failure was substantially justified or is harmless.'").

For the same reason, if you identify new witnesses in the course of discovery and/or your own internal investigation, you would be wise to supplement your Rule 26(a)(1) disclosures to include those individuals lest your opponent claim "surprise" and attempt to exclude their testimony.

B. Documents

Parties are responsible under Rule 26(a)(1)(A)(ii) for providing copies or descriptions of documents, as well as electronic information and tangible items, that they may use to support their claims or defenses. Like the requirement for disclosure of witnesses, the rule was changed in 2000 to require only a listing of documents that may be "used" by the disclosing party. A party is not required to produce its documents, but the rule allows for production rather than a listing and description if a party so desires.[9]

In practical terms, it may be a good strategic plan to produce documents rather than providing a listing in your initial disclosures. If you have done a thorough job of gathering your information prior to formal discovery, you may have available to you a good number of documents that you know will be relevant and will, ultimately, be used in your case. A production of these documents can potentially be useful in getting settlement discussions going early. For instance, in a case where there is a trade secret misappropriation claim, documents that make it clear that the opposing party acknowledged that its information was publicly known can be invaluable in avoiding prolonged and expensive discovery on that issue.

Because business tort cases tend to be heavy (often very heavy) on documentary evidence, it may not be possible to produce in your initial disclosures all documents you may ultimately use, but the rules require that you produce or describe documents "then known" to the party. Thus, there is the potential for providing the opposing side with many of your good documents (i.e., the ones you know you will use) that may allow for an opportunity to limit claims and contentions.

If you are producing a list as part of your initial disclosures, it need not be itemized. The list should describe and categorize documents "sufficiently

---

9. FED. R. CIV. P. 26(a)(1)(A)(ii).

to enable opposing parties 1) to make an informed decision concerning which documents might need to be examined . . . and 2) to frame document requests in a manner likely to avoid squabbles."[10] Providing a description and location of documents in initial disclosures does not, of course, waive the party's right to object to production of the actual documents on the basis of privilege or the burden or expense of production.

C. Damages

Subparagraph (C) of Rule 26(a)(1) acts as a standing Request for Production under Rule 34. If a party claims damages it must, under this rule, provide a calculation of the damages that are reasonably known to it at the time of the disclosures, as well as make available the documents supporting such damages. This rule also allows for protection of privileged and work product documents, and does not require a party to provide a calculation of damages where the information supporting the damages would be in the possession of an opposing party or other person.[11] The advisory notes give a patent infringement action as an example of this, but many business tort cases, including trade secret misappropriation, breaches of covenants not to compete, and derivative claims, will fall in this same category of cases where information identifying and supporting damages will be in the hands of another party or person. For this reason, it is rare in many business tort actions that initial disclosures on damages provide much useful information.

D. Insurance Policies

The final piece of the initial disclosure puzzle is the provision of liability insurance policies for inspection and copying to the other side.

E. Conclusion on Initial Disclosures

Initial disclosures are an important first step in reviewing and assessing the witnesses, information, and documents that the other side views as material and "useful" to its case. While parties are not required to have done an

---

10. *Id.* 26 advisory committee's note (1993 amendments to subdivision (a)(1)).
11. *Id.*

"exhaustive" investigation, the initial disclosures must be based on information reasonably available to the party. Furthermore, supplementation is required as a party's "investigation continues and as the issues in the pleadings are clarified."[12]

IV. THE PAPER CHASE: WRITTEN DISCOVERY
A. Interrogatories

Once you have carefully planned out your discovery, you will have a good sense of how you should use the various discovery devices with one another, and in what order you want to use them. While there is no perfect way to proceed with discovery in a business tort case, interrogatories will usually be (along with requests for production of documents) the first tools used in your discovery arsenal. Keep in mind that interrogatories may only be served on parties to the litigation, as there is no provision in the rules for serving nonparties with interrogatories.

The drawback to interrogatories, of course, is that in most business tort cases the answers are colored (and usually fully prepared) by counsel, who can carefully formulate answers that give away little in the way of real information. Unlike personal injury cases, however, where the key issue may be the eyewitness and party accounts of the accident in question—information much better obtained through an early deposition—business tort cases tend to revolve around multiple critical and complicated issues that focus on the legal implication of an individual or entity's actions. These issues are therefore often somewhat obscure in the early stages of a case. Thus, beginning your discovery with carefully focused interrogatories that are intended to flesh out contentions and refine and focus the information obtained from your informal investigation is the key to building the foundations to support your case.

The benefit of using interrogatories, rather than depositions, to get at initial information is that they are, by design, focused and controlled by the rules of civil procedure. A failure to disclose information requested in an interrogatory is much easier to see (and show) than a failure to disclose

---

12. *Id.*

126

in a rambling 450-page deposition where a topic is raised multiple times. Because each business tort case tends to be unique in its combination of claims and factual and legal issues, there are no "form" interrogatories that work in such cases. Interrogatories need to be specifically formulated for each specific matter.

In federal court, initial disclosures act as the closest thing to traditional "form" interrogatories, requiring the disclosure of the names of individuals with information, locations of documents, insurance, and damages. Taking the "belt and suspender" approach to damages and expert discovery in business tort cases, however, is the safe way to go. Among other things, sending out an initial set of interrogatories seeking information about damages and experts creates a definitive ongoing obligation on your opponent to supplement its responses and helps to focus on those critical issues.

The primary information sought through interrogatories in many business tort cases is often financial, accounting, and similar information that lends itself to summary explanation in ways that are far preferred to trying to obtain the information through document review or in depositions. For example, in an interference with contract or trade secret case, you may seek information related to every sale made by your opponent as a result of the interference or misappropriation. In some cases, that could amount to thousands of purchase orders, bills of lading, invoices, and other related documents. In those cases, an interrogatory that asks for a summary of the sales using either a chart or specific measures (e.g., how many purchase orders issued) can often be the best way to get at the information in an easy-to-digest form. While Rule 33 does allow a party the option of producing business records where the answer to an interrogatory may be "determined by examining, auditing, compiling, abstracting, or summarizing a party's business records," the burden of figuring out the answer using these methods must be "substantially the same for either party."[13]

Contention interrogatories are also useful in many business tort cases as a means of forcing your opponent to identify the basis for its claims or defenses. As the name suggests, contention interrogatories should be

---

13. FED. R. CIV. P. 33(d).

directed at each of the major contentions of your opponent, seeking the facts, documents, witnesses, and information your opponent believes supports those contentions. Damages contentions are particularly helpful, as they force the opposing party to tailor and identify specific elements of its damages. In many business tort cases, the damages will be presented and determined by experts. Thus, while many parties will try to defer providing damages contentions until after expert reports are due, it is still important to serve damages interrogatories to ensure that the party is obligated to fully disclose their theory of damages before trial.

Overall, if used wisely, interrogatories are unlikely to uncover much previously unknown evidence, but they can marshal information and provide helpful direction for narrowing later discovery in the form of depositions and document requests, and they provide a great avenue to seek information that would be difficult to obtain in a deposition. A final piece of advice: remember that in federal court, and many state courts, there is a limit to the number of interrogatories you may propound. Be sure to save some interrogatories for use later as you never know what will come up as discovery progresses.

B. Requests for Production of Documents, Tangible Things, and Entry onto Land

"Rule 34 is a direct and simple method of discovery."[14] As such it does not need much in the way of discussion. Requests for production generally go hand in hand with the initial interrogatories served on opposing parties. If documents were not produced with initial disclosures, the first documents requested will likely be those identified in the Rule 26 disclosures.

Parties in business tort cases are often asked to produce a large variety of business papers in response to document requests. Such requests for production need not give specific detail as to each particular document requested but can be quite general. As the Supreme Court explained more than a century ago, "We see no reason why all such books, papers, and

---

14. Fed. R. Civ. P. 34 advisory committee's note (1946 Amendments) (citing Olson Trans. Co. v. Socony-Vacuum Oil Co. (E.D. Wis. 1944); and 8 Fed. R. Serv. 34.41, Case 2).

correspondence which related to the subject of inquiry, and were described with reasonable detail, should not be called for and the company directed to produce them. Otherwise, the [Party] would be compelled to designate each particular paper which it desired, which presupposes an accurate knowledge of such papers, which the tribunal desiring the papers would probably rarely, if ever, have."[15]

Since 1970, the requirement to produce electronic information has also been in play when the description of "documents" was revised to include electronic data.[16] The rule was further revised in 2006 to make the procedures and requirements of electronic production more clear.[17] These requirements make responding to Rule 34 document requests far more burdensome than before the days of email and other electronic documents.[18]

Particularly in business tort cases, what to ask for in the way of documents is a unique and case-by-case determination. Like interrogatories, the advent of initial disclosure requirements has made traditional "form" requests a thing of the past. Requests in business tort cases must be specifically formulated to call for as much relevant information as possible, while avoiding the kind of data dump that can result from overly broad requests.

Rule 34 inspections, sampling, and testing, though rarely used in business tort cases, should not be completely overlooked. The opportunity to walk through the opposing party's warehouse, factory, or offices can yield unexpected riches. For example, in a trade secrets case, if you find that you are not subject to security when you arrive at the facility, the product is kept in unlocked buildings, and/or marketing plans are written up on whiteboards for everyone walking through the facility to see, you will have ample evidence that the information was not subject to reasonable efforts to protect its secrecy.

Unlike interrogatories and requests for admission, Rule 34 requests are typically not limited in federal (or many state) courts. Thus, if you are subject to a limitation on interrogatories, the use of requests for production

---

15. Consolidated Rendering Co. v. Vermont, 207 U.S. 541, 543–44 (1908).
16. FED R. CIV. P. 34 advisory committee's notes (1970 Amendments).
17. *Id.* (2006 Amendments).
18. *See infra* Section V.

can effectively get around that constraint by creatively framing requests to get at information that you might traditionally ask for in an interrogatory.[19] There is a lot of ground you can cover with Rule 34 requests and they should be used to gather as much relevant information as possible, in a controlled and careful manner.

C. Requests for Admission

Requests for admission are calculated to "define and limit the matters in controversy between the parties."[20] Further, "[a]n important purpose of the rule is to reduce the cost of litigation by narrowing the scope of disputed issues, facilitating the succinct presentation of cases to the trier of fact, and eliminating the necessity of proving undisputed facts."[21] They allow a party to request admissions by their opponents of matters that "relate to statements or opinions of fact or of the application of law to fact."[22] As such they do not permit requests that seek concessions of pure questions of law and have traditionally been limited to matters that would not require an adversary to admit to ultimate facts that would undermine the basis of the claims. In other words, you cannot properly ask "admit that you should lose the lawsuit."[23]

Rule 36(a) also affords the responding party limited options for answering a request for admission. "If a matter is not admitted, the answer must specifically deny it or state in detail why the answering party cannot truthfully admit or deny it. A denial must fairly respond to the substance of the matter; and when good faith requires that a party qualify an answer or deny

---

19. *E.g.*, "Produce documents evidencing the date and state of incorporation of the plaintiff."
20. 8A CHARLES ALAN WRIGHT ET AL., FEDERAL PRACTICE AND PROCEDURE § 2252 (2d ed. 1994) (citing Ted Finman, *The Request for Admission in Federal Civil Procedure*, 71 YALE L.J. 371, 376 (1962)).
21. Thalheim v. Eberheim, 124 F.R.D. 34, 35 (D. Conn. 1988).
22. FED. R. CIV. P. 36.
23. *See* Disability Rights Council of Greater Washington v. Washington Metro. Area Transit Auth., 234 F.R.D. 1, 3 (D.D.C. 2006) ("In 1970, Rule 36 was amended to allow for requests applying law to fact. It is still true, however, that one party cannot demand that the other party admit the truth of a legal conclusion. . . . For example, it would be inappropriate for a party to demand that the opposing party ratify legal conclusions that the requesting party has simply attached to operative facts.").

only a part of a matter, the answer must specify the part admitted and qualify or deny the rest. The answering party may assert lack of knowledge or information as a reason for failing to admit or deny only if the party states that it has made reasonable inquiry and that the information it knows or can readily obtain is insufficient to enable it to admit or deny."[24]

A responding party may also object to a request for admission, but not "solely on the ground that the request presents a genuine issue for trial."[25] A matter admitted under Rule 36 is deemed "conclusively established unless the court, on motion, permits the admission to be withdrawn or amended."[26]

Additionally, Rule 36 expressly permits the requesting party to move a court to determine the sufficiency of an answer or objection to a request for admission. If the court finds that an answer does not comply with the Rule, it "may order either that the matter is admitted or that an amended answer be served."[27]

V. A WORD (OR MEGABYTE) ON E-DISCOVERY

With the ubiquitous use of computers, the internet, email, and social media in business in the 21st century, no chapter on discovery in business torts cases would be complete without a discussion of the discovery of electronically stored information (ESI). E-discovery is a subject that evolves and changes so quickly, however, that whole books can be, and are, written on the topic.[28] This chapter does not attempt to cover all or even a majority of e-discovery issues, but will address a handful of issues that commonly arise in business tort cases.

A. How Much ESI Is There?

According to one study, more than 99 percent of information that was generated by businesses in 2004 was created and stored in an electronic

---

24. Fed. R. Civ. P. 36(a)(4).
25. *Id.* 36(a)(5).
26. *Id.* 36(b).
27. *Id.* 36(a)(6).
28. A.B.A. Section of Litigation, Managing E-Discovery and ESI: From Pre-Litigation through Trial (Michael D. Berman et al. eds., 2011).

format.[29] This includes everything from PDF documents stored on a hard drive, to voice messages on a smart phone or VOIP system, to vast amounts of archived data that your clients keep on backup tapes. Market research tells us that the average employee sends or receives about 105 electronic messages per business work day.[30] This translates into more than 2,635,000 electronic messages a year for a company with 100 employees. Thus, as a business tort lawyer who will be tasked with finding the five emails out of those millions that show, for example, that your opponent was given access to your client's trade secrets, you will want to start any case by getting a handle on how and where your clients and your opponents are maintaining their ESI.

Production of ESI is addressed in Federal Rule 26(f), which requires that parties consider and negotiate early in the discovery process the method and format by which ESI is to be produced. While the rules have certainly added more predictability to the production and use of ESI in litigation, they cannot, and do not, solve the many challenges that every business tort lawyer, in particular, will face in corralling and managing such a vast amount of information.

B. Preservation and Litigation Holds

An initial step to any litigation or contemplated litigation should always be a litigation hold letter reminding your client of its obligations to preserve and maintain documents and ESI that may be relevant to the lawsuit. Where litigation is contemplated but has not yet been filed, it is also often a good idea to send a letter early on to the opposing party or its counsel reminding them of their obligations to maintain documents. Such a letter will definitely pinpoint the latest possible time that "litigation was contemplated," so as to impose on your opponent the duty to preserve its documents. That date can otherwise be a moving target and open to debate.

---

29. David K. Isom, *Electonic Discovery Primer for Judges*, 1 FED. CTS. L. REV. 1, 26 & n.1 (2006).
30. The Radicati Group, Inc., Email Statistics Report, 2011–2015.

C. Get a Handle on IT

Someone from your legal team should also sit down with a member of the client's IT department to ensure a full understanding of the technology used in the business, and the client's policies for maintaining and managing its ESI. The involvement of IT personnel and document management software is inevitable with ESI, but it adds yet another level of complication to already complex cases. An understanding of how business records, for your client or the opposing party, are created, stored, and maintained, including the time period for which the records exist (whether current, archived, backed up, or destroyed), is important to ESI discovery.

Getting technical personnel on board early in the process ensures as smooth and efficient a production as possible. Your legal data support team (LDS) should be intimately involved in consultations with your client's IT personnel and legal team before they meet and confer so that you will know what you can, and cannot, promise in the way of electronic production. LDS should also see, and approve, case management reports and agreements related to the production of ESI. Likewise, once discovery begins in earnest, LDS should see requests for production and should be involved in the process to retrieve and prepare the information for production.

D. Sourcing Your ESI

Identifying the sources that are the most readily available and easiest to preserve and retrieve where there are multiple copies of documents is key to ESI production that is efficient and effective. While you are obliged to produce multiple copies of responsive documents if they are drafts, or contain handwritten notes, there is no need to produce 25 copies of the exact same contract from each person who maintained it. In a business tort case you can guarantee that you will be faced with reviewing, interpreting, and sorting out a room (or more) full of phantom documents; why add to the piles if you don't have to? The fewer documents you have to manage, the better.

One important limitation to always keep in mind is that if production of certain ESI would impose an "undue burden" it is not required.[31] If your

---

31. FED. R. CIV. P. 26(a)(2)(B).

opponent files a motion to compel you will be required to show that the cost and burden of production outweighs the relevance of the information, while in response, your opponent will have to show that its need for the information is greater than the costs of producing it.[32] To "split the baby" courts may grant some of the discovery, but shift the costs by applying certain factors outlined in one of the many Zubulake opinions issued by Judge Scheindlin in the Southern District of New York.[33] These opinions are wonderful resources for ESI battles.

E. Processing and Reviewing the Data

The processing of information collected is also best left to the technical team. While processing data can be expensive, removing duplicates, performing key word searches, and filtering the documents to reduce volume and organize it for review saves time and money in the long run and helps ensure that the legal team is reviewing the most important data.

The review process tends to be the most onerous and time consuming of all aspects of discovery. Reviewers must tackle multiple tasks: assessing relevance, identifying privilege, highlighting helpful (and hurtful) documents, and assigning documents to categories for later use and retrieval. For that reason a "review protocol" that gives a short background, identifies issues, and gives tagging categories and criteria is invaluable. A review protocol also allows identification of possible privilege areas. While the federal rules, and most protective orders, include clawback provisions that allow inadvertently produced privileged documents to be retrieved, no practitioner can rely on those provisions to protect privileged documents. No one wants an opponent to see a privileged communication about litigation strategy, or identifying bad facts; even if you do get the document back you cannot, as they say, "get the toothpaste back in the tube." Furthermore, if your

---

32. *Id.*
33. Zubulake v. UBS Warburg LLC, 217 F.R.D. 309 (S.D.N.Y. 2003). *See also* Zubulake v. UBS Warburg LLC, 230 F.R.D. 290 (S.D.N.Y. 2003); Zubulake v. UBS Warburg LLC, 216 F.R.D. 290 (S.D.N.Y. 2003); Zubulake v. UBS Warburg LLC, 220 F.R.D. 212 (S.D.N.Y. 2003); Zubulake v. UBS Warburg LLC, 229 F.R.D. 422 (S.D.N.Y. 2004); Zubulake v. UBS Warburg LLC, 231 F.R.D. 159 (S.D.N.Y. 2005); Zubulake v. UBS Warburg LLC, 382 F. Supp. 2d 536 (S.D.N.Y. 2005).

opponent wants to be difficult you may have to go to the court to get your information back and the court could deny the clawback. Better to have a detailed discovery plan, review plan, and review protocol that prevents you from disclosing privileged documents in the first place.

VI. THE MEAT OF THE MATTER: DEPOSITIONS
A. The Basics

An effective deposition can be the single most powerful tool in a lawsuit. Depositions not only shed light on the credibility and jury appeal of witnesses, but can provide your best opportunity for developing the factual record and discovering previously unknown facts, witnesses, and documents. As part of the initial discovery plan, counsel should identify the witnesses to be deposed, the purpose of each deposition, and where they fit in the overall strategy of the case. In the initial plan and actual preparations for depositions, the focus should be on planning for the most effective and efficient depositions possible. This is particularly important in federal court where, barring special circumstances, depositions are limited to one day of seven hours.[34] In addition, there is an implied (and often actual through local rules and case management orders) limitation of ten depositions per side.[35]

Some initial questions to ask yourself as you determine how to make the best use of your depositions are whether the individual (or entity) you want to depose will be available for trial, whether you can get the information needed from this person through an informal conversation rather than a formal deposition, and what documents you should seek from this person. Once you have decided on a plan for your depositions, including the order of deponents, each deposition should be approached with a detailed outline including a set of exhibits and documents to be reviewed or authenticated by the witness. Business tort lawyers may approach depositions very differently in terms of specific procedure. For some cases it may be best to jump right in to the meat of the matter and dispense with the niceties that typically precede hard questioning. For others using the documents to frame

---

34. FED. R. CIV. P. 30(d)(1).
35. *Id.* 30(a)(2)(A)(i).

the questioning may be preferred. The individual outline is less important than having a clear goal and view of why you are taking the deposition and what you need to accomplish.

Although an outline will help you focus, it is equally important that a deposing attorney remain open to letting the deposition go where it will. The goal is to maximize information and then clarify it. The best way to get a witness to open up and to understand what that person is saying is usually to be a good listener, make the witness feel comfortable, and treat them with respect. Ideally you want a deposition that flows naturally, where you take a genuine interest in what the other person has to say.[36] This is not to say you want a deposition that becomes a conversation, with a quick back and forth. Instead, you want a witness that listens carefully and answers truthfully, and a transcript that helps your case, whether you are taking or defending the deposition.

B. Getting Your Witness Ready

Allowing an opposing attorney to question your witness can sometimes be a frightening prospect for the witness and the defending attorney. One major concern, of course, is the loss of control. But careful preparation can limit potential damage and allow your witness to have a sense of ownership and power over the deposition. To create that feeling of control a laundry list of rules is unnecessary and can be counterproductive. Witnesses in a business torts case are, typically, businesspeople. Providing a long list of rules can overwhelm and confuse witnesses and take them well outside the comfort zone they should be in to be an effective and believable witness. There is only one definitive rule: be honest. While there are a number of "lesser" rules—such as "don't volunteer," "don't speculate," "don't try to win the case"—that most business tort lawyers will want to impress on their deponents, there will likely be occasions in every deposition when the witness will be asked to speculate[37] or will need to volunteer information

---

36. Edward G. Connette, *How to Take Better Depositions and Perhaps Improve Your Marriage*, A.B.A. J. LITIG. SEC., Spring 2005, at 6–10.

37. Cincinnati Insurance Co. v. Serrano, No.11-2075-JAR, 2012 WL 28071 (D. Kan. Jan. 5, 2012) (holding that "calls for speculation" is a foundation objection, not a form objection,

to clarify an answer. These are not cardinal sins and can be fixed. Lying cannot. Not only is it perjury, but it signals to your opponent that this witness lacks credibility, will be a bad witness at trial, and will likely be easy to impeach. The goal should be to make sure the witness gives truthful, accurate answers that are difficult to impeach. To reach that goal, a good deposition prep will include a thorough review of documents the witness is likely to be asked about, the important facts, topics, and issues in the case, and some "practice" answering likely questions. There is no substitute for a good deposition prep in ensuring that your witnesses understand their role and responsibilities both at the deposition and in the case.

Ideally your deponents should understand that the deposition is theirs to control. They can decide how to answer, how long to answer, in what tone to answer, and whether to answer in a way that enhances the ultimate goal or in a way that simply provides a "yes" or "no." One good rule of thumb for preparing your witness in a business tort case where many issues are particularly nuanced is to ensure that where a witness has an explanation it does not get lost behind a "yes" or "no." Providing qualifying information first and then the "yes" or "no" answer is often the best practice.

C. Speaking for the Corporation

Because business tort cases tend to be heavy on corporate parties and witnesses, they also tend to result in many more 30(b)(6) depositions than many other types of cases. The 30(b)(6) deposition is one of the most powerful tools in the arsenal of a business tort litigator. The pressure on a business to designate the right person(s) to address the issues designated can be high—particularly in a large business, or in a case where the pertinent events happened so long ago that a witness with personal knowledge is unavailable. The general procedure set forth in Rule 30(b)(6) is found in many similar state statutes. The word "shall designate" in the rule is mandatory. A company may have no current employee with significant knowledge

---

which need not be stated at the time of the deposition and "tends to coach the witness to respond that she does not know the answer"). In other words, asking questions that call for speculation at a deposition is not improper—though you may still want to caution your own witnesses not to speculate in their answers if they can help it.

137

on a designated subject, but it cannot refuse to designate a representative.[38] Nor can a company simply present a human body to the deposition and be in compliance with the rule.[39] The corporation has a duty to "make a conscientious good-faith endeavor to designate the persons having knowledge of the matters sought by [the requesting party] and to prepare those persons in order that they can answer fully, completely, and unevasively the questions posed."[40]

Even when the topic goes beyond the designated deponent's personal knowledge, the deponent must be prepared to discuss it based upon information available to the corporation.[41] The designee has a duty to gather and review information reasonably available to the company on the designated topics, including from documents, depositions, past employees, or other sources.[42] A corporation's failure to educate its representative may be treated the same as a failure to respond to an interrogatory.[43]

The purpose of a 30(b)(6) deposition is for the testimony to bind the corporation itself. The word "binding" in the context of Rule 30(b)(6) does not mean, however, that the testimony is akin to a judicial admission—a statement that conclusively establishes a fact and estops an opponent from controverting the statement with any other evidence.[44] Rather, "testimony given at a Rule 30(b)(6) deposition is evidence which, like any other deposition testimony, can be contradicted and used for impeachment purposes."[45]

This does not mean, however, that the party may retract prior testimony with impunity. An attempt to directly contradict earlier 30(b)(6) testimony through an affidavit or otherwise can be met with a refusal to consider the later affidavit if there is no valid and reasonable explanation for the

---

38. *See, e.g.*, United States v. Taylor, 166 F.R.D. 356, 361 (M.D.N.C. 1996).
39. *See, e.g.*, Quantachrome Corp. v. Micrometritics Inst. Corp., 189 F.R.D. 697, 699 (S.D. Fla. 1999).
40. Protective Nat'l Ins. Co. of Omaha v. Commonwealth Ins. Co., 137 F.R.D. 267, 278 (D. Neb. 1989).
41. Bank of New York v. Meridien Biao Bank Tanzania Ltd., 171 F.R.D. 135, 151 (S.D.N.Y. 1997).
42. *Id.*
43. Plantation-Simon Inc. v. Al Bahloul, 596 So. 2d 1159, 1160 (Fla. Dist. Ct. App. 1992).
44. WRIGHT ET AL., *supra* note 20, § 2103 (Supp. 2007).
45. A.I. Credit Corp. v. Legion Ins. Co., 265 F.3d 630, 637 (7th Cir. 2001).

reversal of position.[46] Likewise, a failure by a 30(b)(6) deponent to take a position or respond to questions can result in a trial court refusing to allow evidence on that point.[47]

Under Rule 30(b)(5), a party cannot issue a subpoena *duces tecum* upon a corporate party designee but can attach a request for documents, items, or things in accordance with Rule 34 so long as 15 extra days' notice beyond the 10 or 15 days required by 30(b)(1) is given. This is a great tactical way to get documents that an opposing party might otherwise be able to avoid producing for 30–60 days given liberal extensions of time granted by the court.

If you are serving a 30(b)(6) deposition notice, the rules require that the areas of inquiry be designated with "reasonable particularity." This is undefined, but has generally been held to require more than a generic notice or a nonexclusive list of topics.[48] Some courts require the requesting party to "designate, with painstaking specificity, the particular subject areas that are intended to be questioned, and that are relevant to the issues in dispute."[49]

Importantly, the prevailing view is that the examining party may ask questions outside the scope of the notice, though the answers will not necessarily bind the corporation.[50] This is a particularly important point in many

---

46. Hyde v. Stanley Tools, 107 F. Supp. 2d 992, 993 (E.D. La. 2000); Rainey v. Am. Forest & Paper Ass'n, Inc., 26 F. Supp. 2d 82, 95 (D.D.C. 1998) ("[T]he Kurtz affidavit's quantitative assertion works a substantial revision of defendant's legal and factual positions. This eleventh hour alteration is inconsistent with Rule 30(b)(6), and is precluded by it.").

47. United States v. Taylor, 166 F.R.D. 356, 362 (M.D.N.C. 1996) ("[I]f a party states it has no knowledge or position as to a set of alleged facts or area of inquiry at a Rule 30(b)(6) deposition, it cannot argue for a contrary position at trial without introducing evidence explaining the reasons for the change."); QBE Insurance Corp. v. Jorda Enters., Inc., 277 F.R.D. 676, 688 (S.D. Fla. 2012) (citing Great Am. Ins. Co. v. Vegas Constr. Co., Inc., 251 F.R.D. 534, 539 (D. Nev. 2008)).

48. *See, e.g.,* Alexander v. FBI, 188 F.R.D. 111, 121 (D.D.C. 1998).

49. *See, e.g.,* Prokosch v. Catalina Lighting, Inc., 193 F.R.D. 633, 638 (D. Minn. 2000).

50. King v. Pratt & Whitney, 161 F.R.D. 475 (S.D. Fla. 1995) ("The Rule is not one of limitation but rather of specification within the broad parameters of the discovery rules."); Detoy v. City and County of San Francisco, 196 F.R.D. 362 (N.D. Cal. 2000). *See also* Cabot Corp. v. Yamulla Enters., Inc., 194 F.R.D. 499 (M.D. Pa. 2000) (holding that Rule 30(b)(6) does not limit the scope of deposition to contents of deposition notice); Overseas Private Inv. Corp. v. Mandelbaum, 185 F.R.D. 67 (D.D.C. 1999) (the scope of inquiry of a Rule 30(b)(6) witness is limited only by Rule 26(b)(1)'s general discovery standards). *But see* State Farm Mut. Auto. Ins. Co. v. New Horizont, Inc., 250 F.R.D. 203, 220 (E.D. Pa. 2008) ("[I]f a Rule 30(b)(6) witness is asked a question concerning a subject that was not noticed for deposition

business tort cases, so many of which revolve around 30(b)(6) depositions. The ability to ask questions beyond the scope allows the deposing attorney to delve into areas that may come up as part of questioning on designated topics, but that are outside their scope. This, in turn, can result in additional information to follow up on in future depositions or written discovery.

It is a relatively common practice in business tort cases for a party to take the deposition of individual witnesses in the case, including individual officers of a corporate party, and then seek to shore up the issues in the case through the use of a Rule 30(b)(6) deposition. The case law, though very limited, supports this tactical plan and consistently rejects any argument that the deposition of an individual officer can prevent the later deposition of the company.[51] The fact that individually named witnesses have testified concerning a subject is no obstacle to a 30(b)(6) deposition on the same subject.

There is a split of authority in the federal courts as to whether a party who has once taken a Rule 30(b)(6) deposition on certain designated issues may re-notice another Rule 30(b)(6) deposition on different issues without first seeking leave of court. In the Eastern District of North Carolina, no leave of court was required for a second Rule 30(b)(6) notice.[52] The court in that case noted that the topics in the two deposition notices related to different subject areas and stated, "Rule 30(b)(6) depositions are different from depositions of individuals" and observed that "no aspect of the Rules . . . either restricts a party to a single 30(b)(6) deposition or restricts the allotted time for taking a 30(b)(6) deposition."[53]

This decision was expressly rejected in the case of *Foreclosure Management Co. v. Asset Management Holdings, LLC.*[54] The court there held that leave of court is required before a party may take a second

or that seeks information not reasonably available to the corporation, the witness need not answer the question. Moreover, certain questions may seek details so minute that a witness could not reasonably be expected to answer them.").

51. Miller v. Union Pacific RR Co., No. 06-2399-JAR-DJW, 2008 WL 4724471 (D. Kan. Oct. 24, 2008); ICE Corp. v. Hamilton Sundstrand Corp., No. 05-4135-JAR, 2007 WL 1500311 (D. Kan. May 21, 2007).

52. Quality Aero Technology v. Telemetrie Electronic GMBH, 212 F.R.D. 313 (E.D.N.C. 2002).

53. *Id.*

54. No. 07-2388-DJW, 2008 WL 3895474 (D. Kan. Aug. 21, 2008).

Rule 30(b)(6) deposition of a corporation or other entity because the generic word "deponent" in Rule 30(a)(2)(A)(ii) makes clear that the drafters must have intended to include not only individuals but also corporations and other entities where leave of court is required for a second deposition.[55]

One important point to remember in federal court, and many state courts, is that regardless of where the law comes down on a second deposition, a deposition longer than one seven-hour day, a list of overly broad topics, or other issues related to a deposition notice, "unless [a deponent] has obtained a court order that postpones or dispenses with his duty to appear, that duty remains."[56] As a practical matter, it may be that your opponents will agree to postpone the deposition if you have filed a motion for protective order with legitimate grounds for objection, but tread carefully if all parties do not agree to the postponement as there are courts that will issue sanctions for failing to appear even where a motion for protective order has been filed.[57] Because

---

55. *Id.* (citing Ameristar Jet Charter, Inc. v. Signal Composites, Inc., 244 F.3d 189 (1st Cir. 2001)).

56. Pioche Mines Consol., Inc. v. Dolman, 333 F.2d 257, 269 (9th Cir. 1964). *See* Hepperle v. Johnston, 590 F.2d 609 (5th Cir. 1979) (court's inaction on plaintiff's motion for protective order to postpone taking of its deposition did not relieve plaintiff of duty to appear for deposition); Kelly v. Old Dominion Freight Line, Inc., 376 F. App'x 909, 913 (11th Cir. 2010) ("The district court's inaction on a party's motion for a protective order to postpone the taking of his deposition does not relieve the party of the duty to appear for the deposition."); Pioche Mines Consol., Inc. v. Dolman, 333 F.2d at 269 ("Rule 30(b) places the burden on the proposed deponent to get an order, not just to make a motion"); Alexander v. FBI, 186 F.R.D. 78 (D.D.C. 1998) (plaintiff entitled to award of fees against defendants for defendants' failure to appear for deposition and fact that defendants filed a motion for protective order did not excuse failure to produce witness for deposition); White v. McHugh, CIV.A. 3:09-1559-MJP, 2010 WL 4340399 (D.S.C. Sept. 3, 2010) ("A deponent is relived of appearance only if the protective order is issued prior to the scheduled deposition."); United States v. Fesman, 781 F. Supp. 511, 514 (S.D. Ohio 1991); WRIGHT ET AL., *supra* note 20, § 2035 (3d ed. 2012) ("At least with regard to depositions, the [protective] order should ordinarily be obtained before the date set for the discovery, and failure to move at that time has been held to preclude objection later. . . .") (footnote omitted); *see also* Albert v. Starbucks Coffee Co., 213 F. App'x 1, 1 (D.C. Cir.), *cert. denied*, 551 U.S. 1118 (2007) (unpublished per curiam order) (citations omitted) ("Appellant cites no supporting authority for the proposition that the mere filing of a motion for protective order *requires* the court to excuse a party's failure to obey a court order compelling attendance at a deposition. Indeed, the published authority addressing the issue suggests the contrary.").

57. *In re* Hollar, 184 B.R. 243, 246 (Bankr. M.D.N.C. 1995) (dismissing action under FED. R. CIV. P. 37(b)(2)(c) and noting "[i]t is well-settled that the filing of a motion for protective order does not automatically operate to stay a deposition or other discovery"). *See*

many business tort cases involve a large number of depositions, it is common practice for counsel to work together to come up with a deposition schedule, which may alleviate this issue, but if this is not the case the wise business tort practitioners will be prepared with a motion for protective order (or to quash) very soon after receiving notice.

VII. WHO ELSE TO INVITE TO THE PARTY? THIRD-PARTY DISCOVERY

Third-party discovery in business torts practice may be the most untapped of all the gold mines of information available in a lawsuit. While many litigants may work to avoid production of documents that might hurt their case or help yours, many third-party subpoenas are answered quickly and quietly, and provide substantial information that might otherwise have required discovery motions and untold time and effort. Many nonparty witnesses simply have no dog in the fight between you and your opponent. Thus, if you are looking for information on communications by your opponent to its customers, ask the customers. As long as the information is not overly sensitive, many will not want to bother fighting over the production, and will simply produce the responsive documents.[58]

Third-party discovery can also be a great way to obtain various kinds of financial information, phone records, and internet-based information (including social media). Although large phone and internet provider companies will often assert some grounds for resisting subpoenas, the subpoenas can prove to be very useful and will usually be enforced with some effort on your part. For an excellent article on specific practice pointers for creative third-party discovery specifically in business tort cases, see Daniel J. Winters' article, "Practice Pointers for Creative Third-Party Discovery in Business Torts Cases."[59]

---

also Albert, 213 F. App'x at 1 (dismissing case as sanction for failing to appear at deposition notwithstanding filed protective order).

58. Of course, subpoenas to current customers of your own client, or former customers that your client wants to continue in the future to do business with, should be approached with caution and it should be a client business decision as to whether to subpoena such entities.

59. Daniel J. Winters, *Practice Pointers for Creative Third-Party Discovery in Business Tort Cases*, A.B.A. BUS. TORTS J., Fall 2005.

The Federal Rules do not require that parties "meet and confer" with nonparty recipients of subpoenas in a case where you are moving to compel production or attendance. Some courts or states do have such requirements[60] while others do not.[61] Contacting the nonparty to discuss burden, form of production, cost, retention of important information, scope, and duration of a litigation hold either prior to or immediately after issuing a subpoena is, however, the best practice.[62] Rule 45(c)(2)(B) also authorizes nonparties to file written objections to the subpoena within 14 days after service. The filing of a timely objection to a subpoena requires the subpoenaing party to move to compel production—and to bear the burden of persuasion on the motion to compel.[63]

Additionally, Rule 45 provides nonparties with financial protections that parties are not offered in their production of documents. The party issuing a subpoena must take "reasonable steps" to avoid imposing undue financial burdens on the nonparty.[64] Rule 45's protections do not mean, however, that the party issuing the subpoena must bear all of the expense of a nonparty's production. While generally there is a presumption that the responding party must bear the expense of complying with discovery requests, the presumption is not always controlling.[65] Courts look at a variety of factors to determine whether cost-shifting is necessary in a particular case. If the documents can only be obtained from the nonparty, then a court may order production, but require the subpoenaing party to bear the costs.[66] However, if a nonparty is likely to have information that could be

---

60. C.D. CAL. L. CIV. R. 45-1 (meet and confer required for Rule 45 motions).

61. *See, e.g.,* Travelers Indem. Co. v. Metro. Life Ins. Co., 228 F.R.D. 111, 115 (D. Conn. 2005) (meet and confer not required for Rule 45 motions).

62. The Sedona Conference, *The Sedona Conference Commentary on Non-Party Production & Rule 45 Subpoenas* (April 2008), *available at* https://thesedonaconference.org/system/ ...Rule_45_Subpoenas.pdf.

63. Fed. R. Civ. P. 45(c)(1). *See also, e.g.,* Whitlow v. Martin, No. 04-3211, 2008 WL 2414830 at *4 (C.D. Ill., Nov. 19, 2008), order supplemented by No. 04-CV-3211, 2008 WL 5511178 (C.D. Ill., Nov 19, 2008).

64. Guy Chemical Co. v. Romaco AG, 243 F.R.D. 310, 313 (N.D. Ind. 2007) ("it is fundamentally unfair for nonparties to bear the significant litigation costs of others").

65. *Id.* (citing Oppenheimer Fund, Inc. v. Sanders, 437 U.S. 340 (1978)).

66. FED. R. CIV. P. 45 advisory committee's note (2006 amendments) (if good cause is shown for the materials, then an order compelling production can issue "on terms that protect a nonparty against significant expense.").

particularly important to your case, then an early offer to pay "reasonable" costs, subject to discussion about what is reasonable, can be an important move to get you the documents you want. Keep in mind, if your client is on the receiving end of a subpoena seeking the production of significant documents, most cases have held, as do the Federal Rules, that when and if "costs" are awarded, including costs for production of documents and ESI, they do not include attorneys' fees.[67]

VIII. WRAPPING UP

Discovery in business tort cases has many similarities to discovery in other litigation, but with unique aspects that warrant attention. Because many business cases are resolved before trial, discovery is a significant and important tool leading to resolution. Careful planning in the use of available discovery tools is often the key to putting clients in the best possible position for settlement—or for trial—the position in which every business tort practitioner wants to be at the end of discovery.

---

67.   Fed. R. Civ. P. 54(d) ("Unless a federal statute, these rules [of Civil Procedure], or a court order provides otherwise, costs; see Racing Tires Am., Inc., v. Hoosier Racing Tire Corp., 674 F.3d 158, 163 (3d Cir. 2012). (other than attorneys' fees—should be allowed to the prevailing party."); 28 U.S.C. § 1920. Although Rule 54(d)(1) stipulates that "costs . . . should be allowed to the prevailing party," Congress, in 28 U.S.C. § 1920, specified the litigation expenses that qualify as taxable "costs."

CHAPTER 8

Expert Witnesses

Nelson A.F. Mixon
and
Catherine M. Cameron

I. OVERVIEW

Litigating without the use of expert witnesses is almost inconceivable in many areas of the law. This is especially true in the area of business torts litigation, which almost always involves complicated liability questions and complex damage calculations. This chapter addresses two principal subjects: the types of experts likely to be encountered in business torts litigation, and how to work with, and against, those experts.

To any experienced commercial litigator, much of the material in this chapter is likely well known. The use of experts in commercial litigation generally shares much in common with the use of experts in the more specialized area of business torts. Nevertheless, business torts litigation presents specialized, and often subtle, concerns that not only impact the choice of expert witnesses, but also the approach to working with one's own experts and against the opposing side's experts. Fundamentally, this is because business torts litigation, perhaps more than other forms of commercial litigation, is often focused on deeply human narratives of right and wrong, rather than simple contract interpretation.

As an initial matter, it is important to answer the question, "What is an expert witness?" The term "expert witness" is most frequently used to describe a retained witness who gives opinion testimony under the rubric of Rule 702 of the Federal Rules of Evidence, or state equivalents. The term expert witness, however, may also include witnesses who give no opinions on the facts of a particular case, but who testify about more general matters that the witness has personally observed and may have expertise upon, such as standard industry practices. It is unclear that FED. R. EVID. 702, or state equivalents, governs such witnesses' testimony, although these witnesses certainly testify on the basis of their expertise, and are frequently seen in business torts litigation.

II. TYPES OF EXPERTS IN BUSINESS TORTS LITIGATION

The varieties of expert witnesses used in business torts litigation are largely divided into "liability experts" and "damages experts." In addition, in recent years, expert witnesses are being used to litigate discovery disputes, even though these experts will not likely be called at trial, absent spoliation instructions. This section addresses damages experts first because they are present in almost every business torts case. A discussion on the various types of liability experts follows. This section concludes with a few words about the use of expert witnesses in discovery disputes.

A. Damages

Except in the rarest of cases, almost every party to business torts litigation at some point retains an expert witness to calculate the economic damages claimed or defended against. Such experts typically include forensic accountants, economists, or appraisers.

1. Forensic Accountants

A party's economic damages are most often calculated by forensic accountants or forensic economists. Recognized qualifications for forensic accountants and forensic economists include Certified Public Accountant (CPA),[1] Certified Management Accountant (CMA),[2] and Chartered Financial Analyst (CFA).[3] Forensic accountants/economists with such

---

1. American Institute of Certified Professional Accountants, http://www.aicpa.org.
2. Institute of Management Accountants, http://www.imanet.org.
3. CFA Institute, http://www.cfainstitute.org.

qualifications must adhere to professional standards of practice determined by their respective governing body. Professionals with a doctorate in economics may also prepare damages calculations using their particular expertise in market analysis.

Each qualification has a particular focus that should be considered when hiring a forensic accountant or economist. CPAs focus on financial reporting for external entities, such as public companies, institutional investors, banks, and other businesses. CMAs focus on accounting and management skills required to enhance business performance. CFAs focus on enhancing investment portfolio performance. And, of course, PhD economists focus on industry market analysis.

In addition to selecting an appropriately qualified forensic accountant or economist, his or her specific experience should also be reviewed and considered. For example, has the expert worked primarily in professional offices (such as accounting or consulting firms), in academia, or in industry? The assignment may require expertise in a particular industry, such as real estate, manufacturing, securities, healthcare, construction, retail, mining, software, or professional services. Generally, specific experience within these categories is not required except for specialized areas such as precious metals, fine art, or similar niche categories. For example, if an expert has experience in the retail industry, the identity of the items sold in any specific case is less important. This is because, from a financial standpoint, the relevant calculations do not change significantly whether the item sold is clothes or food, although there are nuances that must be taken into account.

The calculation of damages will vary depending upon the case. Some fraud cases, for example, may only require the expert to calculate the actual amount of money or goods misappropriated. Such damages calculation may require little more than simple addition.

Other torts, such as various shareholder liability or partnerships disputes, have a more complex damages component that necessitates calculating the profits that the claimant would most probably have earned if the alleged tort had not occurred. These projected profits are based upon assumptions and projections calculated by the expert. Those projected profits are compared to the profits actually earned, or losses actually incurred, and the difference represents the claimant's lost profits or damages. This analysis is often referred to as a "But-For" analysis and hinges upon the assumptions used to hypothecate the But-For world in which the alleged tort did not occur. The damages calculations prepared by the expert will be analyzed at length by opposing counsel and opposing experts. If the assumptions are unreasonable or lack support in the evidentiary record or literature in the field, those flaws will be magnified, undermining the credibility of the profit projections in the But-For world. Experts will develop the assumptions used in the But-For world by analyzing historical financial data, industry data, economic data, and expected events absent the alleged tort. Ultimately the determination of the profits that would have been earned in the hypothetical But-For world will require a certain amount of subjectivity, but that subjectivity needs to be based on realistic factual assumptions.

Regardless of how they are calculated, damages calculations must be brought to present value. Because the losses were incurred in the past and may be ongoing into the future, forensic accountants and economists use present value calculations to ascertain the amount of damages as of a specific date, irrespective of when the injury actually occurred or may occur.

Future damages are reduced to present value using a discount rate. The discount rate incorporates the time value of money, which takes into account inflation and the lack of access to money. The discount rate also incorporates the risk that future damages may not occur as projected (i.e., the inherent uncertainty of future profits). Simply using the time value of money as a discount rate is seen as a "risk-free" discount rate—often the rate of United States treasury bills or bonds. Depending upon the particular calculation, future damages may be damages occurring after the alleged tort or damages occurring after the present date. The discount rate used by the expert can have a significant impact upon the amount of damages calculated. For example, $100 expected to be received in ten years has a present value of $61 using a 5 percent discount rate,[4] but has a present value of $11 using a 25 percent discount rate.[5] Determining the appropriate discount rate requires reasoned subjectivity, but with realistic assumptions.

---

4. $100.00 \times 1/(1+0.05)10$.
5. $100.00 \times 1/(1+0.25)10$.

2. Business Valuation

Business valuation experts are most often used in cases where the claimant alleges a total loss of a business or of a proportionate ownership share. In some cases, tortious conduct can completely destroy a business, such that the appropriate damages calculus is the value of the business rather than the amount of lost profits. It should be noted that the value of an entire business is not necessarily higher than damages based on lost profits. In other cases, a business owner may be deprived of his ownership interest in a business as a result of tortious conduct, such that his economic damages are the value of the claimant's fractional ownership interest.

The value of an ownership interest in a business is impacted by the level of control enjoyed by the interest holder. Where the plaintiff owns less than 50 percent of the ownership interest of an entity, for example, an appraiser may, under appropriate circumstances, discount the value of that minority interest to account for the fact that the minority owner's rights are qualitatively different from the rights enjoyed by a majority or entire owner. As one tax court explained:

> The minority discount is recognized because the holder of a minority interest lacks control over corporate policy, cannot direct payment of dividends and cannot compel a liquidation of corporate assets.[6]

In addition, an ownership interest that can be easily sold is more valuable than a shareholding that cannot be readily sold. As a result, all else being equal, shares that are publicly traded are more valuable than shares in privately held companies. An appraiser will discount the value of a privately held company compared to a publicly held company by applying a lack of marketability discount. As explained in another tax case:

> The lack of marketability discount reflects the absence of a recognized market for closely held stock and accounts for the fact that closely held stock is not readily transferable.[7]

---

6. Ward v. Commissioner, 87 T.C. 78, 106 (1986).
7. Mandelbaum v. Commissioner, 69 T.C.M. 2852 (1995).

Minority interest discounts typically range from 35 to 50 percent and lack of marketability discounts are typically 15 to 35 percent. Such large discounts will obviously have a significant impact on the value of the ownership interest in question.

It is important to understand the world of certifications for business valuation experts. Recognized qualifications for business appraisers include Certified Business Appraiser (CBA),[8] Certified Valuation Analyst (CVA),[9] accreditation by the American Society of Appraisers (ASA),[10] and Accredited in Business Valuation (ABV).[11] Experts with these qualifications must adhere to professional standards of practice determined by their respective governing bodies.[12] The standards all have certain nuances that must be considered by the attorney and expert, but they generally require an appraiser to have integrity; use objectivity; be competent for the assigned task; use due professional care; and plan, control, and record the work performed. Each qualification has a different focus and that focus should be considered when hiring a business appraiser. CBAs only appraise closely held businesses, ASAs may value real property and personal property in addition to businesses, and CBAs and ABVs must also be CPAs.

Following the savings and loan crisis in the 1980s, the leading appraisal organizations in the United States and Canada created the Appraisal Foundation, which established the Uniform Standards of Professional Appraisal Practice (USPAP). USPAP is legally mandatory for real estate valuations, but business valuations do not have the same requirement. Only ASAs are

---

8. CBAs may apply to become Master Certified Business Appraisers after a minimum of 15 years of business appraisal experience. http://www.go-iba.org.
9. National Association of Certified Valuators, http://www.nacva.com.
10. American Society of Appraisers, http://www.appraisers.org.
11. American Institute of Certified Public Accountants Accredited in Business Valuation Credential, http://www.aicpa.org/interestareas/forensicandvaluation/membership/pages/abvcredentialoverview.aspx.
12. National Association of Certified Valuators and Analysts Standards, http://www.nacva.com/association/nacva.asp. American Society of Appraisers Business Valuation Standards, http://www.appraisers.org/Files/Professional%20Standards/bvstandards.pdf. Institute of Business Appraisers Professional Standards, http://www.go-iba.org/files/iba_s_new_professional_standards_effective_6-1-2011.pdf. American Institute of Certified Public Accountants Statement on Standards for Valuation Services, http://www.aicpa.org/interestareas/forensicandvaluation/resources/standards/downloadabledocuments/ssvs_full_version.pdf.

required by their professional body to adhere to USPAP for business valuations, although other certified appraisers should be aware of the USPAP sections that relate to the valuation of business interests.

The value of a business depends upon the standard of value used and the date of valuation. These determinants are often a matter of law. The most common standard of value is fair market value, which is defined in U.S. Treasury Regulation § 20-2031-1(b) as

> [t]he price at which property would change hands between a willing buyer and a willing seller when the former is not under any compulsion to buy and the latter is not under any compulsion to sell, both parties having reasonable knowledge of relevant facts.[13]

In many cases the law requires that the fair market value standard be used when determining the value of a business. When use of the fair market standard would be inequitable, the fair value standard may be used. For example, if the case involves minority interest shareholder oppression the fair value standard is often mandated. Fair value is defined in the Revised Model Business Corporation Act as follows:

> (4) "Fair values" means the value of the corporation's shares determined:
>
> i. immediately before the effectuation of the corporate action to which the shareholder objects;
>
> ii. using customary and current valuation concepts and techniques generally employed for similar businesses in the context of the transaction requiring appraisal; and
>
> iii. without discounting for lack of marketability or minority status except, if appropriate, for amendments to the articles pursuant to section 13.02(a)(5).[14]

---

13. Treas. Reg. § 20-2031-1(b) (1966).
14. REV. MODEL BUS. CORP. ACT. § 13.01(4).

Both an expert and counsel should understand the applicable state law on fair value or fair market value, as well as minority discounts. Many states interpret fair value to mean fair market value of a minority interest without application of minority or marketability discounts, thus providing the minority shareholder with a proportionate share of the business entity without any restrictions to selling his interest.

Investment value may also be the appropriate standard of value in many cases. Investment value is the value to a particular investor. If the value of the business is higher if owned by the plaintiff than it would be if the business was owned by another party because of the plaintiff's particular expertise, it would be unfair to use fair market value to compensate the plaintiff.

The date of the valuation is also often prescribed by the law and different states may prescribe different dates for the same tort. An expert's use of the wrong valuation date may lead to exclusion of the expert's testimony.[15] The date of valuation has a significant impact on the calculated value of a business. Consider the value of a real estate development business before and after the real estate crash of 2008—before the crash, it was likely very valuable, but a few months later, its value likely diminished significantly. It is, therefore, important to define the standard of value and date of valuation before the expert starts work.

Business valuations are affected by the same subjectivity in determining underlying assumptions and discount rates as damages calculations generally. These factors should be rigorously questioned to ensure they are fundamentally sound, as any flaws will likely be identified and exploited by the opposing counsel and expert to either seek exclusion of an expert's opinion or discredit the expert on the stand.

3. Appraisers

Aside from business valuation experts, appraisers of many varieties are used in business tort cases to testify to the value of property. These are usually real estate appraisers, although other appraisers may also be used, most often within the context of conversion claims.

---

15. *E.g.*, Haddad v. Rav Bahamas, Ltd., 589 F. Supp. 2d 1302, 1307–08 (S.D. Fla. 2008).

Under the Financial Institutions Reform, Recovery, and Enforcement Act of 1989, real estate appraisers must be licensed by the state in which they work, in accordance with The Real Property Appraiser Qualification Criteria, a set of national guidelines and standards established by the Appraiser Qualifications Board.[16]

Generally, all real estate appraisals should be conducted in accordance with the Uniform Standards of Professional Appraisal Practice (USPAP), a series of guidelines and requirements published by the Appraiser Standards Board.[17] USPAP's preamble indicates that, in and of itself, it is not mandatory and does not contain the force of law. Some states may require compliance with USPAP, however, and it remains the accepted national standard. That being the case, USPAP itself recognizes that *some* of its standards are non-mandatory guidelines, while other standards are mandatory rules that must be followed in all cases in which USPAP is being applied. As a result, appraisers may give USPAP-compliant opinions so long as they follow the USPAP mandatory rules, even if they do not follow the non-mandatory guidelines. An appraiser that does not follow the non-mandatory guidelines, however, should be prepared to explain why the USPAP guideline was not followed.

Appraisers of property other than real estate are often not required to be licensed, although there are still a myriad of professional associations that may set best practices standards, such as the American Society of Appraisers,[18] Appraisers Association of America,[19] National Association of Independent Fee Appraisers,[20] Appraisal Institute,[21] and the International Society of Appraisers.[22]

---

16. As of the writing of this chapter, a copy of The Real Property Appraiser Qualification Criteria may be downloaded at https://appraisalfoundation.sharefile.com/d/s5a51edc02a64131a.
17. As of the writing of this chapter, a copy of USPAP may be downloaded for free at http://www.uspap.org.
18. American Society of Appraisers, http://www.appraisers.org.
19. Appraisers Association of America, http://www.appraisersassoc.org.
20. National Association of Independent Fee Appraisers, http://www.naifa.com.
21. Appraisal Institute, http://www.appraisalinstitute.org.
22. International Society of Appraisers, http://www.isa-appraisers.org.

B. Liability Experts

1. Forensic Accountants/Fraud Examiners

Although the term forensic accountant is often associated with fraud analysis, a forensic accountant is any accountant that provides services for the legal system. Not all forensic accountants undertake fraud analysis. CPAs may perform fraud analyses and may be Certified in Financial Forensics (CFF)[23] to denote their specialty. Certified Fraud Examiners (CFE)[24] specialize in fraud examinations, but may not be qualified accountants.

Proving fraud is often a long and expensive process requiring extensive time on the part of the experts. Fraud analysts are usually engaged when there is a suspicion of fraud to determine if any fraud actually occurred. After extensive analysis by the expert, it may be determined that there was no fraud, but only after significant attorneys' fees and expert costs have been incurred. Thus, it is wise to be sure that there is a concrete basis to suspect fraud before undertaking a thorough fraud investigation.

In addition, even after extensive financial analyses, the findings may be inconclusive. There may be indications of fraud, including suspect transactions that require explanation, yet no solid proof that fraud occurred. The financial expert may suggest that additional expertise would be helpful, such as computer experts or handwriting experts. Other circumstantial evidence may be gathered from such sources as deposition testimony, information on industry norms, and personal financial information of the alleged perpetrator. After the findings of a fraud investigation are ascertained, the findings should be assessed against the level of proof required in a particular case—usually clear and convincing evidence in the case of fraud claims, but a preponderance of the evidence standard for most other torts.

Because there is usually no "smoking gun" in fraud cases, allegations of fraud are usually contested by experts hired by the defendant. The job of a defendant's fraud analyst is usually a simpler process, often described as "poking holes" in the claimant's case. The defendant's expert is presented

---

23. American Institute of Certified Public Accountants Certified in Financial Forensics Credential, http://www.aicpa.org/InterestAreas/ForensicAndValuation/Membership/Pages/certified-in-financial-forensics.aspx.

24. Association of Certified Fraud Examiners, http://www.acfe.com/.

with the case as assembled by the plaintiff's expert and legal team, which he can then assess to determine whether he finds the case convincing or not. If he does not find the fraud allegations convincing, it is his goal to explain why the evidence does not prove fraud.

2. Business Ethics/Industry Practice Experts

Business torts cases are especially ripe for the use of testimony by persons who are experts in a particular industry or business, sometimes known as "business ethics" experts. These experts may testify about the way in which a certain type of business is typically conducted, using standard industry practices and procedures as a guide. A local real estate broker or investor may testify, for example, about the enforcement of standard clauses or the sort of information that is material to most real estate investors in the community.

These business ethics experts should not be overlooked in the business torts context. Their testimony, when used properly, tends to reinforce the themes of right and wrong behavior that inhere in business torts litigation. These experts are particularly useful for prosecuting or defending claims of breach of the covenant of good faith and fair dealing because these experts can assist the jury in understanding the normal and commercially reasonable practices and standards of conduct within an industry that are likely alien to the jury.

When selecting a business ethics or industry practices expert, particular care should be taken to ensure that the expert is well qualified. These experience-based experts—whose testimony often amounts to little more than "because I say this has been my experience"—will arouse particular scrutiny by opposing counsel, the court, and the jury.

3. Other Liability Experts

While often overlooked in business torts cases, a variety of other expert witnesses may be relevant depending upon the specific facts of a case. For example, in a negligent misrepresentation case based upon a misrepresentation about the makeup of concrete sold by the defendant, a concrete composition expert may be required. In an unfair trade practices or Lanham Act case, market research experts may be called to testify to the likelihood that consumers may be confused by the defendant's advertising, promotions, or trade name. Or a software programmer may be needed to establish the defendant's software is so similar to the plaintiff's that it must have been intentionally misappropriated.

C. Experts in Discovery Disputes

Expert witnesses are increasingly used to help prosecute or defend discovery disputes, particularly in the business torts arena. It is not uncommon for courts to hold hearings on discovery disputes in which opposing experts may testify about the availability of evidence, or the ease with which it can be located and processed, as well as the impact of that evidence (or lack of evidence) on the liability or damages experts' ability to formulate opinions.

A key area that experts are becoming involved in is e-discovery disputes. While a full discussion of e-discovery and the use of experts in that arena is outside the scope of this chapter, it is worth a few comments. Computer forensic experts are increasingly retained to evaluate the availability of documents or other data, the ease with which they can be, or could have been, accessed or located by searches or otherwise. In the digital age, judges frequently appreciate expert help in sorting out technical matters about the ability of old data to be recovered or accessed, or whether certain data claimed to be unavailable would, in fact, be available. Expert opinions on these issues are used, by way of affidavit, deposition, or live testimony, to support the contentions made in a discovery motion.

Disputes over the availability of electronic data are especially likely to occur in business tort cases where the failure to preserve evidence takes on special meaning, as the failure to preserve or turn over relevant evidence can show a wrongful mental disposition or attempt to conceal malfeasance, which are frequently elements of business torts, or at least common case themes. In fact, a frequent goal of these disputes is to obtain a spoliation of evidence sanction in which the court instructs the jury that a party failed to preserve relevant evidence, or to otherwise allow the parties to present the spoliation case to the jury so that it can draw its own conclusions as to what the unavailable evidence would have shown and whether its unavailability was intentional.

The use of expert witnesses outside the e-discovery context is also significant. In particular, a party's liability and damages experts can help show

156

the prejudice (or lack thereof) involved in a discovery dispute by explaining how the evidence in question is, or is not, likely to impact the ability to form opinions on key issues. Using experts in this way is, of course, a strategic decision to be made by counsel, as there is always the risk that the experts may need to give opinions without the supposedly necessary data. There are also times when an industry expert or a damages expert may be able to testify about the likelihood that certain documents would have been kept by a party that claims not to have kept such documents.

III. WORKING WITH EXPERTS
A. When to Involve Experts

In business torts litigation, the traditional wisdom is that experts should be involved as early as possible in the process. From both sides' perspectives, experts are an additional expense that clients often resist incurring up front, thinking that the expert will merely say what the client thinks or already knows. This is a false economy.

Involving damages experts early in a case can be particularly helpful with assessing the potential damages so that neither party unwittingly spends a large fortune on legal fees to chase after or defend against a much smaller damage award. This necessitates early involvement by the expert to estimate damages, where possible. This is sometimes more practicable from the plaintiff's perspective, as a business that has lost money or a recently dispossessed owner are likely to have access to the financial documents necessary to calculate damages.

Retaining liability experts before commencing litigation is also advisable. Attorneys have ethical obligations to conduct reasonable factual and legal investigations before bringing claims or defenses. In the business torts context, many claims will require a forensic tracing of various transactions before the claim is evident. It may be that the client has performed some of this work already and can demonstrate to the attorney that an apparent impropriety has occurred, but in many cases the client either has not performed the work or lacks the skill and ability to perform it adequately. Hiring an expert witness to engage in a prelitigation analysis can assist the attorney in evaluating the client's claim and whether a lawsuit is advisable.

From the defense perspective, it is not always feasible to retain an expert to evaluate a potential claim before it is brought. In some instances, however, it may be evident that a claim is likely to be made, either as a result of the findings of an internal investigation or awareness of dissatisfied parties to a transaction. In such circumstances, early-retained experts can assist not only with planning the defense, but with ensuring proper document retention and claims evaluation.

B. Vetting Experts' Qualifications

If you decide to hire an expert after determining the qualifications and experience required for your particular case, you should take the time to scrutinize the expert's CV and check on references. Searching Westlaw or Lexis can also unearth opinions admitting or barring the potential expert's testimony. This research is important to ensure that no information comes to light during the litigation that may undermine the expert's credibility, which could have adverse, or even devastating, consequences for your case. Similarly, it is important to check a potential expert's references on testimonial ability, because an expert who does not present well, even if intelligent and well qualified, may be worthless at trial. The same research should be conducted for opposing experts. Finding an error in an opposing expert's resume or an undisclosed sanction against the expert can be very helpful to your case.

Professional bodies of which the expert is a member should be contacted to ensure that the expert is a member in good standing and that there is no history of complaints or sanctions against the member. There are numerous online databases that can uncover useful information about the expert. However, it is mandatory to verify information obtained online, as such online data is not always accurate. *Merck v. Vioxx*[25] is often cited as a reminder to check an expert's qualifications. In that case, the court overturned a verdict after an expert's qualifications were found to have lapsed.

In addition to checking an expert's background for inaccuracies or embarrassing sanctions, articles he or she has published should also be reviewed to ensure that the expert's opinions in your case do not contradict his or

---

25. 489 F. Supp. 2d 587, 591–92 (E.D. La. 2007).

her previous writings. For example, if an expert authored an article arguing that a particular method of calculating a discount rate was the most appropriate, but used a different method in your case, the inconsistency could easily become an issue.

C. Scope of an Expert's Work

Even before hiring an expert, the scope of his or her work should be considered. The scope of an expert's work should always be discussed and defined up front, regardless of whether the scope appears obvious (calculating damages, valuing a business, appraising real estate) or more complex (establishing liability). While it is important to define the scope of work with your expert, you should avoid documenting the scope, if possible. Opposing counsel may use any documented scope to attempt to show that the attorneys controlled the expert's work, or that the scope was insufficient to form an adequate basis for the expert's opinions.

If you represent the plaintiff, before disclosing the expert, it is always advisable to obtain an estimate of what the expert believes the level of damages might be. It is useful to initially hire the expert as a consultant to get a preliminary damages calculation. In some cases, the expert might find that the damages are minimal or non-existent. If that is the case, you may wish to contact another potential expert or re-assess the entire case.

If you represent the defendant, you may want a potential expert to review the opposing expert's opinion (if it is available) before engaging him. If the opposing expert's opinion will not be available before you must engage an expert, it may be useful to initially hire the potential expert as a consultant to get a preliminary damages calculation. You should also consider if you want your expert to rebut the opposing expert's opinion, prepare an alternative damages calculation, or both.

Regardless of which side of the aisle you are on, the scope of your expert's work should generally include becoming involved with the discovery process and developing case themes. The heart of a business torts claim is business and experts tend to know business better than attorneys, even experienced commercial litigators. Involving experts with discovery helps ensure that they receive the necessary documents for their opinions and that complete records are obtained through the discovery process. Experts should also be used to help prepare discovery requests and deposition questions for opposing experts and other key witnesses. Involving experts with developing case themes helps ensure that the expert's opinions and trial presentation fit in flawlessly with the attorney's overall presentation.

Because expert analysis on liability issues in business tort cases may be extensive, with no guarantee of the expert's ultimate opinion, it is useful to ask the expert to prepare a staged plan of work. A fraud analysis, for example, could involve an extensive investigation with no way to know the results up front. Having the expert take a staged, step-by-step approach will give you a better ability to make informed decisions about the viability of the case before the costs spiral out of control.

D. Should an Expert Prepare a Report?

In federal court, most every testifying expert must prepare a report.[26] This is not true in all state courts, meaning that a decision must be made in those cases as to whether to prepare a report or disclose opinions.

With respect to forensic accountants, business valuation experts, or appraisers, a report is almost always recommended. These experts' opinions are usually detailed and fact-intensive, such that a report does not involve much additional work, and the process of preparing the report can be an effective way for the expert and counsel to "check the math" through each step of the calculation.

A report may not always be desirable for other experts, particularly those whose testimony is less mathematical and does not involve significant tracing. Specifically, business ethics and industry standard of care experts might become too tied down in their opinions were they to prepare a report. These experts' opinions may require more fluidity than a report can accommodate. On the other hand, a report can help keep an expert from becoming too fluid or contradictory. Before making these decisions, an attorney should consider the sort of opinions the expert will be giving, the degree of flexibility needed or desired, and the testimonial abilities of the expert.

---

26. FED. R. CIV. P. 26(a)(2).

E. Ensuring Compliance with Evidentiary Standards

Counsel must always keep in mind that an expert's reports, disclosed opinions, and deposition testimony must pass muster under the applicable evidentiary standards. In federal courts and many state courts, this requires compliance with the twin *Daubert* standards of reliable principles and methods and reliable application of those principles and methods, now enshrined in FED. R. EVID. 702. Keeping these evidentiary requirements in mind from day one is the best way to ensure that an expert is not excluded from trial.

While the *Daubert* standard is often thought of as being a way to exclude "junk science" from the courtroom, its applicability to the sort of expert testimony commonly found in business torts cases must not be overlooked. With the exception of some of the more esoteric market analysis opinions of economists in certain cases,[27] it is rare that an attorney will be able to successfully challenge the reliability of a damages expert's methodology. The exception to this is when an expert simply applies the wrong methodology.[28] Thus, the expert fights in business torts cases tend to revolve around the reliability of an expert's application of his methodology. Such challenges often take the form of challenges to the expert's failure to consider certain evidence,[29] departure from accepted methodologies,[30] or mathematical errors (they do occur).

Challenges to liability experts are often more fruitful. A frequent challenge to the admissibility of liability expert's opinions is that the expert's opinions are nothing more than impermissible legal conclusions, in other words, they tell the jury how to decide the case.[31] Other times, these experts'

---

27. *E.g.*, In re Williams Sec. Lit.-WCG Subclass, 558 F.3d 1130 (N.D. Ill. 2009) (excluding plaintiffs' economist for unreliable methodologies in determining effect of fraud disclosures on value of company).

28. *E.g.*, United States v. 25.202 Acres of Land and building affixed to land located in Town of Champlain, Clinton County, N.Y., 860 F. Supp. 2d 165 (N.D.N.Y. 2010) (excluding property owner's real estate appraiser for improper application of income capitalization valuation method when the comparable sales method was available).

29. *E.g.*, Parsi v. Daioleslam, 852 F. Supp. 2d 82, 88–90 (D.D.C. 2012) (excluding testimony of expert who selectively reviewed some of the defendant's sources and none of the background sources).

30. *E.g.*, Bricklayers and Trowel Trades Intern. Pension Fund v. Credit Suisse First Boston, 853 F. Supp. 2d 181 (D. Mass. 2012) (excluding economist's damage calculations where he departed from accepted methodology and standards).

31. *E.g.*, Webb v. Omni Block, Inc., 166 P.3d 140, 146 (Ariz. Ct. App. 2007); Greenberg Traurig, P.C. v. Moody, 161 S.W.3d 56, 100 (Tex. App. 2005).

opinions are challenged as unscientific or unreliable *ipse dixet* ("because I am an expert and say so").[32]

IV. EXPERT DISCOVERY
A. Privilege Issues

Under the current federal rules, and many state equivalents, testifying experts' draft reports and communications with parties or counsel are generally not discoverable absent a showing of substantial need.[33] The federal rules previously allowed broader discovery into such materials because they constituted "facts or other information" considered by the expert.[34] This language was recently narrowed to the "facts or other data" considered by the expert, so as to limit discovery to the facts considered by the expert and to provide greater protection for counsel's mental impressions.[35] Despite the change, communications between experts and the attorneys or parties remain discoverable to the extent that those communications relate to compensation for the expert's services, identify facts or data for the expert's consideration, or identify assumptions provided for the expert's opinions.[36]

The federal and many state equivalent rules also exempt a party's consulting experts, as well as their opinions and work product, from discovery absent a showing of "exceptional circumstances under which it is impracticable for the party to obtain facts or opinions on the same subject by other means."[37] As noted above, this is an important consideration when retaining an expert and gives counsel the option to retain consulting experts whose identities and opinions can generally be kept confidential.

B. Scope of Discovery on Experts

The scope of discovery in federal and most state courts is broad—anything reasonably calculated to lead to the discovery of admissible evidence. The same is true of expert discovery.

---

32. Zenith Elec. Corp. v. WH-TV Broad. Corp., 395 F.3d 416, 420 (7th Cir. 2005).
33. Fed. R. Civ. P. 26(b)(4)(B)–(C).
34. *Id.* 26 advisory committee's note (2010).
35. *Id.*
36. Fed. R. Civ. P. 26(b)(4)(C).
37. *Id.* 26(b)(4)(D)(ii).

One area that may be particularly fruitful for expert discovery is evidence of possible bias. One prominent Arizona case recently affirmed the right to request an opposing expert's financial information—in the form of tax returns and other itemized financial information—via a subpoena *duces tecum*.[38] While such financial information may prove to be of little interest, it may reveal biases, such as the fact that an expert testifies almost exclusively for the plaintiff or defense, or does most of his work for opposing counsel.

Every expert who testifies in federal court must disclose a list of his prior cases for the previous four years.[39] In addition to this list, attorneys should request copies of the opposing expert's prior reports, deposition transcripts, and any articles or other published materials. Experts will usually object strenuously to producing prior reports and deposition transcripts from other cases as they may be subject to confidentiality agreements or protective orders. This is one area where an attorney should not be afraid to file a motion to compel, absent clear proof that some reports or deposition transcripts are the subject of a valid confidentiality agreement or protective order that would bar production of the materials, even pursuant to a court order.

In addition to formal discovery, informational research should also be conducted through various expert witness databases and the internet to find additional information on the expert. These can yield a wealth of possibly critical information. Research may disclose, for example, opinions in other cases or articles that are inconsistent with the expert's opinions in your case. In a business torts case, where honesty and dishonesty are usually key themes, a party's case can be seriously undermined if the party's expert is perceived as having changed his or her views to reach a desired outcome.

C. Expert Depositions

A complete guide to taking or defending an expert witness's deposition is beyond the scope of this chapter. But there are a few considerations within the business torts context that are worth highlighting.

---

38. *E.g.*, American Family Mut. Ins. Co. v. Grant, 217 P.3d 1212, 1217 (Ariz. 2009).
39. Fed. R. Civ. P. 26(a)(2)(B)(v).

First, an attorney must decide if an expert should be deposed. The conventional practice is often to "depose everyone," or "depose all experts, always." While usually deposing an opposing expert is helpful and important, it is not always advantageous. The federal and many state rules of civil procedure require detailed disclosure of an expert's opinions, usually in the form of a report. Because of this, an attorney should consider not deposing an opposing expert whose disclosed opinions may not pass muster under *Daubert* or state equivalents, to avoid giving the expert more time to establish the reliability of his or her work. Similarly, an attorney may not wish to depose an opposing expert whose disclosed opinions suffer from significant flaws, or do not address certain issues, to limit that expert's trial testimony to the disclosed opinions. Using a deposition to expose flaws in an expert's report may also do little more than disclose your cross-examination strategy and give the expert and your opposing counsel the chance to better prepare for trial.

V. EXPERTS AT TRIAL

Expert witnesses play a prominent role in most business torts trials. While general trial presentation of business torts cases is reserved for a later chapter, two expert-specific issues are discussed below: the extent to which attorneys should rely upon their expert witnesses and the presentation of expert opinions.

A. Reliance on Experts

Attorneys are often tempted to allow the experts to take over the presentation of the case. Do not do this. While experts are very important to presenting a business torts claim or defense, the experts' opinions must fit into a factual narrative that makes sense to the trier of fact. This factual narrative is most compelling when told by the people involved in it, rather than by experts. The parties and other witnesses can supply critical details about the persons and transactions at issue, as well as the "human interest" that the experts simply cannot give. Such details are important to establishing the improper nature of the transactions, rather than the mere existence of "sloppy accounting." Put another way, showing improper motives is often key in a business tort case—indeed, it is often an element of the claim.

164

Expert testimony can add to the evidence of improper motive, but, by itself, can seldom prove that improper motive.

Case presentation aside, relying too much on an expert can be dangerous in a jury trial. Juries frequently place less importance on an expert's testimony than the testimony of the parties actually involved in the transactions, given the perceived economic incentive of the expert to say whatever is most advantageous for his or her client. And when both sides present opposing expert testimony, juries are sometimes inclined to simply cancel the experts out, effectively ignoring them. Because of this, your trial presentation should focus on the witnesses who were involved in the events at issue, with support from the experts, rather than the other way around.

B. Presentation of Expert Opinions

The sort of expert testimony commonly called for in business torts cases can be difficult to present in an engaging manner. The testimony often requires going through numerous transactions, financial documents, or complex damages calculations that may be difficult to explain to an average juror with no experience in the subject matter. There are, however, some things you can do to make expert testimony more interesting and effective.

A good expert witness takes on the role of a teacher or professor, whose job it is to help the jury understand complex transactions and concepts with which the jurors may have little or no experience. It often helps for an expert to begin his testimony by summarizing his opinions and to give a few brief examples of the transactions or data supporting his opinions. This will help orient the jury to the expert's opinions and methods early in the testimony.

Second, an expert should illustrate his or her testimony with demonstrative exhibits, slides, and charts that illustrate the testimony in a simple way. These demonstratives serve as anchor points for the jury to understand the expert's analysis and conclusions. Without such anchor points, a jury can quickly become lost in a sea of numbers and transactions. This not only will lose the jury, but will impact the expert's credibility because the jury is less likely to believe something that they could not follow or do not understand.

When presenting testimony of a forensic accountant or other expert witness who has analyzed a series of transactions or performed other analysis to identify fraud, counsel should consider having the expert witness testify about his methodology and then give a sample of the transactions analyzed, rather than go through each and every one. This is especially effective when combined with charts illustrating the number of transactions analyzed, so that the jury can see that the expert has "done the math."

VI. EXPERT APPELLATE ISSUES

Expert witnesses are generally unable to be of assistance within the context of an appeal. Nevertheless, the admissibility of an expert's testimony is frequently an issue on appeal. Generally, a trial court's evidentiary rulings are entitled to deference and are reviewed for an abuse of discretion. Appellants generally stand a better chance of obtaining a reversal of a trial court order allowing or disallowing expert testimony if the appellant can shift the issue from an issue of fact to an issue of law. One way to do this is to argue that the expert's opinions are typical of a broader methodology or area of science that will be a recurring issue for trial courts, who could use guidance on the boundaries of such opinions. Another effective avenue is to focus on the consistency or inconsistency of the expert's opinions and methods with established bodies of case law on specific damages calculations, methodologies, or valuation dates. To illustrate, it is more effective to argue that an expert's testimony was improperly excluded because "the expert's methodology has been specifically approved of by this court" than because "the expert's methods were sufficiently reliable."

CHAPTER 9

Summary Judgment

Peter J. Boyer

In the business torts litigation world, most cases are resolved before an opening statement or selection of a jury. A motion for summary judgment is, in many cases, the pivotal battle in the litigation. Discovery has usually been completed, preliminary motions addressing venue, jurisdiction, and the sufficiency of the pleadings have been resolved, and the issue remaining for determination is what claims and issues, if any, will be presented to a judge or jury for determination at trial. For the defense, summary judgment may be the last opportunity to avoid a trial on particular claims and issues. For the plaintiff, it is an opportunity to demonstrate that it has marshaled sufficient evidence to persuade a judge or jury that its claims are meritorious and that it should be given the opportunity to present its case at trial. The summary judgment determination will influence important decisions to follow: whether to settle the case and on what terms, and if settlement is not in the cards or not on the agenda, formulating the plan of attack for trial.

I. THE MODERN VIEW OF SUMMARY JUDGMENT
In federal court, the standards applicable to motions for summary judgment were reshaped by a trilogy of cases issued by the United States Supreme Court in 1986. In *Celotex Corp. v. Catrett*,[1] *Anderson v. Liberty Lobby,*

---

1.   477 U.S. 317 (1986).

Inc.,[2] and *Matsushita Elec. Indus. Co. v. Zenith Radio Corp.*,[3] the Supreme Court opened the door to the modern era of summary judgment practice by redefining the standard to be applied by federal courts in hearing and deciding summary judgment motions. Much has been written about this trilogy and its impact on summary judgment practice. A review of the changes wrought by these decisions is beyond the scope of this book and this chapter. However, it is worth touching on two areas in which summary judgment practice has been changed by these decisions.

A. Emphasis on the Role of Summary Judgment

Prior to 1986, there had been a growing sentiment in some federal courts that summary judgment should be disfavored because it denies a litigant the opportunity to prove its case at trial. In *Celotex*, the Supreme Court went out of its way to counter this trend in declaring that

> [s]ummary judgment procedure is properly regarded not as a disfavored procedural shortcut, but rather as an integral part of the Federal Rules as a whole, which are designed "to secure the just, speedy and inexpensive determination of every action."[4]

Applying this restated standard, the Court held that summary judgment should have been granted (1) in *Celotex*, based upon the failure of plaintiff to come forward with evidence sufficient to meet its burden of proof, (2) in *Anderson*, based upon a finding that the evidence relied upon by plaintiff was insufficient to meet a heightened evidentiary burden of clear and convincing evidence, and (3) in *Matsushita*, where the Court found that the evidence of record demonstrated that the plaintiff's antitrust claim was "inherently implausible."

---

2. 477 U.S. 242 (1986).
3. 475 U.S. 574 (1986).
4. *Celotex*, 477 U.S. at 327.

B. Burden of Proof and Summary Judgment

The Supreme Court clarified confusion that existed previously in the federal courts with respect to the issue of burden of proof. Prior to 1986, there were reported federal court decisions holding that the moving party on a motion for summary judgment has the initial burden of demonstrating an entitlement to relief. As a result, parties sometimes found themselves in the difficult position of having to prove a negative by coming forward with affirmative evidence that a particular factual assertion relied upon by the adverse party (and as to which that party would bear the burden of proof at trial) was not true. *Celotex* directly addressed this issue and held that a party may move for summary judgment without offering *any* evidence on a particular issue as to which the non-moving party bears the burden of proof, and thereby force the non-moving party to come forward with evidence sufficient to meet its burden. That holding has been referenced in many federal and state court decisions since *Celotex*, and is referenced in the 2010 amendments to Rule 56 of the Federal Rules of Civil Procedure. The Official Comment to Rule 56(c)(1) expressly states that

> [s]ubdivision (c)(1)(B) recognizes that a party need not always point to specific record materials. One party, without citing any other materials, may respond or reply that materials cited to dispute or support a fact do not establish the absence or presence of a genuine dispute. And a *party who does not have the trial burden of production may rely on a showing that the party who does have the trial burden cannot produce admissible evidence to carry its burden as to the fact.*[5]

In state court, it is important to know whether the standard for summary judgment differs from the modern federal standards. Some states have expressly adopted the new federal standards either legislatively or judicially, while other states have expressly disavowed the approach articulated in the *Celotex* trilogy. Obviously, it is essential to know and understand what

---

5. Fed. R. Civ. P. 56(c) Committee Notes on Rules, 2010 Amendment (emphasis added).

standard will be applied in your case and in your jurisdiction, and to tailor your summary judgment strategy accordingly.

II. STRATEGIC CONSIDERATIONS
A. Timing of the Motion

While typically a summary judgment motion is filed near the end of the pretrial proceedings in the case, under the rules there is no prohibition on filing the motion earlier. There are issues that may be appropriate for an earlier motion, such as statute of limitations defenses, UCC defenses, and standing issues. However, an early motion will likely be met with an assertion that discovery is needed,[6] and a likelihood that a judge will want to give the adverse party every opportunity to prove its contention. A party witness who has not yet been deposed may be able to craft an affidavit sufficient to create a factual issue, a step that will be more difficult after a deposition has been taken and that party's testimony is of record. In most cases, the best time to file the motion is after discovery is complete, when the evidentiary record has been set, the testimony of the witnesses is of record through depositions, and the issues have been joined and framed for determination by the court.

B. Showing Your Cards

A well-crafted summary judgment motion will lay out your case (or particular portions of your case) in considerable detail in advance of trial. There is always the possibility that doing so will educate an adverse party and counsel who may not otherwise have focused on issues or evidentiary considerations and may, as a result, be better prepared to deal with the issues by having them aired in advance of the trial. There may have been a time when holding your cards until trial was an effective litigation strategy, but in most courts those days are gone. Pretrial disclosure requirements are such that it is now very difficult to employ a litigation strategy that includes springing a surprise argument or piece of evidence at trial. Moreover, in

---

6. Rule 56 and most equivalent state court rules expressly provide that a party opposing a motion for summary judgment can assert, through an affidavit of counsel, that discovery is needed to properly respond to the motion. *See, e.g., id.* 56(b).

the litigation of the business tort case, in which actual trials to verdict or judgment are few, consider whether it is a bad thing to give your adversary a concise summary of your case and the strength of your arguments. Holding back key evidence or argument for a trial that never occurs means that such evidence or argument is effectively lost as a tool to secure the best possible result for your client.

The flip side of this consideration is that a well-crafted summary judgment motion may flesh out your adversary's theory and view of the key arguments and evidence, information that may assist you in formulating a strategy for settlement and/or trial, regardless of the outcome of the motion. A motion may also have the benefit of educating the judge and reinforcing legal and factual arguments supporting your position on issues that will live on at trial and in post-trial motions, if the motion for summary judgment is not granted.

C. The Forum and the Judge

In some jurisdictions, or before some judges, there is a predisposition against summary judgment, notwithstanding the legal standards set forth in the rules and the cases. If you are in a court or a jurisdiction in which you know who the judge will be, find out what you can about that judge's philosophy and track record on summary judgment motions and factor that into your analysis of whether to file such a motion, and how to approach the crafting of the motion if the decision is to file it.

D. Expense and Cost Benefit Considerations

To move or respond properly to a motion for summary judgment, a detailed analysis of and reference to the record will be required. Preparing that motion and the supporting exhibits will take time and cost your client money. As with most strategic decisions made in litigation, a cost-benefit analysis needs to be considered and discussed with the client. While a successful summary judgment motion will save what could be the far greater expense of a trial, an unsuccessful motion will add a significant amount to the ultimate cost of the case. The decision of whether, when, and on what issues to move for summary judgment is an important one that should be made jointly by the client and counsel.

171

III. PRACTICE POINTERS
A. Understand and Follow the Applicable Court Rules

While always true, it is especially important when filing a potentially dis-positive motion, such as a motion for summary judgment, to ensure that relief is not lost or hindered by a failure to comply with the applicable court rules. In addition to the state or federal rules of procedure applicable to motions for summary judgment, many courts have local rules requiring a separate "Statement of Material Facts Not in Dispute," with numbered paragraphs and specific citations to the record.[7] Most such rules require the non-moving party to file a responsive statement, with specific citations to the record responding to the moving party's contentions. The failure to file a proper response typically means that the moving party's facts will be deemed admitted for purposes of the motion. Some courts impose strict deadlines on when a summary judgment motion can be filed so as not to delay a scheduled trial.

B. Present a Clear and Organized Record

In most business tort cases, the record presented to the court in support of and in opposition to a motion for summary judgment is quite large. Par-ties typically rely on numerous documents, as well as affidavits, deposition transcripts, interrogatory answers, and other evidence in support of their respective positions. With this volume of material, it is important to provide a clear path for the court to find and review the key evidence.

One of the keys to success on summary judgment is to articulate clearly the material facts that you are contending are or are not disputed and to support those assertions with clear and precise citations to the record. Fac-tual assertions without a citation to the record are likely to be disregarded by the court on the assumption that they lack evidentiary support. A gen-eral reference to a lengthy exhibit is usually a waste of time and paper. It is unreasonable and unrealistic to expect a judge or a law clerk to take the

---

7. Even if such a requirement does not exist, it can be a useful technique to focus the court on the facts relied upon and the specific evidence of record supporting those facts. It also makes it more difficult for the opposing party to counter those facts without specific ref-erences to evidence of record.

time and/or have the familiarity with the issues to locate the relevant portion of a lengthy multiple-page exhibit.

Organizing and simplifying a voluminous record is also important. A compelling argument can quickly lose its impact if a judge or law clerk has to spend an inordinate amount of time combing through multiple affidavits, declarations, or packages of exhibits to find the critical evidence at the heart of the argument. Instead of multiple affidavits or declarations each containing multiple exhibits, consider one bound appendix of exhibits, with a uniform lettering or numbering system. Distinguishing Exhibit A to the Affidavit of John Jones from Exhibit A to the Affidavit of Sally Smith is cumbersome, confusing, and time consuming. Having one Exhibit A in a bound set of exhibits is far easier, clearer, and more efficient. Similarly, distinguishing your Exhibit A from your opponent's Exhibit A can be easily remedied by adopting a different scheme from your opponent. If your opponent uses letters, use numbers. In a large case involving multiple parties, consider whether a joint appendix can be agreed upon and used by all parties.

C. Consider the Admissibility of Evidence Relied Upon

While it stands to reason that evidence bearing on a motion for summary judgment should be admissible evidence, it has not always been clear that that is the case.[8] In federal court now, there is no room for ambiguity on this point. FED. R. CIV. P. 56(c)(2) expressly provides that a party may seek exclusion of material cited to support or dispute a fact if it cannot be presented in a form that would be admissible in evidence. For example, while an affidavit is itself hearsay, it is admissible for summary judgment purposes on the assumption that the affiant will be competent to testify to those facts at trial. However, the affidavit has to be based upon personal knowledge. Hearsay within an affidavit is not admissible (e.g., affidavit of John Jones saying Mary Smith told him that she took confidential business information with her). Where a case may turn on expert testimony,

---

8. This confusion likely results, in part, from the fact that while an affidavit is ordinarily not admissible at trial, it can properly be considered on summary judgment.

a summary judgment motion may provide an opportunity to challenge the sufficiency of the expert's report and the admissibility of the expert's opinion testimony.

Most evidence is not self-authenticating, so care must be taken to ensure documents relied upon have been properly authenticated. An affidavit or declaration by the author of the document is best, but may not be available in every case. Depending upon the basis for admissibility, an affidavit from the recipient of the document or the custodian of records (if the document may be admissible as a business record) may also suffice. An expert's report should be offered together with an affidavit signed by the expert to ensure that it is properly considered.

IV. SUMMARY JUDGMENT OF BUSINESS TORT ISSUES

At first blush, a claim grounded in tort would not seem to be well suited for summary judgment. At the heart of most common law tort claims is the concept of the reasonableness of the defendant's conduct and the foreseeability of the resulting harm, both of which, on their face, would seem to present classic fact questions for the jury.

In business tort cases, however, the elements of the claims and defenses, and the burdens of proof with respect to them, are generally more complicated. While that complexity can result in more potential factual issues, it can also raise more questions about the ability of each of the parties to sustain its burden at trial. In evaluating the potential for summary judgment, consider the following:

(a) What are the elements of the cause of action or defense?

(b) Is there sufficient evidence to demonstrate a prima facie case as to each element?

(c) Who has the burden of proof and what is the applicable standard for meeting that burden?

(d) Is expert testimony required to establish compliance with the applicable standard of care and, if so, does the expert's testimony meet the standards for admissibility and does it meet the burden of proof of the party proffering the expert?

174

(e) Is there opposing evidence that raises a genuine issue of material fact for trial?

While every case is different, there are some issues that are common to many business tort cases that may be especially well suited to summary judgment. Some examples are discussed below.

A. The Contract Case Dressed Up as a Business Tort

Most initial pleadings assert alternative theories of relief. At the outset of the case, such alternative pleading is permitted under the rules and is strategically beneficial because discovery may reveal facts that support some claims more than others. Discovery may also reveal, however, that the claim is primarily grounded in a written contract and that there is language in the contract that may itself be dispositive of the claim. If the contract has an integration clause expressly providing that it supersedes all prior oral and written discussions and communications, there may be a basis for arguing that the dispute can and should be decided as a matter of law based upon the language of the contract. Even if the contract claim cannot be determined as a matter of law, the court may be persuaded that the issue to be determined is one of contract, not tort, and that the alternative tort claims should be dismissed. Stated in some jurisdictions as the "gist of the action" rule, this can form the basis of an effective motion that can significantly narrow the issues for trial, or eliminate the need for a trial altogether.

B. Claims of Fraud or Fraud in the Inducement

Where a claim of fraud or fraud in the inducement is asserted, analysis of both the elements of the cause of action and the level of proof required may suggest areas of attack that are appropriate for summary judgment. For example, many jurisdictions require proof of fraud by "clear and convincing evidence," a higher burden than the ordinary "preponderance of the evidence" standard. If the case were being tried, one would expect that at the close of plaintiff's case, a motion would be filed asserting that, as a matter of law, plaintiff has not presented sufficient evidence to meet its burden to allow the case to move forward. A motion for summary judgment can be an effective means of securing a resolution of that issue in advance of trial.

175

For example, if the claim is that a party was misled into believing and relying upon statements that turned out not to be true, but discovery reveals that the plaintiff was aware of the true facts from other sources, summary judgment may be appropriate on that claim.

C. Breach of Fiduciary Duty Claims

Various elements of the claims and defenses in a breach of fiduciary duty case may also be susceptible to summary judgment. For example, whether the defendant owed the plaintiff a fiduciary duty often comes down to an issue of law that the court can decide on summary judgment in light of the undisputed facts of record. In many states, there is established precedent holding that banks, insurance companies, or companies in other particular industries do not owe fiduciary duties to their customers, while partners in a partnership, for example, owe such duties to each other as a matter of law. Such duties may or may not be owed in the context of a limited liability company, depending upon the enabling statute and the language of the operating agreement. The same is true with one of the common defenses in such cases, the business judgment rule, which may or may not be available to a particular defendant depending on its status or position. State law may also provide protection where a fiduciary is permitted to take certain action by the express terms of the parties' contract, which can override more general common law duties.

D. Misappropriation of Trade Secrets

Trade secret claims often raise legal issues that can be disposed of on summary judgment, particularly once the facts are developed through discovery. Trade secret status may have been lost, for example, through disclosure. Or the facts may show that the plaintiff failed to meet its duty to take reasonable steps to protect the confidentiality of the information. On the other hand, summary judgment may be available to the plaintiff where forensic computer evidence shows that a former employee downloaded your client's legitimate trade secrets and used them to compete improperly against the company. While each case obviously turns on its own facts, careful review of the record and the elements of the claim or defense may reveal opportunities to dispose of all or large parts of the case before trial.

176

E. Tortious Interference with Actual or Prospective Contractual Relations

Consider whether the elements necessary to establish a claim of tortious interference have been established. If it is a claim of intentional interference, is there sufficient evidence of intent to get to the jury? For example, a company that hires an employee who is subject to a restrictive covenant from his former employer may be deemed to be intentionally interfering with the contract if it can be shown that it had knowledge of the contract. Even where the evidence supports a finding of intentional interference, the conduct may be subject to a defense of legal justification or privilege, such as where the conduct was a bona fide exercise of a party's own rights, or the defendant has an equal or superior right in the subject matter of the claim. Analysis of the elements of the claims and defenses and the burdens of proof with respect to those claims and defenses may provide opportunities for disposition on summary judgment.

F. Unfair Competition and Statutory Remedies

Most states have enacted statutes, such as Unfair Trade Practices Acts and Consumer Fraud Statutes, intended to protect consumers from unfair business practices. In addition, there are statutes protecting businesses that regulate trade and the use of deceptive and unfair practices in advertising and marketing, such as the federal Lanham Act. Careful review of the statutory language and the case law interpreting that language may provide opportunities for a pretrial adjudication, through summary judgment, of such claims and appropriate defenses. Among the issues that may be appropriate for summary judgment are whether (1) the plaintiff is a "consumer" for purposes of a statute providing remedies to consumers; (2) the defendant is a party or business regulated by the statute; (3) the statute requires prefiling action as a prerequisite to the lawsuit or requires the action to be instituted within a particular period of time; and (4) the necessary steps were taken to exhaust administrative remedies, if any.

G. Statutory Preemption of Claims

Some claims commonly asserted in business tort cases may be the subject of state or federal statutes that provide the exclusive remedy for the claims asserted. Where that is the case, a motion for summary judgment may be effective in eliminating common law claims that are preempted by the statutory provisions. For example, the Uniform Trade Secrets Act, as adopted in most states, preempts common law claims for misappropriation of trade secrets and commercial business information.

H. Statutory Claims Providing for Enhanced Recovery and Attorneys' Fees

Claims that carry the potential for recovery of treble damages and/or attorneys' fees can significantly enhance the value of the case and the risk to the defendant of going to trial. Summary judgment is an opportunity to test the viability of those claims in a manner that gives each side the chance to react, evaluate its position based upon the court's determination, and factor the ruling into its settlement analysis. Most statutes providing for enhanced damages and/or recovery of counsel fees have specific elements and burdens of proof that are well suited for summary judgment adjudication. For example, if a claim has been asserted under the Federal Racketeer Influenced and Corrupt Organizations Act (RICO), the party asserting that claim will have to prove, among other things, specific predicate acts falling within the statutory definition, a pattern of racketeering activity over a defined period of time, and an enterprise that is separate and distinct from the persons who committed the predicate acts. Claims under franchise practices statutes or unfair trade practice statutes similarly have very specific statutory requirements for claims asserted thereunder. Summary judgment is an opportunity to test the sufficiency of the proofs offered as to each of these elements in a more thorough and orderly way than will likely be possible at trial.

A successful result on summary judgment requires a careful analysis of the claims and defenses asserted, the elements of each, and the evidence that is available to be presented by each side. This analysis, while time consuming and expensive, will be needed for trial in any event. Moreover, a well-crafted summary judgment motion can narrow or eliminate issues and reduce the risk and expense of a trial on the merits.

CHAPTER 10

Trial Preparation

Matthew J. O'Hara

Getting ready to try a business torts case is an exercise in planning themes that are supported by the stories your witnesses and your documents will tell. Even though most cases settle, these are questions you should be thinking about early in the case, and certainly no later than when you begin to take and defend depositions. If you wait to think about the themes of your case until you have an order setting the case for trial in a few months, and about how the witnesses and exhibits fit with that theme, you may well have imposed limitations on your case, both big and small, that could have been avoided by thinking about trial preparation much earlier. Of course, no one can anticipate two or three years in advance every issue that will come up at trial, but starting to think about and plan for trial early on in the case and continuing throughout the process will put you in the best position to be ready once the trial begins. This chapter considers both early-case trial preparation and the kind of meticulous trial planning required in the last two or three months before trial.

I. EARLY IN THE CASE

Careful planning at the beginning of discovery will help ensure that you have as much as possible of the facts and testimony you will need down the road and that you can get your case smoothly into evidence. Holes in the prosecution or defense of a case become hard to fix when trial is near, and logistical problems caused by lack of preparation can eat up valuable time and erode your credibility with the judge and jury if you struggle with displaying evidence or winning its admission into the record.

A. Themes

A cause of action for a business tort does not make for a theme. Nor do elements of causes of action. A theme tells the judge and jury what happened and why. If your case is a fraud case, who will explain why the people involved, who have such great credentials, would tell a lie? If you are defending a claim of breach of fiduciary duty, and your client acted with the highest degree of loyalty and integrity, why is the other side pressing this case? If the case involves tortious interference, why would the other side interfere in your client's contract?

Answering questions like these early in your case helps you ask for the right documents from your opponent. Thinking about these issues locks down testimony from people who might be beyond the reach of the court's subpoena powers when trial comes, and allows you to know what your adversaries will say about your key points. If you cannot tell a consistent narrative from beginning to end, and rebut your opponent's narrative, you will have a hard time winning when you get to court.

B. Exhibits

All things being equal, judges and juries who decide cases believe documents, especially when it comes to questions like duties and truthfulness and motives. Thinking about exhibits before the first witness gets deposed can save a lot of time and difficulty when you get close to trial. The larger the universe of documents in a dispute, the more important this exercise is. It is also worth trying to reach agreement with your opponents about the logistics of handling documents in the case.

As simple as it may sound, the way in which the lawyers number exhibits in a case may well affect how smoothly the trial goes. Should you have one sequential exhibit list that both sides will use throughout the case? This has its advantages, as neither side is necessarily thought of as the proponent of particular exhibits that will be relied on by both sides. It also helps avoid duplication, where the same document gets assigned different exhibit numbers by both sides. Where many parties and nonparties produce the same document with different Bates numbers, you may be able to agree that the same document with the same Bates number will be used for that exhibit. A variation on this idea is that each side will keep its own sequential set of exhibits, with Plaintiff's Exhibits from 1 through 100 and Defendant's from 1 through 200, rather than re-marking the same document "Smith Exhibit 5" and "Jones Exhibit 10" and "Green Exhibit 15," or worse yet, calling the first exhibit in each deposition simply "Exhibit 1." Sequential numbering aimed at reducing duplication is most easily adhered to when there is generally no more than one deposition in the case on a particular day; a frenetic schedule will work against your desire to achieve this kind of streamlining.

Why does this matter? If your trial lasts a couple of weeks, everyone will come to learn key exhibits by number—all of the lawyers, the paralegals, the judge, and the jurors. No one should need to keep straight whether the version of the contract you are discussing is Defendant's 10 or Plaintiff's 25, or whether it is the version of the document with the plaintiff's Bates prefix on it or that of its auditors, when the documents are substantively the same. When you want to impeach an opposing witness, you should want to avoid having to explain to the witness or the court or the jury that Watson 22 in the deposition transcript is really Plaintiff's 418, or worse yet, spend time getting a reluctant witness to agree with you about such mundane things as a precursor to what would otherwise be your devastating cross.

C. Litigation Technology

It is also important to think about producing documents in a format that both sides can use throughout the case and especially at trial. In what format will you want electronic documents so you can use them in your electronic database? Will that format translate well into your trial presentation software? There is no reason to spend time and money later fixing formatting glitches or converting file formats that you could have anticipated at the inception of the case.

The same ideas apply if you will be taking video depositions. If it's worth the investment to put a witness on video, be sure that the court reporter and the videographer have synchronized their work so that you can easily create segments of testimony of unavailable witnesses to play at trial, or to create clips of the most important testimony that can be used for video impeachment. When you are so fortunate as to have a key witness give you such an opportunity, be sure that you can easily put it to use.

These issues are worth discussing with your opposing counsel. You may find that your opponent uses different software than you, but with the help of your paralegals and information technology professionals, there is a way to find a common denominator that saves everyone time and money.

II. AFTER DISCOVERY CLOSES
AND TRIAL IS SCHEDULED

A few months out from trial, you'll want to make a high-level task list of things that need to be done to be ready for trial, and who is responsible for each. Methodical preparation during this time will help you pace what needs to get done in your case, as well as whatever else you need to accomplish in the rest of your practice and in your life away from work. How will you get your case into evidence? How will you attack your opponent's case? When you get to talk to the judge or jury about your case, what will you say?

A. How Will You Get Your Case into Evidence?

It is one thing to have an interesting and compelling story, but it is another to get it into evidence. If something cannot be admitted because it is hearsay, or a witness lacks personal knowledge, or it is not relevant to something that someone has to prove, it will not help you. There are two key components to answering how you will get your case in—witnesses and exhibits.

1. Witnesses

The foremost issue in preparing for trial is who will be your trial witnesses and what will they say. Juries may believe documents, but documents cannot get on the witness stand and raise their right hands and testify. Having the right people testify convincingly about the key documents is crucial.

You will probably want to divide the witness list for your case into "will call" witnesses and "may call" witnesses. The court may require you to do this by rule, or the judge may require it. In any event, you will want to know if there are people whose testimony is essential, and if there are others who will only be necessary if the trial moves briskly, or if the court rules against you on a certain motion in limine, or if the other side elicits testimony from someone else about that issue.

While it is good to know who knows what, you will need to plan how to get each witness to appear at your trial. Witnesses under your control—your clients or their employees—give you the greatest flexibility, but even they need advance notice to make sure they are available when you need them. If you have nonparties who are within the court's subpoena powers, you will need to be sure that your subpoenas are prepared and served in a timely manner. In some cases, you will want the other side to bring its people to testify as your witnesses in the case, but you will need to give the required notice under the applicable rules of procedure. If a witness cannot be made to come to trial, you will need to consider if you have deposition testimony taken in a way that is admissible for your jurisdiction. Video to play for the court and jury is best, but whether you are working with video or just a cold transcript, you will need to do deposition designations.

Most importantly for the witnesses in your case, you should meticulously plan what each witness will testify to. Start with a high-level outline of topics for each witness. As you get further into your preparation for trial, you can drill down into your outline, making it more detailed. You can arrange the points in the outline in the order that is most effective. The principles of primacy and recency are the most important guidelines for organizing witness testimony. That is to say that your audience remembers best the things they see and hear first, and the things they saw and heard most recently. You want your witnesses to start and end strong. You should think about what is a strong opening subject for your witness, and what is the strongest and most important point you want the witness to talk about right before you sit down. Even for each individual topic on your examination outline, try to start strong and end strong. A corollary to these concepts is that the best place to bury things that you need to front or admit, but don't want to dwell on, is in the middle of a witness's testimony.

2. Exhibits

Making an exhibit list is an important task to start on at the beginning of your intensive trial focus. Make a list that you can keep your own work product in, and when you are done, you can create a version that excludes columns in the spreadsheet that contain work product. You can give that version to the other side and to the court. So, for example, you can have a column that shows which witness or witnesses will testify about each document. If you were unable to avoid duplication in the numbering of exhibits throughout the case, another column may show other exhibit numbers for the same exhibit. In another column, have a hot link to a digital image of your document so that you can call them up on your computer as you work from now until the end of the trial. Some exhibits may be easy to get admitted while others may not, so you might track in another column particular evidentiary issues relating to each exhibit.

In most courts, you will be required to put every exhibit you want admitted on your exhibit list, at the risk of having it excluded if you do not. You will want a method that makes sure you have considered everything you need. Obviously, your key documents will jump right onto your list. Beyond that, you will want to look at the deposition exhibits marked in discovery. There may be some basic building blocks that no one bothered about in discovery, but are necessary to tell your client's story from the beginning, so be sure to consider if you need exhibits that were produced but never marked. You may even need to use documents that were not produced. If so, determine whether those documents were the subject of discovery, and if so, make a supplemental production as soon as possible. If you are using new documents not produced in discovery, you should be prepared to explain why they were not produced before.

The exhibit list may need to reflect contingencies as well. Judges generally consider it fair play for the other side to make use of your documents, and are not impressed by the argument that the other side did not list the document themselves. So, for example, you may be bound and determined to keep a certain issue out of your trial, and if you succeed, you will not want any documents about it on your list. On the other hand, if you lose a motion in limine on that score, you will still want to put that issue in its best light. In that case, consider a contingent section of your list that says a certain subject should be excluded at trial, but if it is not, here are the documents that you will want on your list.

Making a list of demonstrative exhibits, though usually much shorter than your exhibit list, is just as important. What do you want to use to show the jury what you are talking about? You may consider summaries of voluminous evidence or charts that show a timeline or statistical trends. Or you may want to build a list of persons on the other side who knew the facts your client is accused of hiding. As you develop this list, it will grow into a list for working with your graphics consultants as well as to present to your opponent and the court.

As you build your exhibit list, consider how you will handle exhibits in the courtroom. If you do not know what your judge requires or prefers, find out. Will you use paper or computer screens, or both, to show exhibits to witnesses, to the court, and to the jury? Will you pass out copies during the trial? Do you want to? Will you do so one at a time, or in binders of exhibits that are already assembled? Each method has its own advantages and disadvantages. Handing around paper takes time and is distracting—but do you want the jury to have stacks of documents to peruse when you're not talking about them? Jurors may look at one document when you want them to look at another. The judge may or may not think this idea is a good one, and you certainly won't be able to distribute in advance exhibits whose admissibility is contested. In addition, you will need to consider what technology you will use in the courtroom, what it requires to work, and who will run it at trial.

B. How Will You Attack Your Opponent's Case?

While you cannot control many things about how your opponent puts on its case, you can and should devote just as much preparation to undermining that case as you do in preparing your own. In fact, if you represent the defendant, you will need to be prepared for this to come first.

1. Cross-Examinations

There are some witnesses whose testimony makes a damning case against the other side during their direct examinations. If only they could stop there; many of those same witnesses look as bad during cross as they looked brilliant on direct.

It helps to think of witnesses whom you will cross-examine just as you think of the witnesses you will present. What subjects will you question each about? Again, think of organizing the subjects of testimony. You want to start strong and end strong. The same applies during the questioning on each subject. The subject areas you build into an outline also help with transitions you can use to headline changes of direction that are helpful to your audience.

After you have outlined the cross for each witness, you will need to carefully outline what you are going to say. Of course, technically, you will be asking questions, but really you are making your own statements during cross. Your statements end with question marks, but you want each to be an assertion with which the witness will be forced to agree.

Everything about your cross-examination needs to be about control. The most fun you can have as a trial lawyer is an effective cross, and the worst disaster is to let the witness you are crossing start discoursing, telling his stories, and giving his explanations. The best way to maintain control is to ask questions based on answers from that witness's deposition or from documents he or she authored when he gave favorable testimony. Even when the witness was asked longer questions or gave longer answers during the deposition, break each favorable statement into bits to ask short, leading questions. Prepare your outline so that you have instantly available at trial the page and line of the witness's deposition testimony, and the exhibit number and page of a particular document, that will help you force the witness to say what you expect. At each juncture, you will need this to decide whether to press the witness to go your way gently, or with a soft impeachment or a forceful one. You can't assess this at trial if you don't know exactly where the testimony you are relying on is.

When it comes to preparing for cross-examinations at trial, you will also need to consider whether to do video impeachments when you have a witness's deposition on video. Since you will already have had your transcripts and video synchronized at the time the depositions were taken, you can pre-select video clips to use for impeachment. You can have bar codes created that correspond to particular questions, which you can trigger yourself if you like, or someone assisting you in the courtroom can be prepared to play.

Among your video clips, you need to know which ones are the most devastating. To do that, try to anticipate where the witness will push back. Often, this is where he gave the most helpful admissions to you in his deposition.

Then you need to look at the clips of those questions and answers. Some video impeachments will be better than others; some impeachments are sufficient without video if they are just a building block of your cross. If you have the time, you can even edit the clips so that they start or end with a particular expression on the witness's face. Given that digital video can be edited to the thousandth of a second, you have the ability to capture a pained or quizzical expression on the witness's face. If the witness fights you on cross and you are so fortunate as to be able to impeach him with video, that pained expression is something you can show the jury again in your closing.

2. Objections to Exhibits and Deposition Designations

At some point ordered by the court or negotiated with your opposing party, you will exchange your exhibit list and deposition designations with the other side. Often court rules or simple practical considerations dictate that you must first preserve your objections here. It is most efficient for you and your adversary to exchange these documents in digital format. You can then add your own objections in another column. It is helpful, and may be required, to note the basis of your objection, often by reference to the rules of evidence. With documents, in some cases your objection may be directed only to a particular portion of a document, which may be inadmissible hearsay while other portions are not. In those cases, you should make clear that your objection only goes to a portion but not all of a document.

These principles also apply to deposition designations. In addition, one important thing to consider with designations where the witness will not appear at trial is counter-designations. You may want to include part of your opponent's questioning that didn't go so well, or other times you want to include your cross at the deposition. You can expect your opponent will be one-sided in his or her designations, so only you can be sure that the record is as complete as it should be. If you will be playing video at trial, you will want guidance about when the court will rule on objections so that the proponent of the testimony can prepare the segments to be played at the right time and the other side can verify that it was prepared in a way that is fair and consistent with the court's rulings.

3. Motions in Limine

Pretrial motions about important evidence that is likely to be disputed at trial are vitally important to your preparation. Motions in limine have a number of important functions. Once the court has ruled, they help you to craft your opening statement. They save the jury's precious time during trial. They allow you to assess your case on the eve of trial and your settlement posture. Even if you do not prevail as a preliminary matter, you can begin to educate and persuade the judge about an important issue for your case, before the evidence begins to be presented.

The court will likely set a schedule for filing and opposing motions in limine. Often, the court does not decide these before you will need to prepare many other aspects of your case, from witness examinations to witness and exhibit lists. The court's rulings may make whole categories of exhibits or subjects of witness testimony out of bounds. You will need to plan for as many different contingencies as you can, especially when you see what the other side is looking to exclude or get admitted.

Remember, if you lose any motions in limine, you still need to preserve your objections at trial to avoid a waiver. If you are the proponent of testimony that the court excludes, you need to make an offer of proof during the trial before you rest your case.

C. Preparing to Talk to the Judge or Jury

If you will be trying your case to a jury, your first opportunity to talk to jurors will come before opening statements. What questions do you want to ask during voir dire, or if lawyers are not allowed to ask, what questions do you want the judge to ask? This is your opportunity to make a good first impression with people who will end up on your jury and to learn important information about how they think. You will also need to know how the judge will seat jurors in the box and handle strikes for cause.

While preparing for trial, you must be preparing your opening statement. You need to consider what you want to say, and consistent with the themes you have developed throughout the case, what themes you will use to hang your facts on. You will also need to consider what to show the jury—and you had better be sure it will get into evidence before you dwell on it in opening statement. You also need to plan how you will show it to a jury. More often than not today, jurors will expect to see documents or visuals presented on digital monitors. Are you going to use PowerPoint or trial presentation software of some kind? Will you show a video clip of a witness whose deposition will be played during the trial?

Once you have decided these things, you need to practice. Your goal should be to keep boiling down whatever you have written so that it fits on one piece of paper. And then you should be able to put that paper down at trial and not rely on it, feeling reassured that it is close by if your mind completely blanks out on you. When you feel comfortable that you can tell your story in a natural way without being tied to your notes, you know you are ready. Try out your themes formally and informally, in whole and in part, on your colleagues and on your family—and especially on people who are not lawyers. If you have kids, do they understand your case? If not, you might have to go back to work on it some more.

There is a theory that says you should know what you will say in your closing argument when you file your complaint or your answer and affirmative defenses. That's a nice theory, and it has some sound reasoning behind it. Nevertheless, as a practical matter, you will not be able to fully plan this until the evidence comes in during the trial. At best, as the trial wears on, if you are giving the closing you can hope to take advantage of times when a colleague is preparing and presenting a witness to start accumulating your key moments from the trial to build into the closing. It is then you will know how you can best reprise your opening, and how you can best show the fact-finder that you delivered on your opening promises.

D. Jury Instructions

If you are trying your case to a jury, you have to propose jury instructions as part of the pretrial submissions. Depending on the jurisdiction, many will be prescribed by pattern jury instructions. Often, however, when trying cases about business torts, you will not have pattern instructions to work with, or any patterns that do exist will be less than fully established in your jurisdiction. You want to write instructions in plain English, include your key points, and draft something that you can imagine your judge will actually be willing to give. At the same time, these are a staking out of your position on legal issues that will govern the trial and will be reviewed *de novo*

189

on appeal. So if you have a good faith basis for contending for something that the judge will not agree on, but is worth preserving for appeal, now is the time to include it.

Typically, the jury instruction conference will not happen until shortly before the close of the evidence. Nevertheless, if you anticipate a jury instruction on a key issue will affect your opening statement, you can ask the court to rule on such instructions before trial begins. For those arguments, you want to be organized, with case law, statutes, and other authorities at your fingertips for each instruction.

III. WORKING WITH CONSULTANTS AND SUPPORT STAFF

Though a law license is required to speak in the well of the courtroom, some of the most important contributions to your case will be made by people who are not lawyers. The more that is at stake, the more likely it is that you will be working with outside consultants.

If you are going to pick a jury in a business torts case of any significance, chances are you will want the benefit of jury research. Jury consultants provide different degrees of juror research and testing, depending on your budget. If you only want some research about attitudes in the venire and insights about how those attitudes may impact your case, you will want to build in time for your consultant to read key case materials and give you insights. If you plan to go so far as a complete mock trial—with opening statements, presentation of witness testimony on video or even clients in person, closing arguments, and juror focus groups—that requires significant advance planning as well as a lot of lawyer time to prepare the presentations. In addition, you will want time to understand the results and decide how to incorporate them into the presentation of your case.

Visual presentations are an important part of your ability to persuade and educate a jury, and even, to a lesser degree, a judge in a bench trial. If you are thinking that you do not want to look too well-heeled to a jury by having high-quality digital graphics, or if you have a senior partner who tells you that, think again. You need to give jurors what they expect. Jurors like other people spend their lives looking at screens, from smartphones to televisions to computers. If you are going to take up their valuable time, give them the kind of show that your case is worth.

You may have some good ideas for how to show the fact-finder key points about your evidence, but talented graphic arts consultants with experience in trials can bring your ideas to a new level and contribute vital ideas of their own. Lawyers' primary tools are words, but graphics professionals think in visual terms and think about how jurors who are not lawyers will see a case—literally and figuratively. Your preparation should include graphics for your opening and closing, and also visuals to demonstrate important witness testimony concerning complicated technologies, finance, and industries that will not be readily familiar.

Another important part of educating your fact-finders is to show them what they need to understand. For example, if you have a case involving software, it's not sufficient for your witnesses to just talk about it. Have them show the jury how the software works. Hand the witness a computer that is connected to a display screen, with your software loaded and ready to roll, and explain in both words and images how it works. You will need to work with your own IT staff and the court staff to make sure this is ready to go without glitches in real time. The same is true in a case about other kinds of products. What do you need to do to show the jury the products that your client makes that are at issue in the case? Your preparation should include what you will bring into the courtroom and how you will use it.

Another vital aspect of the trial that will require you to work with consultants and support staff is the use of technology at trial. A business torts case is by definition document intensive. You will need to plan how to display your documents to the judge and jury. This includes planning for the software you will use to display documents, video, and photos. Once you have done that, make sure all of the documents and other materials are loaded and can be readily displayed at trial. On this score, part of a smooth presentation means that the people who are responsible for putting your documents up—right now—at trial know where you are going. They should have your outline, whether for a direct or a cross, for starters. But beyond that, you should discuss with them, preferably the night before, which pages in a document you want to ask about, in what order, and what paragraphs and sections you want circled, highlighted, or called out during testimony. For cross examinations, they should also be familiar with your video clips for potential impeachment. The people running your courtroom technology can make you look really good, but they need to know where you are going.

IV. LOGISTICS OF THE TRIAL

A jury trial is a show. Even a bench trial is a production. For everything to run seamlessly from one act to another, without wasting anyone's time or fumbling around, your stage has to be prepared. If you know what the backstage of a theater looks like, or you have watched a band get set up to play, you know you have to sweat all of the behind-the-scenes details.

In the first instance, some member of your team needs to get in touch with the court and judge's staff before the trial starts. Most likely, they will welcome your contact and be anxious to help. Some courtrooms are modern workshops built to anticipate every trial lawyer's need, while others are beautiful monuments to a long-ago time. Where can you set up your monitors? How will you get your equipment into the courthouse and up to the courtroom? Does the court have equipment that you can use? Where are the electrical outlets? Does the courtroom have Wi-Fi? What can you store in the court when the trial recesses? You will need to answer these questions and many more of the same nature.

Nothing can be worse than looking up imploringly at the judge, while you have a jury in the box, to ask for time, or even a recess, to make something work. You are the director of the show, and you need to make sure it runs like clockwork. The safest thing is to have a backup for everything: backup laptops loaded with exhibits, extra batteries, extra electrical cords, duct tape—whatever you need to be completely self-reliant.

Beyond technology, you will also need to plan for case materials in the courtroom. You need to have a courtroom library, whether it's in books or stored on your computer. You will need your research files, your pleadings, your written discovery and responses, and your exhibits. When you decide what you need to try your case, you need to organize it in the courtroom and know where everything can be found at a moment's notice.

A good trial has the energy and proficiency of a show, but it may call for you to be on your feet and using your voice for up to six hours a day. You and everyone working with you need energy to make it through each day. Each day will be tightly scripted in terms of time, and you won't have any time to waste. So someone will have to plan for your team your human needs, from meals to water to mints to pain medications to lodging and transportation. Any well-oiled trial team will make sure that the people involved in the production, including clients and witnesses, have what they need to endure and excel.

Every trial will have its glitches. Being ready for trial will help you deal with them. The more your preparation shows in the courtroom, the more the judge and the jury will forgive you when something doesn't go as planned. Notwithstanding glitches, your preparation will help your witnesses, your themes, your case, and you to stand out.

In a well-run trial, you will get your exhibits and your testimony into evidence. You will make a record whenever you need to do so. You and your witnesses will be on time, and will be considerate of the time spent by everyone in the courtroom who is not there to win your case, from the judge to the jurors to the courtroom deputy to the court reporters and the court clerk. You will put on a good visual show using modern technology. You will have all the materials you need to make your legal arguments. When you have done the best you can, as always, the result of the trial is not in your hands. When all of this work is done, you hand it off to others and hope for the best.

CHAPTER 11

Presenting the Business Torts Case to a Jury

David B. Graeven, PhD

On first impression, the particulars in a business torts dispute may seem clearly in favor of one side, but by no means is the "case closed" and the verdict a "done deal." Using carefully crafted themes, a relevant story, properly prepared witnesses, and strategic jury selection, attorneys can present their clients' account of events to optimize success at trial.

I. THE IMPORTANCE OF CASE THEMES IN A BUSINESS TORTS CASE

The consensus among jury consultants and experienced trial attorneys is that to prevail in business litigation, it is imperative to develop persuasive themes. Jury research in a variety of types of litigation has demonstrated the significance of themes in organizing information and making decisions.[1]

In business torts, the complexity of the case, tediousness of the trial, or lack of juror familiarity with case issues makes this type of litigation challenging for trial attorneys. It often requires educating jurors about issues, terms, and concepts because not everyone has experience with the subjects being explored. For example, in a personal injury case, people often know

---

1. Brian H. Bornstein & Edie Greene, *Jury Decision Making: Implications for and from Psychology*, CURRENT DIRECTIONS IN PSYCHOL. SCI., Feb. 2011, at 63.

someone who has been injured, whether on the job or in an accident. However, they do not always have the same connection with, or even know what constitutes, a breach of fiduciary duty or tortious interference with contract.

Jurors develop their own narratives for the dispute. As the case unfolds, jurors try to fit the facts of the case to their own point of view, accepting more readily the facts that conform to something they can understand or that helps them make sense of events, and scrutinizing carefully the facts that do not. Jurors inflate the facts on their side and deflate the facts that disagree with their personal interpretations.

The construction of these individual narratives is influenced by the frame of reference each juror brings to the case. Life experiences, the experiences of close family and friends, and even knowledge of current or historical events can impact and predispose a juror one way or another. Luckily, these frames of reference are not immutable. Attorneys can employ case themes to introduce their client's story and impact jurors' understanding and analyses of case facts.

Establishing case themes from the outset helps attorneys build an effective and well-articulated strategy that tells their client's story while organizing facts, events, and evidence, including witness testimony. Themes provide a frame of reference for the matters at hand, allowing counsel to present the essence of the business dispute to jurors in a way that they can understand and relate to, while informing jurors on issues such as responsibility, blame, and in many cases justice or fairness.

A. Tools for Building Themes

While case theme development is a deliberate and analytical exercise, its creative aspect should not be overlooked. Metaphors and analogies provide compelling imagery to supplement case facts. If a large corporation is being sued by a person, small company, or town, to transform the David and Goliath image in jurors' minds, counsel could preface the dispute by first acknowledging the disparity between them, then presenting a history of the company and its origins. If presented effectively, case themes can convey an alternate view and humanize a company, even if it is seen as Goliath.

The basic approaches to theme development include the story model, attribution theory, and counterfactual thinking. The story model has always been a tool that attorneys use, but the other two approaches, attribution theory and counterfactual thinking, while used intuitively by counsel, are now recognized psychological principles for building case arguments.[2] These psychological concepts are routinely used explicitly by attorneys when developing themes.

1. The Story Model

Stories are ingrained in our culture through myth, fable, and mass entertainment. Since litigation began, trial attorneys have used the story model in crafting case presentations. This strategy is based on the fact that jurors organize the evidence of a case into a coherent explanation or story. The narrative structure is then compared to the verdict categories to determine the best match.[3] Jurors are not passively sitting and listening during a trial, they are actively engaging in creating their own story about a case, and their individual narrative may or may not include the attorney's version of the story. The story model helps jurors make sense of what happened and, most importantly, why it happened.

In addition to helping the jurors make sense of the case, the process of working with the facts and crafting them into a story helps the attorney to "get it." It is very helpful for the attorney in the role of storyteller to talk and play with the narrative format and share it with others. When an attorney puts the case into story format and starts talking with all sorts of people about the story, that experience often helps the lawyer see different perspectives, which, in turn, can lead to a better crafted story.[4]

In a dispute over a real estate development, for example, jurors were told one party on a project did most of the work. He found the land, negotiated the purchase, and put in the time to obtain the necessary permits. The other party was a fiduciary and controlled the capital. The party with the fiduciary responsibility never completed those tasks he was designated to

---

2. Linda Heath & R. Scott Tindale, *Heuristics and Biases in Applied Settings, in* APPLICATIONS OF HEURISTICS AND BIASES TO SOCIAL ISSUES 8–10 (Linda Heath et al. eds., 1994).

3. INSIDE THE JUROR: THE PSYCHOLOGY OF JUROR DECISION MAKING 3–37 (Reid Hastie ed., 1993).

4. Tom Galbraith, *Storytelling the Anecdotal Antidote,* LITIG. Spring 2002, at 17.

perform, and as a result, the project was in danger of failure. The hardworking partner went ahead and spent considerable time and money completing all the tasks and the project was a huge success. When the project was sold, the fiduciary partner tried to claim the majority of the profits.

These facts fit the classic story of the "Little Red Hen." In that fable, the little red hen did all the work to make the bread, and when the bread was made, the other animals wanted a share. The Little Red Hen said, "No." The attorneys for the hardworking partner in the dispute used this fable to convey their client's story. In fact, they showed an animation of this fable during closing arguments. This story fit the facts and jurors were more inclined to see the success of the project as due to the efforts of the hardworking partner and that the fiduciary failed to fulfill his obligations. Despite many weeks of testimony, jurors felt the animation factored in the defense verdict and was a great tool for tying everything together.

2. Attribution Theory/Choice Theme

Attribution theory says that when a person or entity makes a choice to do something, that person or entity is then seen as responsible for the consequences of that choice. To the extent that the plaintiff or defendant is seen as having a choice in his conduct, jurors will feel the plaintiff or defendant is responsible for the result.

Consider a case involving claims of misrepresentation and fraud against a developer of a major shopping center brought by a business with a long term lease at that shopping center. The business was an anchor tenant and the first to go into the project with the developer. The business operated for several years during which time the shopping center was not expanded. Due to a lack of customers, the business terminated its lease based on the misrepresentation and fraud by the developers. The business said the developer never intended to build out the development. Because the shopping center was never expanded, the business did not have enough customers to become profitable. The developer sued for rent and breach of the lease.

The business used the choice theme to explain what happened. The developer had promised to continue to develop the project. When sales slowed, the developers halted construction because it might not be financially successful. The business argued that the developer misrepresented its intentions, making the choice not to develop, never intending to do what it promised, and therefore had to accept the consequences. Jurors felt it was reasonable for the business to expect the project to be completed and that the developer's repeated misrepresentations and failure to meet its promises caused the business to fail, and thus the business had the right to terminate the lease.

One of the critical ways to analyze a case using attribution theory is to evaluate whether the parties have alternatives to their chosen paths. When judgments of responsibility and blame are being made, it is important to know whether or not there was any choice involved. In the example above, the question is, did the developer have any options that could have changed the outcome of the dispute? The conclusion was that it did have other choices, but it chose to protect its bottom line. In doing that, the developer broke its promise to develop the project and create an environment where an existing business could succeed.

Most attorneys use a version of the choice theme when they introduce the notion of personal or corporate responsibility. When a decision facing a company or individual is presented to jurors using the choice theme, jurors are allowed to conclude on their own what the choice means. In other words, if a company chooses to engage in fraud or negligent misrepresentation, its responsibility is inferred.

3. Counterfactual Thinking

Yet another strategy to develop case themes is the use of counterfactual thinking. Counterfactual thinking occurs when a person evaluates an event by how easily it could have been undone to create a different, usually more positive, outcome. The ease with which a party can undo a negative event with a counterfactual affects the amount of blame jurors attribute to that party.

If it is hard for jurors to develop reasonable counterfactuals, or "if only" statements, it will be harder for them to attribute responsibility, and thus blame, to the person or company. On the other hand, the more counterfactuals jurors can create to prevent the negative outcome, the stronger their feelings of blame are toward the party who they feel could have changed the outcome of the event.

The question answered by a counterfactual usually takes the form "if only . . ." or "what might have been . . ." An example of a counterfactual would be, "If only the owner of the business had said the lease requires you to keep this building in first class condition and you are not doing that, we would have done more maintenance," or "If the title company had only disclosed to buyers the fraudulent acts and churning of property sales by the developer, the fraud would never have occurred." A counterfactual creates an alternative way of looking at a situation, an alternative reality.

The way to use counterfactuals for case themes is to consider what "if only" arguments the plaintiff and defendant could make in a case. Often the plaintiff will have several "if only" arguments. Other examples from a business fraud or misrepresentation case include:

- If only the other side had said they never had done this kind of business before, we never would have agreed to invest our money.
- If only the other side had said they were in other pending litigation, we never would have gone into business with them.

The defendant, of course, can develop its own themes by employing arguments using the "if only" form. "If only you had done your own due diligence, you would have learned there are risks in this type of business."

One way for a company to defend against counterfactuals is with an "even if" argument. "Even if we had done further investigation, we never would have learned you were about to be sued." "Even if we had included that disclosure in our agreement, it wouldn't have made any difference, because you admit you never read the agreement."

Counterfactuals and the choice theme are two different ways of thinking about blame and judgments of responsibility. Since they both focus on responsibility, they often deal with the same set of facts. For example, in a securities case, the defendant could argue:

- *Choice Theme*: "The plaintiffs assumed the risk involved in investing in limited partnerships when they purchased a share of the venture."

- *Counterfactual*: "If only the plaintiffs had more carefully read the prospectus and the accountant's report, they would have been aware of the problems facing the company in the next fiscal year."

4. Hindsight Bias

Business disputes arise in situations where things have not gone right. One side or the other has been left with a bad outcome or unfulfilled expectations. Another very powerful psychological phenomenon, hindsight bias, often comes into play. Hindsight bias is one of the errors in judgment affecting jurors' decision-making when attributing cause and responsibility to an individual or company for a bad outcome. Hindsight bias refers to the tendency to see events as expected after they have occurred, even when they were seen as unlikely prior to their happening. This after the fact knowledge tends to increase feelings of confidence in judgment after the fact, and can lead to continued use of faulty decision strategies.[5]

Attorneys are well aware of "Monday Morning Quarterbacking" and the way it can be used to second guess a decision by a party. A number of studies have shown that hindsight bias is very difficult to overcome, even among sophisticated decision-makers. If hindsight bias is present in a case, one of the few things that can be done is to educate jurors about it. The hope is that if counsel points out the bias and how it plays out in the case at hand, at least one juror will understand that idea and bring it up during deliberations.

B. Power of Language

Jury research supports the importance of introducing persuasive phrases, images, and metaphors for the jury to use in thinking and talking about the case. The language serves as a filter through which they process the evidence. Some questions to consider include: What persuasive phrases, images, or metaphors will be used by the jury? What images will be most powerful? Which side's images/metaphors will jurors find most compelling?

---

5. Heath & Tindale, *supra* note 2.

The language needs to be simple enough to understand. It is especially important to look at business terms that jurors remember, as well as terms they may stumble over. In the heat of trial it is very easy to forget that jurors can get confused by the use of acronyms and technical terms. These are important questions to keep in mind as you are presenting the case.

C. Teaching Opportunities

Post-trial juror interviews indicate that attorneys generally earn credibility when they become teachers rather than advocates. Jurors appreciate the opportunity to learn new concepts and that learning is often motivation for them to work to understand the more complex elements of the case. Teaching is especially important if the law and legal concepts are inconsistent with how jurors feel about the case.

Teaching about the law is often an effective tool to neutralize sympathetic or inflammatory case facts. Jurors may not like the high interest rates charged by a finance company that caters to low-income consumers. Jurors may instinctively feel the company takes advantage of poor people. In that situation the attorney has to acknowledge to jurors that they may not like his client's business model, but the model they use or the way they represent and sell their services does not amount to misrepresentation or breach of fiduciary duty. Jurors often comment on the difference between their negative feelings about a party and their decision-making in a case. Jurors will say, "I never thought I would be on the side of a business like that, but we had to make our decision based on the law, not on whether we liked the company."

II. WITNESSES IN A BUSINESS TORTS CASE

In business tort cases, the "characters" an attorney has to work with—the witnesses testifying on behalf of the company—present a series of problems that are often unique to each specific company and industry. In a business tort involving professionals, juries have higher expectations of the parties than a case in which one side is a lay person with no professional training.

Business tort trials are surprisingly as much about the players as they are about the conflict. Since jurors are often trying to determine the motives, honesty, and intent of the parties, witness performance can be critical to the outcome of a business torts dispute. For example, in a trial involving a financial institution accused of negligent misrepresentation about an investment, the financial officer's testimony had a multiplier effect on jurors. Jurors felt that the corporate officer showed no compassion for the investors who lost their money. Jurors also felt that the corporate witness did not show a willingness to see how his disclosures could be misleading. The performance and testimony of the witness was seen as so unethical and negative that it transformed a case that on its merits and legal basis would have been a likely defense verdict into a case with liability and punitive damages.

A. What Jurors Say About Witnesses in Business Cases

How something is said by a witness is just as important as what is said. As one juror put it, "I didn't believe his testimony because of the way he looked. He may be a big business guy, but he was lying about all of it. He seemed sleazy and nervous."

1. What They Like

Generally, there are no marked differences between business cases and other types of litigation when it comes to witness performance. Jurors like witnesses who give clear, direct answers and use ordinary language. In terms of demeanor, jurors believe in the adage "looking someone in the eye" and comment, when witnesses maintain eye contact, they appear confident. Jurors are less suspicious when a witness shows even temperament on direct and cross. While a credible business executive can be assertive, they are not combative, while appearing confident. Jurors also like witnesses who take responsibility for decisions or actions. Corporate witnesses who assign blame are usually evaluated poorly.

2. What They Do Not Like

Jurors sometimes feel that corporate witnesses appear arrogant or cold. Other behaviors mentioned include witness impatience, combativeness, and irritation. An unfeeling witness, or one who acts superior, can turn off jurors.

In comparing behavior on cross and direct, jurors with negative impressions of a witness have mentioned that during cross examination the witness avoided giving a straight answer or appeared to lose his or her memory

203

with a lot of "I don't recall" answers. In these situations, jurors are left with the impression that the witness seemed to be hiding information or fighting with opposing counsel.

B. Overcoming Witness Problems

There are techniques for preparing witnesses that can help even the most experienced trial teams. Practice and witness work is the answer for a witness who presents problems. Although the importance of preparation appears obvious, both attorneys and witnesses often talk themselves out of this essential part of trial preparation. Counsel has been overheard on the morning of trial saying, "We can meet for breakfast and talk about your testimony," or "You know the case."

Even though businesspeople can be familiar with legal proceedings, the best way to reduce anxiety and improve performance is preparation. There is no substitute for practice. Telling someone what to do when they are a witness, such as instructing them to "just answer the question yes or no," is not sufficient.

Preparation takes resources, but it is time well spent. It is seldom the case a witness says about preparation, "This doesn't help me!" Witnesses can be upset about the fact that there is a lawsuit and irritated that they have to devote resources to it, but most often they find one or more practice sessions to be of value.

For witnesses who need to rein in their behavior, such as a business executive who is used to being in charge, or a fast talking salesman type, or for a witness who does not have an understanding as to how he or she will be seen by jurors, it is good to include video feedback in the preparation. Even well-heeled executives will be their best critic when their testimony is played back to them.

Use of video feedback should be judicious as there are times when it can be more damaging than beneficial. For example, witnesses who lack confidence and need support to present their story may become overly self-conscious and uncertain when they view a playback of their performance. By contrast, witnesses who are overly confident, argumentative, or uncooperative may be helped to see their own behavior on video.

If a rigorous cross examination is anticipated at trial, a preparation session with a different attorney can be a great experience for a witness. Using an outsider is preferred for cross examination because it is a more realistic experience and does not impact the relationship between the witness and counsel. Many witnesses comment on how helpful it was for them to have the preparation for cross examination.

For a business torts case, as well as most other civil litigation, witnesses need to have a safe harbor: an answer they can give when they are in a tough spot. Safe harbors are a great help for a witness because they are easy to recall, are based on the truth, and are usually something simple that reinforces case themes. Safe harbors are unique to every case, but some that have been effective include:

- *Fiduciary duty for company issuing stock*: "We told investors about all the risks with the company, including the possibility that there could be a downturn in the economy."
- *Negligent misrepresentation involving a lease*: "Every one of the developer's executives told us they were going to build out the shopping center. I asked them about that every month. They said they were working on it. They never intended to do more and they used the economic crash as an excuse."
- *Inducing employee to breach confidentiality*: "We never asked their former employees that we hired about confidential information, in fact we clearly told them we didn't want to hear anything about what they did at their previous employer."

C. Tools for Change

Attorneys have a variety of tools to help witnesses improve their demeanor. One technique is to have a discussion with the witness about the goals of their testimony. Find out how the witness wants to be perceived by jurors. Possible goals could include "I want them to see me as a hardnosed but fair businessman," or "I want to be seen as a person who always gives someone a chance, gives others the benefit of the doubt."

Once the witness identifies their goals and how they want to come across, this can be reinforced when going through their testimony.

205

Counsel can point out how the way they are talking or their demeanor supports or undermines their goal. By using the witness's stated goals, the feedback process provides a more effective "buy-in" by the witness and ownership of their performance. Without that commitment, a witness can move into a passive mode and put the burden on the attorney to help them be a better witness rather than accepting that responsibility for themselves.

One of the traditional approaches to working with witnesses involves "wood shedding," the practice of aggressively telling a witness how to answer questions. Attorneys sometimes feel the need to read the riot act to witnesses and tell them to shape up. As a change strategy, wood shedding is rarely helpful and has many limitations. Tension increases and witnesses generally become more anxious and less able to learn from negative feedback. The more effective tool to help improve witness performance is positive feedback. Focus the witness on what he is doing right, on what he should do, rather than emphasizing what not to do.

III. VOIR DIRE AND STRATEGIC JURY SELECTION IN A BUSINESS TORTS CASE

As a general principle, negative attitudes toward the issues favoring your side should be explored in voir dire where possible. Because the goal is to reveal strikes, jurors with biases against you, the most important questions are most often those that relate to any weaknesses or vulnerabilities in your case. Of course there always are case-specific questions covering topics and issues in the case. The following are examples of topics to raise in voir dire for a business tort.

A. Questions About Business Experience

- How many of you have owned or run your own business? Do any of you have family members who have owned or run their own business?
- If yes, how successful was the business?
- Have you, or has someone close to you, had a business that was unsuccessful or failed? Tell me about that.
- Has anyone here ever negotiated a business deal or had someone else negotiate on their behalf? Tell me about that.

- Have you, or has someone close to you, ever felt cheated or defrauded in a business or investment situation? If yes, please explain.
- I'm interested in how trusting you feel you are when you enter any new kind of relationship—personal or business. Would you describe yourself as very cautious when it comes to entering into a business relationship?
- By a show of hands, who feels that you cannot be too careful nowadays in business?
- How many of you would describe yourself as a risk taker when it comes to business dealings?

B. Moral and Ethical Dimensions

- Some people believe that all is fair in business and everyone has to look out for themselves. Others feel that business ethics have to be improved. Where do you stand on the issue of business ethics?
- Which standard statement best describes you? "Follow the letter of the law," or "Follow the spirit of the law."
- Is there anyone here who simply would not want to work in the private sector? Why is that?
- Businesses are in the business of making a profit. How do you feel about that; do you think businesses have become too focused on profits?
- How do you react to the view, "We are living in a tough world and I have to look out for myself and I expect others to do the same"?

C. Strike Characteristics for a Business Torts Dispute

While jury selection in a business torts case will not, by itself, win a case, with the wrong jurors, it can definitely lose the case.

Because jurors are less familiar with the issues, strike priorities are sometimes less apparent for a business torts case as compared to other types of cases. For most business disputes, the core issue for jury selection centers on how jurors feel about contracts, business deals, business experience, trust, and oral agreements.

As mentioned earlier, identifying who is a strike priority in a particular business case is more difficult than it is for some other types of cases such as a product liability case or toxic tort case. Generally jurors have well developed attitudes about issues in a case that deals with topics such as warnings, product safety, or companies accused of polluting. Jurors do not generally have well developed attitudes about arcane issues related to fiduciary duties, trade secrets, or tortious interference with contracts. However that does not mean there aren't jurors who hold biases that will affect how they process and decide the issues in a case.

One consideration when determining strike candidates for a business torts case is the general issue of who brought the lawsuit, and the attendant attitudes jurors have about lawsuits and tort reform. The party bringing the lawsuit for any type of trial has to consider this issue. The topic of lawsuits can be tied to the business world by exploring beliefs about the fact that "some companies would rather sue each other than compete." We have found that those who strongly hold those views are much more judgmental to the party bringing the lawsuit.

Another important consideration for business torts is juror beliefs about written and oral contracts. Business torts claims often involve contract disputes, and for that reason, juror views on contracts need to be explored because they can impact juror reaction to a case. This topic does divide the jury pool in a significant way. There are those who believe the written contract is what rules and oral contracts have little if no merit. Those who hold this view tend to be very judgmental of anyone involved in a business tort who did not have a written contract, anyone who did not read their contract, or anyone who had an objection about a contract and didn't complain. These criticisms are multiplied if one of the parties is seen as a big corporation or someone with special professional training such as an attorney. This expectation that written contracts are of ultimate importance also comes up when jurors deliberate. We often see in deliberations in business disputes jurors pointing to the fact that a business failed to protect itself by having a proper contract. Often they will say, "If they don't want to protect themselves, they should not expect us to do that for them."

A related issue for a strike priority and one that would have to be artfully explored in voir dire is the idea that one's actions can be used to understand how a contract is understood by the parties. Jurors have a difficult time accepting the fact that the behavior of the parties, when it is inconsistent with the terms of the contract, can be used to determine their understanding of the contract. This would be a difficult concept to discuss with jurors, but any given case may require that this be explored.

Another important area of inquiry that should be considered for a business tort is the moral dimension. Often when jurors are evaluating a business tort they look at it in moral terms. If your side of a case will be presented and framed as being less ethical, not sticking to their word, or taking advantage of someone, then it would be important to attend to those jurors who look at the world from a moral perspective.[6] Generally those would be individuals who agree that businesses are not as ethical as they should be and who decide things based on what they think is right rather than what is legal.

D. Use of Juror Questionnaires

The use of written questionnaires to assist in the selection of jurors has become more widespread, particularly in high profile business disputes. Research and experience have shown that potential jurors provide more open and honest answers in response to a written questionnaire than in response to judge or attorney conducted voir dire. Attitudes and experiences, more than demographic attributes like race, gender, or age, drive juror thinking and decision-making. To discover those drivers of decision-making it is helpful to have a questionnaire to point out those who likely hold attitudes detrimental to your case.

To best identify strike candidates it is important to ask the tough questions. For example, if a business dispute involves claims of conspiracy among parties, jurors need to be asked the extent to which they think conspiracies are common in the business world. Belief in conspiracies can be a powerful predictor of juror behavior. If your client has been accused of conspiring against the other side, that question can be tough to ask in voir dire. In that case, it may be easier and more effective to have that question asked in a juror questionnaire.

Judges are more open to use of a questionnaire if a trial is anticipated to be lengthy, has had high publicity in the media, or involves sensitive issues

---

6. Tess Wilkinson-Ryan & Jonathan Baron, *Moral Judgment and Moral Heuristics in Breach of Contract*, 6 J. EMPIRICAL LEGAL STUD. 405, 407 (2009).

that might be more difficult to discuss in open court. Examples of sensitive issues that may be relevant to a business torts dispute are foreclosures, loss of a job, or bankruptcy. There are steps that can be taken to increase the likelihood that a questionnaire will be adopted, including getting counsel from both sides to agree on the idea of using a questionnaire, agree in advance on what questions should be included, and keeping the questionnaire to a reasonable length.

IV. CONCLUSION

Business torts trials present challenges for jurors and for counsel. Good case themes, credible witnesses, and getting the best possible jury are all keys to maximizing chances of success in trial.

TABLE OF CASES

C

D

Miller v. Union Pacific RR Co., No. 06-2399-JAR-DJW, 2008 WL 4724471 (D. Kan. Oct. 24, 2008), 140n51

Mohr v. Bank of N.Y. Mellon Corp., 393 F.App'x 639 (11th Cir. 2010), 55n29

Momenta Pharms., Inc. v. Amphastar Pharms., Inc. 686 F.3d 1348 (Fed. Cir. 2012), 63n56

Montgomery v. Wyeth, 580 F.3d 455 (6th Cir. 2009), 108n45

Moore v. New York Cotton Exchange, 270 U.S. 593 (1926), 112

N

Nat. Mkt. Share, Inc. v. Sterling Nat. Bank, 392 F.3d 520 (2d Cir. 2004), 107n41

New Hampshire Ins. Co. v. MarineMax of Ohio, Inc., 408 F.Supp.2d 526 (N.D. Ohio 2006), 99n24, 100n27

New Valley Corp., *In re*, 181 F.3d 517 (3d Cir. 1999), 62

Nutrasweet Co. v. Vit-Mar Enters., Inc., 112 F.3d 689 (3d Cir. 1997), 63n55

O

Ohio *ex rel.* Celebrezze v. Nuclear Regulatory Com., 812 F.2d 288 (6th Cir. 1987), 54

Olson Trans. Co. v. Socony-Vacuum Oil Co., (E.D. Wis. 1944), 128n14

Oppenheimer Fund, Inc. v. Sanders, 437 U.S. 340 (1978), 143n65

Opulent Life Church v. City of Holly Springs, Miss., 697 F.3d 279 (5th Cir. 2012), 53n21

Original Great Am. Chocolate Chip Cookie Co. v. River Valley Cookies, Ltd., 970 F.3d 273 (7th Cir. 1992), 61n49

Overseas Private Inv. Corp. v. Mandelbaum, 185 F.R.D. 67 (D.D.C. 1999), 139n50

P

Papasan v. Allain, 478 U.S. 265 (1986), 98n19

Parsi v. Daioleslam, 852 F.Supp.2d 82 (D.D.C. 2012), 161n29

People of State of Ill. *ex rel.* Hartigan v. Peters. 871 F.2d 1336 (7th Cir. 1989), 65

Phillip M. Adams & Associates v. Dell, Inc., 621 F.Supp.2d 1173 (D. Utah 2009), 8n7

Pioche Mines Consol., Inc. v. Dolman, 333 F.2d 257 (9th Cir. 1964), 141n56

Piper Aircraft Co. v. Reyno, 454 U.S. 235 (1981), 15n13

Plantation-Simon Inc. v. Al Bahloul, 596 So.2d 1159 (Fla. Dist. Ct. App. 1992), 138n43

Polymer Indus. Prods. Co. v. Bridgestone/Firestone, Inc., 347 F.3d 935 (Fed. Cir. 2003), 113n63

Porto Transp., Inc. v. Consol. Diesel Elec. Corp., 20 F.R.D. 1 (S.D.N.Y. 1956), 96n15

Prime Contr., Inc. v. Wal-Mart Stores, Inc., No. 06-383-JBC, 2008 U.S. Dist. LEXIS 56449 (E.D. Ky. July 22, 2008), 94n4

Sosna v. Iowa, 419 U.S. 393 (1975), 77n18

Southern Constr. Co., Inc. v. Pickard, 371 U.S. 57 (1962), 113n63

Stanley v. Univ. of S. Cal., 13 F.3d 1313 (9th Cir. 1995), 53n19

State Farm Mut. Auto. Ins. Co. v. New Horizont, Inc., 250 F.R.D. 203 (E.D. Pa. 2008), 139n50

State Farm Mutual Automobile Insurance Company v. Riley, 199 F.R.D. 276 (N.D. Ill. 2001), 99, 100

Steel Co. v. Citizens for a Better Environment, 523 U.S. 83 (1998), 77n18

Stemple v. Board of Educ. of Prince George's County, 523 F.2d 893 (4th Cir. 1980), *cert. denied*, 450 U.S. 911 (1981), 48

T

Taylor, United States v., 166 F.R.D. 356 (M.D.N.C. 1996), 138n38, 139n47

Thalheim v. Eberheim, 124 F.R.D. 34 (D. Conn. 1988), 130n21

Ticor Title Ins. Co. v. Cohen, 173 F.3d 63 (2d Cir. 1999), 51n15

Toll Bros., Inc. v. Twp. of Readington, 555 F.3d 131 (3d Cir. 2009), 78n20

Tom Doherty Assocs. v. Saban Entm't, Inc., 60 F.3d 27 (2d Cir. 1995), 51n16, 53n20

Travelers Indem. Co. v. Metro. Life Ins. Co., 228 F.R.D. 111 (D. Conn. 2005), 143n61

25,202 Acres of Land and building affixed to land located in Town of Champlain, Clinton County, N.Y., United States v., 860 F.Supp.2d 165 (N.D.N.Y. 2010), 161n28

Tyco Fire Prods., LP v. Victaulic Co., 777 F.Supp.2d 893 (E.D. Pa. 2011), 108n49, 109n50

U

United States v. *See* name of opposing party

University of Texas v. Camenisch, 451 U.S. 390 (1981), 50n5, 51n11, 60n47

W

Ward v. Commission, 87 T.C. 78 (1986), 149n6

Webb v. Omni Block, Inc., 166 P.3d 140 (Ariz. Ct. App. 2007), 161n31

Western Water Mgt. Inc. v. Brown, 40 F.3d 105 (5th Cir. 1994), 57n32

White v. McHugh, CIV.A. 3:09-1559-MJP, 2010 WL 4340399 (D.S.C. Sept. 3, 2010), 141n56

Whitlow v. Martin, No. 04-3211, 2008 WL 2414830 (C.D. Ill. Nov. 19, 2008), order supplemented by, No. 04-CV-3211, 2008 WL 5511178 (C.D. Ill., Nov. 19, 2008), 143n63

Williams Sec. Lit.-WCG Subclass, *In re*, 558 F.3d 1130 (N.D. Ill. 2009), 161

Women's Med. Prof'l Corp. v. Taft, 199 F.R.D. 597 (S.D. Ohio 2000), 65n64

W.R. Grace & Co. v. Local Union 759, 461 U.S. 757 (1983), 59n42

Wyandotte Nation v. Sebelius, 443 F.3d 1247 (10th Cir. 2006), 58n36

Z

Zenith Elec. Corp. v. WH-TV Broad. Corp., 395 F.3d 416 (7th Cir. 2005), 162n32

Zimmer v. United Dominion Indus., Inc., 193 F.R.D. 616 (W.D. Ark., 2000), 106n38

Zivkovic v. S. Cal. Edison Co., 302 F.3d 1080 (9th Cir. 2002), 107n40

Zubulake v. UBS Warburg, 220 F.R.D. 212 (S.D.N.Y. 2003), 8n6

Zubulake v. UBS Warburg LLC, 216 F.R.D. 290 (S.D.N.Y. 2003), 134n33

Zubulake v. UBS Warburg LLC, 217 F.R.D. 309 (S.D.N.Y. 2003), 134n33

Zubulake v. UBS Warburg LLC, 222 F.R.D. 212 (S.D.N.Y. 2003), 134n33

Zubulake v. UBS Warburg LLC, 229 F.R.D. 422 (S.D.N.Y. 2004), 134n33

Zubulake v. UBS Warburg LLC, 230 F.R.D. 290 (S.D.N.Y. 2003), 134n33

Zubulake v. UBS Warburg LLC, 231 F.R.D. 159 (S.D.N.Y. 2005), 134n33

Zubulake v. UBS Warburg LLC, 382 F.Supp.2d 536 (2005), 134n33

INDEX

220